Silver Lining

This book is dedicated to my son

Karen Platt's
Silver Lining

Black Tulip Publishing

First published in February 2005 by
Black Tulip Publishing.

British Library Cataloguing in Publication Data.

Platt, Karen
ISBN: 0954576438

35 Longfield Rd
Crookes
Sheffield
S10 1QW
England

Cover concept, Design and Artwork: Joshua Coventry

Printed and bound in Singapore.

Front Cover: Echeveria subridgia
Back Cover: top to bottom
Stachys byzantina, Caladium candidum, Liriope 'Okina',
Osteospermum
Inside front flap: Artemisia 'Powis Castle'

Title Page: Crassula 'Morgan's Beauty'
Page 2: Salvia argentea
Page 3: Stachys byzantina
Page 4: Artemisia
Page 5: Crassula 'Morgan's Beauty'

Other titles by Karen Platt:

Black Magic and Purple Passion
Gold Fever
Seed Sowing and Growing Success
Platt's Plant Synonyms

Future Releases:
Emeralds
Fruit Cocktail
The International Seed Directory

FOUNDER OF THE INTERNATIONAL BLACK
PLANT SOCIETY
To join the soicety and purchase books, please visit
www.karenplatt.co.uk
www.blackplants.co.uk

CONTENTS

INTRODUCTION

Primarily known for my research and writing on black plants which encompasses everything dark in horticulture; the results of which are found in my book 'Black Magic and Purple Passion'. I have also given the same treatment to gold plants in my book 'Gold Fever'. Now, it is naturally the turn of silver.

The modern garden relies more heavily on foliage for lasting colour. Silver in all its tones is attractive for a restful, elegant garden. The book concentrates mainly on foliage, from solid silver to variegated green and white plants. The favourite flowers I have chosen here are white. I know of flowers called silver, but really this is not a flower colour.

These silvered plants are a natural companion to the dark foliaged plants I love so much. They are a perfect foil. Whilst I have included every silver foliaged plant I have ever come across, the variegated plants and flowers are simply favourites and not intended to be a complete source.

I have continued to build upon the popular cool companions and hot partners; thereby rendering it easy to use plants in the garden. It is easy to create handsome vignettes by using these plants together.

Garden designs are once again included to bring ideas for the monotone garden and for using silver in combination; from the classic white garden to innovative style with silver to white. As usual, these ideas are intended to fire your own imagination and creativity and used in combination with the in-depth plant profiles, are all you need to produce your own individual garden.

COOL AND COLLECTED

Silver is highly collectable as a precious metal; it is sought-after in the garden too. Sophisticated gardeners love white to silver and the garden takes on elegant charm in these colours. Used judiciously its qualities are rare indeed. Silver is valued as a highlight in the garden, making other colours appear more intense.

The soft leaves of Ballota are delightful to touch. New leaves are like little rosebuds carved from sugar icing. They are covered in a dusting of silver and the felted stems are virtually white.

SILVER IN HORTICULTURE

WHY IS IT SILVER?

Silver leaved plants are often covered in tiny hairs giving the appearance of silver. Others are covered in farina, a mealy dust. This can wash off in rain, revealing the undertone of green leaves. *Salvia argentea* is cloaked in downy fur to protect from excessive heat and sunlight, in this way it conserves moisture. *Sedum spathulifolium* 'Cape Blanco' is covered in white dust.

Silver is best equipped to reflect heat and light and the hairy, felted or woolly surfaces are designed to keep plants cool or to act as insulation against heat or drying winds. Silver plants are perfect for a dry landscape. Grey is mainly the colour for sunny, dry gardens and is usually intolerant of wet. Many silver plants are suitable for rock gardens but there are also giants for the border such as *Cynara*.

Unlike purple and gold whose colour comes from pigment triggered by sunlight, silver plants have evolved to cope with climate. They usually come from warmer regions of the world and have developed fine hairs, a white wool or powder to survive the climate in which they grow. These features serve to reflect bright light and to keep the plant cool. They are also capable of collecting tiny droplets of water on cooler nights to keep them going through the hot days. This does not mean you have to live in a desert to grow these plants, but most do appreciate full sun and extremely well-drained soil. These plants are for low-water gardens. Tempted to put them in the shade to brighten a dark corner? In most cases this is a no-no, but there are some that will tolerate partial shade, namely the beautiful painted fern *Athyrium niponicum v pictum*, *Liriope*, *Pulmonaria* and *Heuchera* and the blue-toned silver types found in *Hosta*.

Silver plants often look soft. Think of hairy *Salvia argentea* and *Stachys byzantina*. They add great impact in the textural, tactile garden. However, not all silver plants are a soft touch. *Cynara* are eminently structural, the only soft quality here is found in the huge leaves as they cascade. *Agave* are architectural beauties without a soft side at all.

BOTANICALLY SPEAKING

The specific epithet (the second word in a botanical name) gives an indication to the characteristics of a plant. There are several words which indicate silver, grey, white and the farina or hairs found on the surface of leaves.

adenophyllus means hairy leaves; *ciliaris* means fringed with hairs; *eriophorus* means woolly; *hirsutissimus* means very hairy; *hirsutus* is hairy; *hispidus* means bristly or stiff hairs; *lanatus* means woolly; *lanuginosus* is descriptive of a plant with soft hairs; *pilosus* is for plants with long, soft hairs and *tomentosus* means thickly haired

albus means white; *albescens* means turning white; *albicans* becoming white or off-white; *albidus* means whitish; *albomaculatus* is spotted white; *albopictus* means painted white; *albovariegatus* means white variegated; *lactescens* means becoming milky white; *lacteus* is milky white; *lactiflora* means milky; *nivalis* and *niveus* can be used for snow-white; *ochroleucus* means yellowish white; *vestalis* denotes white; *virginalis* is virginal white and *zaleucus* means very white

dealbatus or *farinosus* means white-powdered and *glaucus* means whitish bloom, often blue-tinted

argentatus or *argenteus* mean silver

cinereus means ash-grey; *griseus* means grey or pearly grey; *lividus* denotes lead grey or bluish grey; *margaritus* means pearly; *murinus* can mean mouse grey; *plumbeus* means lead grey and *ravus* means greyish

noctiflorus means night flowering and *vespertinus* denotes evening flowering; both often refer to white flowers or to grey leaves

Do not be fooled by *sylvestris*, it might look like silver, but refers to plants found growing in woods.

This list is compiled from my book Platt's Plant Synonyms.

SILVER HARDSCAPE

The Accenture Garden was designed by Miriam Book in 2002, it was called Through The Ceiling

Silver can be used for hardscaping in the garden. In this garden, tubular steel supports a glass roof, the eye-catching grey slate flooring leads the eye into the garden to the stainless steel chair and the 'trompe l'oeil' windows, the stainless steel water feature cascades down into the pond. Pale flowers team well with the silver hardware.

SYMBOLISM

Step into the ivory tower. Just what do silver, grey and white represent in society?
What are the associations we make with these colours?

My first thoughts when I think of silver are those of jewellery, precious metals; having a silversmith amongst my ancestors and coming from the home of sterling silver and stainless steel probably accounts for this since I am one to collect plants not jewels. However, I have an interest in arts and crafts and silverwork from the Incas to modern day artists working with this precious metal. Ornamentation which is mimicked in the garden in the form of mirrored obelisks reflecting shimmering silver, stainless steel water features, scrollwork and many other artefacts that work well with silver foliage. Grey sounds dull, silver sounds exciting and valuable. I have long designed with stainless steel in the garden and am always attracted to the shiny quality of silvered metals. Sterling Silver, Platinum, Titanium, Pewter and Stainless Steel, the metallic quality blends nicely into the garden. Metallic silvers are equally enchanting when found in foliage.

Grey to white through silver are the elegant colours. Neutral, cool and conservative. Though grey can be seen as moody and cloudy, it rarely evokes strong emotions. It is a colour which does not offend.

Grey is the lighter side of black; a colour that blends well with the darker tones. It is seen as formal for it is the accepted dress or suit colour in the corporate world. Pale greys are light and fairly bright whilst dark, charcoal greys carry some of the qualities of black. Grey is sophisticated without the negative side effects associated with black. Calming yet it can convey a lack of commitment.

Grey has two sides, there are greys which evoke good feelings, namely charcoal, slate, gunmetal, silver, dove grey, powder grey, oyster, pearl, taupe and there are greys which evoke a heavy, doom laden, cloud filled sky, ashen, lead, mousy. Grey is associated with old age, feared by some; but maturity brings its advantages. Grey areas are things we do not understand, the unexplained. Grey is connected with melancholy, boredom and sadness. Grey matter is associated with wisdom and knowledge and the power of those little grey cells, the brain. Jesus is often depicted wearing a grey cloak and this colour is linked with the resurrection of Christ and is associated with rebirth. Mist, stones and ashes are the undefined areas represented by this colour of neutrality. Most of us hate grey skies and withdraw and recoil from them.

White is precise, critical and sincere. The symbol of purity, sprituality and femininity. White is absolute, the reflection of all other colour.

The colour of rebirth, illumination, innocence, knowledge and revelation. It is the colour of shrouds, ghosts and death. In many countries it is the colour of mourning. White flowers are often laid on coffins.

It is also the colour of initiation and enlightenment. It has been used as a symbol of holiness. The colour of angels and gods, it is heavenly and sacred.

White is cleanliness. It represents simplicity, reverence, protection, truth and humility but is also seen as cold and clinical, sterile and is associated with harsh winters, ice and snow; halting life in the garden.

Silver is a metallic grey, but it has a different quality, shining, sleek, ornate. It is a cool metal, lacking the warmth of gold. It is glamorous and distinguished, representing refinement and riches. Silver coins reward good deeds and hard work. Silver can represent security, reliability, modesty, maturity, it is seen as conservative.

Silver was one of the fundamental symbols in Western alchemy and Chaldean practices of associating seven heavenly bodies with seven metals and with human organs and destinies. Luna (silver) was represented by a crescent. In alchemy, silver was dedicated to the moon, the Mother God of ancient religions with female tenets. It is associated with Monday. Quicksilver, a metallurgic compound of liquid mercury that in nature contains amounts of platinum was dedicated to Mercury and associated with Wednesday.

In heraldry, silver is represented by grey or white, symbolising nobility, peace and serenity. It is associated with the qualities of purity and chastity since the metal withstands the test of fire.

In Frank Baum's original story, Dorothy's slippers in The Wizard of Oz, were silver. MGM changed them to red, thereby losing the symbolism of the silver standard as opposed to the gold standard represented by the yellow brick road.

Circ Contemporary Man's Garden designed by Andy Sturgeon 2001. Bold lines make a beautiful outdoor living space

USING SILVER IN THE GARDEN

Subtle writ big. Shadows come to the fore. A hazy, airy atmosphere of mists at dawn. Moondrops, stars falling from the skies at night. Colours appear to capture light particles as they shimmer like icicles and diamonds. The garden almost appears transparent with its ghostly air.

Whilst completely at home in the dry garden, grey can be successfully used in other areas. It is much used in Australia and the Mediterranean. Silver is excellent for breaking up intense colours and is an ideal transition between two colours. Silver and grey can calm hot colours.

The colours work well with black, white, and pastels. Silver is excellent in the dry landscape as the most drought tolerant plants have silver foliage and need little maintenance once established. Do not be fooled by the soft velvet, often drooping texture, they are not in need of water. Neither do they require much fertilizer. These are some of the toughest plants you can grow. They are adapted to reflect the sun's heat thereby keeping leaves cooler in hot sun and loosing less water. They are often salt tolerant too and make good coastal plants.

It is easy to create a high-tech, almost business-like, modern garden with these colours. Yet grey is highly adaptable as the designs included here will demonstrate. Grey has been a favourite for hundreds of years. Jekyll and the French painters Monet and Renoir used grey foliage in paintings and gardens. Monet loved to grow silver foliage and red poppies. Jekyll always punctuated her whites with greys, thereby eliminating any stark quality possessed by too much Persil linen white.

The late Westside architect Robert. M. Fletcher used grey plants in most of his landscapes. His very favourite was *Senecio cineraria*, dusty miller planted in beds of pink, blue and purple such as *Petunia, Viola* and *Verbena*. These schemes are echoed to this day in many public gardens and municipal plantings.

Right: A simple, high tech garden relies on off white walls and hardscaping with silvery slate grey chips. Silver is echoed in the stainless steel container.

Below: Silver breaks up hot colours in this scheme, acting as a soft buffer to cool things down.

THE PALETTE

Three tones to play with: silver, white and grey. Silver and grey form classic neutrals in the garden with a classy look. From grey through silvery tones to white, this is the colour of the cool garden. Leaves can have a pearly quality, some are frosted, others almost appear transparent.

Grey matter

Grey is a serious colour but when grey meets silver it is elevated from cloud to silver lining. It is not doom and gloom. There are no dull standards here.

Grey skies full of clouds often have a silver lining. A silver lining can be used in the garden to great effect. It is useful to edge a path or wind a silver trail through the border. An edging of silvery *Lavandula* is perfect along a winding path, bringing a streak of light in its foliage accompanied by scent which will waft on the air in the gentlest breeze or as you pass by brushing the leaves.

Grey appeals to the intellect. Soft, furry leaves appeal to the senses. They trigger a need to feel. Grey plants are calm; they soothe. Environmentally friendly plants, they appeal to the water conscious.

Grey is the colour of shadow and contrast.

Shimmering silver

A sprinkling of silver is like a sprinkle of fairy dust. A little goes a long way to lift the garden into a magical creation. Highly reflective of light, silver plants shine and glow in the garden like the moon and stars.

Bright lights

Pure as driven snow. Clean whites like laundered linen peep out amongst the dirty greys of unwashed clothes! Diluted black and milky white are chic.

Silvers tend to fall into two categories, blue-green and grey-green. I have concentrated on the latter.

Make a statement with silver and black

THE MOOD

Soothing silver is the colour of relaxation. The choice of the sophisitcated gardener who wants to unwind after work. It is the chill out zone for the mind and the soul. Classical music wafts on the air whilst the ice chinks in the drinks. Perfume is also wafting on the garden as this is the garden of the senses.

Silver is for the person who likes clear-cut decisions, the ones who know where they are heading in life. They make the right choice, then relax and enjoy it.

There is a silver lining in the garden, a happy ending. It is also often a water saving garden so you are doing your bit for the environment when you opt for silver.

THE STYLE

Clean, cut lines suit these colours; they are perfect for modern design. They echo the colours of today's modern garden hardcore of stainless steel and even concrete sits better with grey and silver. It echoes perfectly the house decorated in minimalist style. Cool neutrals bring grace and sophistication, they make the garden a peaceful setting ideal for contemplation and quiet relaxation. Elegance is the keyword.

The urban look is built on neat shapes and simple lines which bring about the controlled mood of the modern garden. The formal look has a cool edge. The hardcore accoutrements are masculine whilst the softcore plantings are feminine.

The look is soft, the tones subtle. It is a return to simplicity, romance and innocence. Uncomplicated colour blends with urban serenity.

One can also expect the unexpected, amongst the soft harmonies it is feasible to inject a shot of hot colour to great effect.

THE PLANTS

Neutrality has its faults, it needs a little oomph, a raison d'être. This is provided by the plants. Texture is of chief importance, it will offer a bold, luxurious quality to quiet plantings. Outstanding variegation adds interest and keeps the pulse beating. Variegated plants can link two colours found in their foliage, and break solid blocks of green and white. Statuesque and architectural plants add focus. The occasional white flower offers purity. With care, plants can be chosen for many scapes and situations not just the dry garden. The colour is quiet and relaxed but the plants are exciting and beckon in drifts of cool colour.

The green leaves look so handsome against white flowers

The green and white garden is refreshing in flower and leaf

Green and white has long been a favourite of florists

Green and white are the elements of this handsome, cool garden

SILVER AND PURPLE

Silver and purples seem to be made for each other. Shimmering grey to white foliage makes a perfect foil for glistening purples. Favourite purple flowers are Alliums, those globe heads are so very fascinating.

Angelica gigas is another must-have in this setting with its large purple flowers and airy Verbena bonariensis.

At ground level, add the fabulous leaves of purple Heuchera and some of the silver ones too.

16

SILVER AND BLUE

At Tatton, Chesire, England silver and blue were used in a formal garden to great effect with a sprinkling of white flowers.

SILVER AND RED

Startling red is cooled by silvery grey at Tatton, Chesire. If you are afraid of using red in the garden, mixing it with grey is a good way to start.

DESIGNS ON SILVER

Silver Strands

Silver or grey make an easy marriage between colours, good for separating two colours which would not sit easily together. Silver-white or grey plants reflect light and act as blenders. Silver can be used like a string of pearls through the garden, dotted here and there. Broad drifts of silver look better punctuated with colour.

Grey is a perfect foil to green and to purple foliage. 20% makes a good balance. Silver and turquoise give jewel-like colours evocative of Caribbean seas.

A classic combination with most colours, perfect for pastels, lovely with lemon, ravishing with red, basic class with black, brow-raising with brown, gorgeous with green, go for it with gold, bold with blue, vivacious with violet. Grey is a great highlight for red verbena, blue campanula or pink mallow. Mellow saturated yellows or magnificent magenta with the proximity of silver leaves. Silver or grey is a punctuation when used with hot colours. Red hot is cooled when placed with silver foliage. Silver makes great show-stopping combinations.

Pastel flowers in the shape of Aquilegia, Iris and Verbascum sit handsomely amongst the grey foliage of Cynara and the bluish Eucalyptus gunnii

THE SENSUOUS GARDEN

Touch me plants, smell me scents, easy on the eye, the sound of water, the taste of edible landscaping. These are plants you want to touch, stroke, feel. Irresistible foliage, soft and silky. Noli me tangere, latin for touch me not, is not on the menu here. Silver foliage is a tactile hot spot. Touch me foliage can be on the rough side too, jagged, hairy or leathery and waxy and these combine well with feathery, hairy and fuzzy plants for an all round awakening of the senses. They combine and contrast well and some release scent into the air which is so important in the garden. Touch me plants are ideal by the pathway, easy to touch. This is sensational gardening that touches all five senses.

Feel Free

Top of the feely charts is lamb's ears *Stachys byzantina* with those soft as lamb's coat leaves. I can never walk past without wanting to feel the velvet quality of this plant. Add *Salvia argentea* for the teddy bear look furry leaves. The rosettes of *Verbascum* are a close second, the leaves much larger and dramatic or you could choose the smaller all round *Verbascum dumulosum* for its tomentose leaves. *Helichrysum petiolare* has felted leaves. The leaves of many an *Artemisia* beckon with their alluring silver filigree lace foliage. *Salix lanata* is a good choice too. Grasses add impact with their silky tassels begging for fingers to stroke, dynamic in the last rays of the evening sun.

This is the sensual garden, feel the touch, let it flow like a breeze from your fingertips to your heart. All gardens speak to your heart. Feel the breeze through the garden, watch those leaves move and sway, let it rock. Reach out and touch, feed your senses.

Water is an important element in any garden but in the silver garden it adds not only pleasurable sight and sound but also a silver effect on a new dimension.

Sous le dome épais où le blanc jasmin
A la rose s'assemble
The Flower Duet, Delibes

In this garden, the scent comes from many white flowers with a backdrop of silver-scented foliage. *Lilium* take centre stage for just one bloom of *L. regale 'Album'* can scent a room. Roses are a close second and can be employed in all their guises; as hybrid teas with their neat blossoms, old white roses with their blowsiness and climbers soaring on high. Clothe a wall or a hefty pergola with white *Wisteria* and plant the annual *Lathyrus*, sweet peas. In summer, *Jasminum* brings the scent of the Eastern Mediterranean with its heady perfume. In winter, sweet box, *Sarcococca* fills the air with sweet perfume.

Scented foliage is found in *Lavandula* and *Artemisia* with grey leaves. This is a romantic garden, so make some space for romantic arbours and quiet places to sit; it is a good idea to incorporate a secret garden.

Walk into the sensuous garden through the rose, jasmine and honeysuckle arch which please the nose with scent on the air all season long. Brush past the lavender hedge as you walk the length of the path, stroking the Stachys, lamb's ears on the other side of the winding path. As you reach the bench to rest, your nose is once more greeted by the sweet perfume of climbing roses and jasmine. In the large pots by the bench and on the deck· or patio are the large trumpet lilies of Lilium regale 'Album' exuding an intoxicating perfume in summer.

WHITE WATER

In silver and white gardens water almost echoes the colour. Transparency is desirable, the rush of silvery water is advantageous for the seductive sound, sensuous quality and sensation it brings to the garden. Rushing water is wonderful if you have the space, but water can also go straight up into the air, and still water has a peaceful quality. A trickle of water can be just as effective as a gush. Water features can be tiny, pebble fountains to enormous features like canals. One of my favourite features is the rill borrowed from Muslim gardens. Water is extremely important in the Arabic garden and perfect examples are found at the Alhambra Palace in Grenada, Spain where one finds the fabulous water feature in the Generalife gardens with its criss-cross fountains and the water feature in the courtyard of the lions. The intricacy of this Palace is found in its architecture and craftsmanship, the water features are simple, elegant and very effective. The key is simplicity, purity. Water is the source of life, let it flow without complication.

Few of us have room for a full-blown waterfall like the one below, but we all stop and admire when we see one. Even morning dew plays a part in the silver garden.

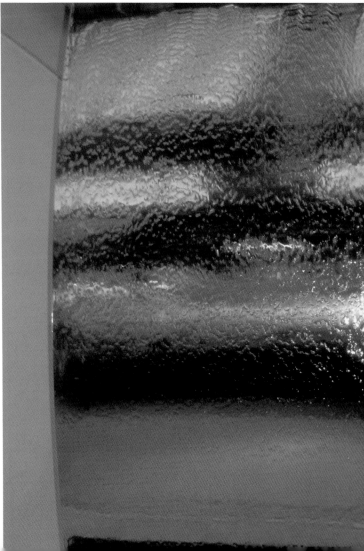

GARDENING WITH CONTAINERS

Use stunning silver to good effect on its own with a structural plant such as Astelia left.

The black containers above were designed by Ravenna Gardens for the Northwest Flower Show in Seattle. They looked stunning against a slate floor with silvery pebbles.

Handsome containers are easily achieved with white flowers, grey foliage and a stunning contrast. The cool green and white theme is very popular and always looks fresh.

Grey, white and black is very modern, try Ophiopogon planiscapus 'Nigrescens' underplanted with Sedum spathulifolium 'Cape Blanco' and a silver Helichrysum. Another favourite combination is Heuchera 'Silver Scrolls' with Ophiopogon planiscapus 'Nigrescens' and Bacopa 'Cabana'.

23

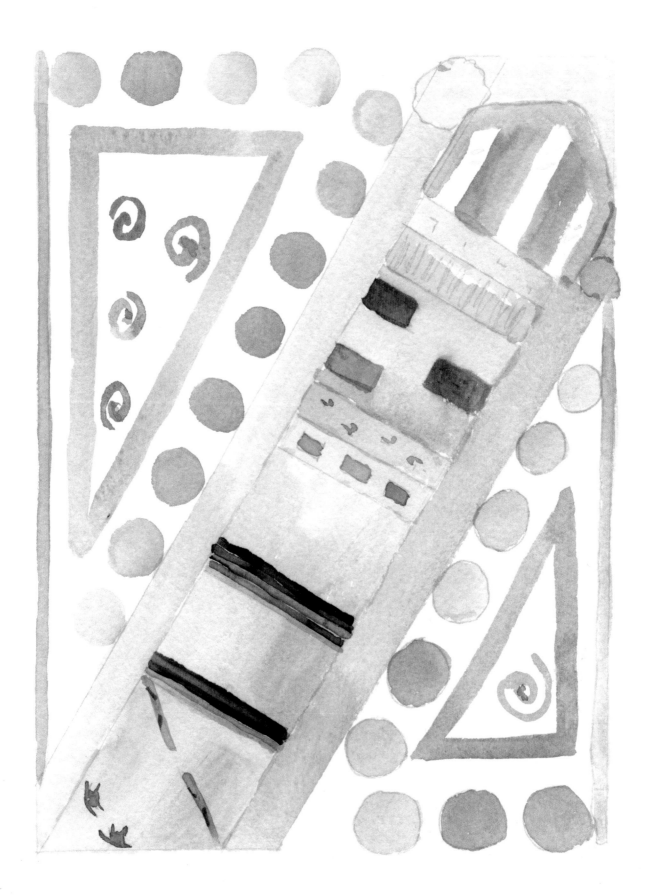

CHILL OUT

Relaxation is the keyword. Reduce stress and enjoy. This garden is the place to unwind, regenerate, relax, rejuvenate. Chill out and escape the pressures of the day, the mad world recedes in this calming, peaceful garden. Its very neatness evokes security.

This is the space for entertaining friends. A space to sit and talk, reminisce, plan, think or even just let your mind go blank and contemplate the garden scenery. It is the third dimension. A silver planet of your own.

The plants are tidy globes, cones and mounds. Twisted topiary adds interest in triangles of low hedges.

The quiet shapes follow clean lines, a clutterless space, everything in its place, neat, clean and tidy. You can go for straight and formal or sensual curves, but the lines are clear cut and bold. The sensual curves are echoed in stainless steel partitions on the first deck and on either side of the garden.

Lighting is important in this garden, there are downlights from the stainless steel partitions and uplights from the deck and the path edges.

The entertainment area is self-contained, everything is at hand. The stainless steel sunhouse has a music centre to lull you into a quiet mood with modern jazz, sublime classics or sophisticated soul.

Neat, rounded mounds and twisted topiaries make decisive plantings, following the clean lines of the garden. *Melianthus major* makes an architectural statement in a prominent position.

The garden of relaxation is where everyone deserves to unwind. Destress, detox, luxuriate in the scents and colours of quiet tones to soothe, calm and rebalance.

Silvery blues with greys, silvers and whites make up the colour scheme. They calm and soothe the senses. We are lulled into a sense of security by the crisp, clean look.

Enter the garden from the French windows of the house onto the patio and outdoor seating area which is cut off from the rest of the garden with a sliding silver aluminium or stainless steel screen with cut out flower shapes. The screen is pulled back on sliders to reveal two further decks each descending to a lower level. The decks can be used for sunbathing, partying or quiet relaxation and contemplation of the garden.

The water feature is made up of three compartments each planted up with ice cool plants such as stately Zantedeschia aethiopica 'Crowborough', water Iris and white Nymphaea.

At the far end of the garden is the stainless steel and glass sunhouse. This is the ultimate chill out house. The doors slide on smooth gliders and this is an inside-outside room, opening fully on warm, sunny days, but double-glazed for warmth in winter. White chairs and grey cushions adorn the inside with handsome pot plants in stainless steel containers.

Outside the sunhouse, a bold clump of Miscanthus stands at the far end of the garden, breaking the view to the house itself. The decks are lined with rounded clumps of Santolina, Artemisia and Lavandula in cool greys. Small clipped hedges of Santolina or Leucophyta surround the swirling topiaries of clipped blue Juniperus or variegated Ilex, holly.

LOW WATER GARDENS

Mediterranean and Californian gardens are low on water usage. Not only environmentally friendly, they are also low maintenance. Mediterranean gardens are full of white flowers and scent whilst the Californian gardens can contain cacti for the south in Mexican, desert style. Australian gardeners have long learned to cope with drought and harsh sun.

THE GRAVEL GARDEN

Dry scapes look good on gravel. The purpose of the latter is to give the perfect habitat for plants which like it dry. Clink your dry martinis as you sit and sip on the minimalist look.

The Beth Chatto gardens are a must for every gardener. Created from a wasteland between two farms, these gardens are a paradise with a difference. Beth Chatto is Queen of right plant, right place, gardens in tune with nature. Her creations are groups of plants ideally suited to their situation. In the gravel garden which has never been artificially watered since its creation in 1991-2, drought tolerant evergreys such as *Lavandula*, *Ballota* and *Sedum* see the year through along with the fabulous bold stature of *Cynara*, cardoon.

At Beth Chatto's the scree garden has been recently built to accommodate plants that would get lost in the main gravel garden. 'Alpine' sun loving shrubs include many silver-greys in low mounds.

Mediterranean plants are well adapted to survive without water. Many Californian natives require the same conditions. Many hardy Australian natives come in greys. Desert gardeners choose silver for its drought tolerant qualities. Use *Eucalyptus*, *Pinus*, *Lavandula*, *Senecio* and *Iris*. Employ raised beds and create shade with vines.

Favourite plants for scree or rock garden include Androsace, Townsendia, alpine Centaurea, Leontopodium, Leucophyta.

MEDITERRANEAN GARDEN

Walk out of the patio doors, down on to the deck and into an oasis of warmth. Even in England, this style of gardening has become popular. Gardeners like to be outdoors, so why not make your garden an outdoor living space? In warm climes, you will not have problems with too much summer rain rotting these Mediterranean plants. The driest, sunniest spot in your garden is the place to create this paradise. *Olea europea*, an olive tree shows its silvery undersides in the slightest breeze; at its feet wafts the scent of *Lavandula*. This is the place to sit and relax and enjoy the perfume.

This garden can take on a French, Italian, Greek or Spanish theme; the choice is yours. Try a golden, peach or terracotta background. *Convolvulus cneorum, Marrubium incanum, Ballota, Perovskia, Stachys byzantina, Salvia argentea* and *Santolina* make a sea of silver. In summer, silver *Begonia* make a wonderful feature with their large, silvered leaves. If you have steps in the garden, make a display with white variegated leaf *Pelargonium*, bedding geranium, they will look spectacular all summer long with their pink or red flowers.

The deck is balanced by a round pond with *Nymphaea* and *Zantedeschia*, linked by a swerving path. Two large blue pots balance the scheme in opposite corners.

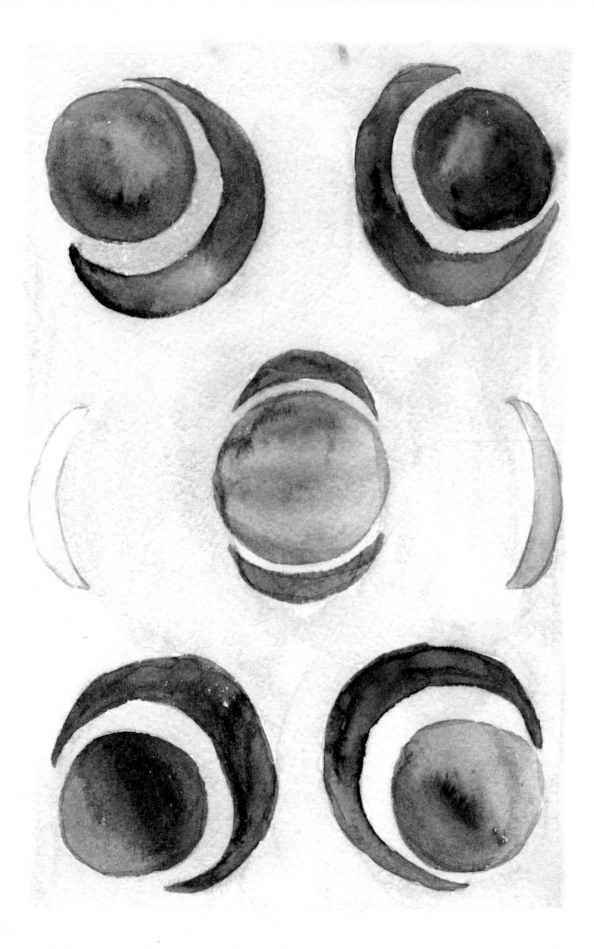

MOON GARDEN

Moon gazing is spectacular, flower gazing by the light of the moon is extraordinary. If you are entranced by the sight of a full moon, if you are unwound by the cool glow of light and the shadows cast, then this is a good idea to follow.

They say that women are ruled by the moon, but these gardens can be enjoyed by men too. What better if you come home late from work, tired from a day of frustration, to unwind in the glow of the evening light. If the only time you have to enjoy your garden is in the evening, it is worth devoting space to a moon garden.

Moon gardens are a popular theme. Be prepared for flowers to take on another form and to appear in a different guise. For example, the golden-green cones on a white coneflower such as *Echinacea 'White Swan'* will recede, leaving a frill of white petals apparently suspended in mid air. Silver foliage becomes silver clouds. At first the plant just ghostly, becomes a whiter shade of pale.

Why create a moon garden? Moon gardens represent peace, tranquility, relaxation, serenity, quiet, privacy and romance. Imagine instead of slumping in front of the television, you soak up the scents of delicious, heady flowers. Blooms need to open at night to be viewed by moonlight, white flowers glow accompanied by silver foliage plants. Many night bloomers are poisonous.

When creating a moon garden, check the path of the moon; many moon gardens are created to find the moon never shines on them. Facing east will see the rising moon, and remember not to plan your garden where large trees surround it. The shadows cast will spoil the effect. Plan your garden where you can sit and admire. Plant close to a patio where you can enjoy the fragance wafting through the evening air. The tapestry of texture and colour and the scent will weave a magical spell. Perfect for night owls, party goers and insomniacs not to mention moon worshippers.
As other areas of the garden recede, moon gardens awaken. These gardens shimmer and shine by the light of the silvery moon.

In the U.S. moon gardens were popular in the nineteenth century in New England. The first documented moon garden in the U.S. was created in Massachusetts in 1833. Two enormous borders, each 700ft long by 12ft wide were filled with white flowered plants.

Other examples on a white theme are China's white sand and pond meditation gardens. India's 'Mahtab Bagh' created for Shah Jahan in 1639 to the most famous white garden of all, Vita Sackville's white garden at Sissinghurst in Kent, England.

The Taj Mahal must be one of the most romantic and mysterious of monuments, appearing as one of the most beautiful palaces, the Taj is in fact a tomb. Mahtab Bagh, now lost, was a purpose-built night garden across the river from the Taj. In plan, proportion and alignment it mimics the gardens of the Taj itself. The garden was a vision of paradise on earth. Its central, octagonal pool held the reflection of the Taj on moonlit nights. The aromatic moonlight garden was a Hindu concept.

I chose slivers of moon for the borders each surrounding part of a circle which represents the full moon. Crescent moons and full moons are filled with white flowers and silver grey leaves. The two quarter moons either side of the centre are seating. This garden is encased in silver hedging in the form of Lavandula, Leucophyta or Santolina. Variegated Buxus would be an alternative.
The garden is sited in the path of the moon, where trees cannot inhibit the glow. Many night-flowering forms are found here; asleep during the day, they glow at night, shining like spectres in the garden. Any night owl would welcome a chance to sit and enjoy this moon garden. Flowers appear whiter and non-white parts, such as the cones on Echinacea recede. New developments in white foliaged plants have led to companions in leaf for this type of scheme. Try Hosta and Liriope and add Caladium in summer or in warmer areas.

At first the plant just ghostly, becomes a whiter shade of pale.

Sedum 'Cape Blanco'

The purpose of evening opening flowers is to attract pollinators, these plants are usually pollinated by moths or other flying insects or mammals. Butterflies will be attracted to the garden too in the daytime especially if white *Buddleja*, not surprisingly called butterfly bush and white *Zinnia* are grown.

The flowers of *Ipomoea alba*, the aptly-named giant white moonflower are shut tight in daytime, opening their petals at dusk and staying open usually until nine in the morning. What a party goer. Clearly seen by moonlight, their delicate, lemon scent also fills the air. At its feet grow the sweet-scented night tobacco, *Nicotiana alata* whose pure white trumpets, 7-10cm (3-4") long open during the evening. *Nicotiana sylvestris* is another tobacco worthy of addition in this setting. Growing them is another kind of addiction, but not at all harmful to your health, but restful to the mind and spirit. The large showy, white flowers of *Datura inoxia* open at night, sometimes up to 20 blooms can open of an evening. Give the *Datura* some room. Both *Datura* and *Ipomoea* are fascinating to watch unfurl, they should be at the top of anyone's list for a moon garden. *Datura* trumpets can be 20cm (8") long and are sometimes scented. These tender perennials are often grown as an annual, but can be cut back and overwintered under glass. Night *Phlox*, *Zaluzianskya* is an excellent choice with its own unusual fragrance, successional sowings and weaving the plant throughout the garden works well. Night bloomers also include *Oenothera*, the tender cactus species *Cereus*, some tropical night blooming water lilies if you are in a warm zone and if you are in that zone a white flowered *Hibiscus* will thrill. *Matthiola longipetala*, night-scented stocks are more suited to cooler areas.

Annual or perennial *Iberis*, candytuft makes attractive mounds and will form good groundcover. The fragrant, long blooms of *Mirabilis longiflora*, sweet four o'clock plant, open in the evening. *Cestrum nocturnum*, even though the flowers of Queen of the Night are nothing to get excited about, will earn its living in fragrance alone. Scent is part of the mystery of the night-blooming garden, the perfume seems more intense by moonlight, the white of the flowers stronger, magic is in the air. White climbing roses, Rosa 'Iceberg' add a touch of romance and elegance. *Miscanthus* 'Morning Light' adds a silver touch to lift the planting into the realm of fairies and dreams. Add a touch of water to the garden, a water flute will add music; a calming effect is thereby achieved. A small pond can reflect the moon. The silvery quality of water is an important part of a white garden. *Sarracenia leucophylla* is great in boggy ground and really will look wonderful by moonlight. Add *Hosta,* especially those with white flowers or the newer white-leaved varieties.

Choose a broad variety of annuals, perennials, shrubs and trees for a long season effect. White bulbs will brighten spring and provide an understory for awakening shrubs and herbaceous perennials. Starting with snowdrops as the harbinger of spring, followed by white *Crocus, Muscari, Narcissus, Scilla* and *Tulipa, Leucojum, Galtonia* and *Nerine* in summer and white *Colchicum* in autumn. *Cleome* will add texture with its spines and white flowerheads, *Gyposphila* for an airy cloud, Oriental lily, *Lilium* 'Casablanca' for purity, *Gaura lindheimeri* 'The Bride' for innocence, *Dicentra spectabilis* 'Alba' white dancing ladies like pearls on a string, night-flowering *Hemerocallis*, the daylilies are for beauty, blowsy *Petunia* well for sheer blowsiness. Climbers include white *Lonicera, Jasminum,* which I simply cannot live without and *Clematis* all with their own perfume. Try to separate strong perfumes, just as you would not yourself wear 'Chanel No. 5', 'Ana Sui' and Worth's 'Je Reviens' together, the garden cannot handle too many confusing fragrances. Use winter bark for a stunning effect in this stark season. *Betula* and *Ribes* will add a sparkle to the winterscape. *Artemisia* will not only add silver foliage, but texture too, *Santolina* and *Senecio cineraria* will serve the same purpose, as will *Salvia apiana*. However, now it is not just silver foliage that can enhance the white or moon garden, one can add incredible white-leaved plants in the shape of *Liriope, Ophiopogon, Caladium* and *Hosta*.

Blue can shine just as glowingly. Pale yellow can have great effect too. A superb look is had by planting golden leaved trees such as *Acer plantanoides* 'Princeton Gold' and *Ginkgo biloba* 'Autumn Gold' which glow in the dark even by just a little moonlight. Downlighting can have the same effect as moonlight. I like the thought of garden flames or candles too on moonless nights. Designer extras could include a Moon bridge.

No garden or space? Create your moon garden in a large container, window box or hanging basket. White *Impatiens, Petunia* and silver-white *Lamium* with trailing *Helichrysum petiolare* look just fine. Pale pinks will work well in this combination and will reflect moonlight too. *Heliotropium* is available in white and excellent in pots by the door or on the patio where you can appreciate its vanilla scent. Another favourite pot plant is *Lilium regale* 'Album', I have often swooned to the exquisite scent of this on my patio and it is much admired by my neighbour too. Allow your garden to glow at night, sit back, relax and enjoy the sparkle and sizzle of a moonlit garden.

If you love someone all the way to the moon and back, but too high the moon, create a moon garden in your own yard

WHITE GARDEN

White, white still as the night. What is it about the purity and innocence of white flowers that can stop you in your tracks?

The most famous white garden and perhaps the most inspiring garden of all time, much copied, is Vita Sackville's white garden created at Sissinghurst Castle and kept up-to-date. Vita was not the first to pull off a white garden, but the way she did it superceded what had gone before and it has remained Queen of white gardens.

The parterre of box hedges are the perfect backdrop for the white garden; green adds something and takes nothing away except the starkness.

White can look washed out in the heat of midday, so plant for effect at dawn and dusk. Silent walks alone are what moon gardens are made for, for contemplation of one's inner self.

Gardenia is ravishingly fragrant, undesirably difficult. Gardeners always tread where wise men fear to go, knowing an angel is at hand, watching over God's land. A *Gardenia* for marginal zones 6 and 7, is G. 'Chuck Hayes' a double. In mild areas, *Gardenia* can remain open all night long.

White *Magnolia* add structure and elegance when in flower, *Camellia* add a touch of upper class refinery, romantic white roses add fragrance as well as romance, such as one of my favourites *Rosa 'Iceberg'*. *Romneya coulteri* and the epitome of elegance, *Zantedeschia aethiopica* are also must-haves in a white garden.

So many white flowers these days, add silvery *Stipa barbata* and silver foliage to link plants. A touch of pale silver blue in the guise of *Eryngium* and *Festuca glauca*. Large white *Lilium* (lilies), *Papaver* (poppies) and *Cosmos* are wonderful. A little wearing on the eye, all white needs a subtle partner in the shade of pale lemon or blue or stunning black for a contemporary touch.

I adore Dicentra spectabilis 'Alba', any starkness in white flowers can be tempered by the addition of grey foliage, here Cynara and Artemisia perform the task admirably.
Below: the author's watercolour of Zantedeschia aethiopica

THE URBAN GARDEN

The busy town gardener needs a low maintenace garden with easy care plants. This simple design caters for four borders brimming with easy plants and a central stunning design to catch the eye. Seating and a water feature add extra dimensions.

There is no better silver tree than *Pyrus salicifolia*, so handsome and debonair in its sweeping foliage that sways in the breeze. With clear 1.5-2m (5-8ft) stems it allows plenty of light into the garden. There is a natural look to this plant, it belongs in the garden with natural drifts of silver, grey and purple and a hint of black amply provided by plants chosen for colour and texture. Here I have combined it stunningly with *Ophiopogon* and if you really want to set the garden on fire, don't paint it red, just plant these two with breath taking *Liriope 'Okina'*.

Keep the edges of the four borders soft. It is up to you whether you create four identical corners or whether you go for four different looks. Safe is found in sameness. *Astelia* makes a dramatic statement at the end of the garden. Two pots by the bench are full of white flowers with *Helichrysum petiolare* trailing over the sides and tumbling down the pot. The water feature is enhanced with plants and a wall statue.

Heuchera shimmer in the garden and can make colour echoes with reds or solid silvers and greens.

Sun loving Santolina chamaecyparissus, Hebe pinguifolia, Lavandula lanata and Senecio cineraria for the greys through silver to almost white. Berberis thunbergii 'Atropurpurea Nana', Aeonium arboreum 'Zwartkop', Iris germanica 'Deep Black', Papaver 'Patty's Plum' and Allium 'Purple Sensation' mingle with Alcea rosea 'Nigra', Angelica 'Vicar's Mead' and Scabiosa 'Chile Black' for the purple to black. Colouring and texture are further enhanced by grasses and grass-like plants, the stiff spider-like Ophiopogon planiscapus 'Nigrescens' and Astelia 'Silver Spear', Phormium 'Platt's Black' and soft swathes of Hordeum jubatum. Variegated grasses such as Arrhenatherum, Carex and Ophiopogon add interest. The striking architectural Cynara cardunculus plays an eye-catching role and Foeniculum vulgare 'Purpureum' provides a fuzz of bronzed foliage. Beneath the Pyrus drifts of Athyrium niponicum 'Silver Ghost' and A. niponicum v pictum echo the colouring with the darkest Helleborus available.

GEOMETRIC POWER

Some town gardens are mainly paved. If you have one of these gardens and still want lots of plants in borders instead of pot plants, go for raised beds to achieve the look. Geometric shapes are powerful, yet so easy to create.

Start in the centre of the plot with a square. I used *Ophiopogon planiscapus 'Nigrescens'* but *Liriope* would give a different look. My darkest and most beloved of grass-like plants contains a circle of *Lavandula 'Goodwin Creek Grey'* for the beautiful grey leaves. The tiny mauve bells of the mondo grass go nicely with the flowers of the lavender. The mondo grass could be underplanted with *Lamium.* For the larger square choose something grey and fairly short. *Cerastium tomentosum* or *Senecio cineraria*, give a bedding effect which I would rather avoid. *Convolvulus cneorum* looks wonderful and much more refined but remember it is tender. At each corner add a touch of blue in the shape of clipped *Juniperus* or *Chamaecyparis.*

At either end is a triangle of *Plectranthus argentatus* with its velvet-like, soft silvered leaves, bordered by *Hebe pinguifolia*. Alternatives for shade include *Athyrium, Heuchera, blue Hosta, Arisaema, Asarum, Arum* and *Corydalis.*

The shimmering silvery foliage of Heuchera 'Stormy Seas' combines well with Acer palmatum Atropurpureum Group

POLAR WHITE

The winter white garden is icy but not frigid. Its versatile foliage offers luxury and warmth, its texture is comforting. This garden really comes into its own in winter, with ice on the ground and frost on the foliage. Your garden is capable of becoming a winter wonderland.

The chief protagonists in this setting are conifers. Include different types for the different texture and shades of silver from mounds, cones and creeping types. The blue spruces and junipers will also look handsome here. Dramatic foliage is enhanced by frost and even a light covering of snow. The outline and silhouette afforded by a group of conifers is well worth the effort of giving consideration to siting. Make the conifer bed an island bed, viewed from all sides for maximum impact. Underplant with white-flowered *Erica*, winter heaths and add *Helleborus niger* for its creamy winter blooms. The silver foliage of some *Helleborus* is a great addition too. A silver *Ilex*, holly would also work well in this scheme, or two as you need a male and female for berries. They are valuable for adding contrasting, spiky texture.

The foliage is soft and touchable for the main part, so one can add hardscaping in the form of stainless steel and metal. It is then possible to soften the furniture with cushions in shades of grey. Choose large Mexican grey pebbles and dark grey slate for paths and features by a pond.

In raised bedding, winter flowering *Sarcococca* will add its scent and small, white flowers. The very silvered foliage of *Astelia 'Silver Spear'* makes an upright accent throughout the year in all but the coldest areas.

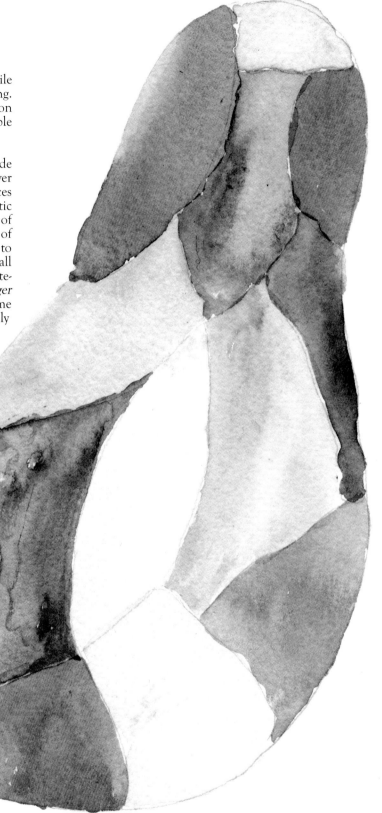

THE HERBACEOUS BORDER

Plant lovers who have to have flowers and long for lush scenery will still opt for the tried and tested herbaceous border, the epitome of the English garden. They tend to be labour intensive, so you need to be a keen gardener to keep this style in tip-top condition and looking at its best. A well-kept herbaceous border in cool greens, icy whites and silver is tremendous.

Variegated plants sit nicely tying the colours together handsomely. *Cornus alba 'Variegata'* is a must-have in this situation planted about half way along the border. *Pyrus salicifolia* or *Salix lanata* make a focal point at each end of the border or use a variegated *Acer*. Fill the border in fluid style with a variety of texture, shape and size and beautiful white flowers.

SHINING IN SHADE

Silver is so excellent for brightening shady areas of the garden. At ground level, plant *Pulmonaria, Asarum* or *Lamium* to make superb, shining silver carpets. Enjoying light shade and making a spectacular display are the *Arisaemas* with silver markings on their leaves. Handsome woodland companions include *Trillium* with their silver-green mottled leaves. In flower we find *Digitalis purpurea 'Alba'* will relish these conditions forming colonies of white spires alongside *Veratrum album*. *Betula* is perfect for its white trunk will focus the eye.

In the author's garden silver Artemisia sits at the side of bluish Eucalyptus gunnii. At their feet are Lamium 'Beacon Silver' and Brunnera 'Jack Frost'

The Herbaceous border is much loved by the English gardener and is often thought of as the very epitome of English gardening.

It is labour intensive, but when well done, you would not notice the thought that has gone into layout, colour and the never-ending succession of flower and foliage that appear like magic all season long until they have earned their rest.

There are a few key tips to getting it right:

Choose your colour scheme carefully, for our purpose here, we are thinking of silver, grey and white, perhaps with the addition of pastels, a touch of blue or black. You could also opt for a touch of red.
The height of plants need to flow in rhythm, rather like a wave. Do not be afraid to plant something quite large near the front of the border.
Plants should not be in regimented lines, but in drifts.
If any plants are summer dormant, be prepared to have something to cover the gap.
Always have plenty of standby plants in pots to fill any area which looks ratty, bedraggled or empty.
Make a break to blot some of the view about half way down the border.

This border is backed by a dark yew hedge which helps the variegated white and green plants and the silvers to stand out.

Clematis montana 'Alba' and Hedera clamber up and clothe the hedge. To either end of the border Cornus alba 'Elegantissima' makes a graceful stand, beneath it in the shade it casts sits handsome variegated white and green Hosta such as H. 'Fire and Ice', or one of the new white foliaged ones such as 'Mostly Ghostly'. Behind is a variegated Iris and behind this a white climbing rose, Rosa 'Iceberg'. A large mound of Artemisia announces its presence with a delicate filigree echoed in lacy Tanacetum haradjanii to the foreground against the solid, strap-like leaves of Astelia 'Silver Spear'. Taking centre stage is the magnificence that is Cynara cardunculus with Hosta 'Silver Scrolls' in the foreground.

Above left: Begonia 'Looking Glass'
Above right: Catalpa speciosa 'Pulverulenta'
Below right: Sorbus wardii
Below: Persicaria 'Red Dragon'

PLANT PROFILES

SOLID SILVER

A sea of silver plants at Eden

ABIES

Long-lived, fast-growing conifers for cooler regions. The firs are highly ornamental in their elegant, pyramidal, symmetrical habit. Young specimens branch almost to the ground; older plants are superb for large landscapes. They make effective silver Christmas trees on rooted stock.

HOW TO GROW
Add organic matter before planting. Abies will tolerate part shade, but full sun is best. Protect from drying winds. Prefer a slightly acidic, moist but well-drained soil. Needle-drop may occur in alkaline soils. They perform poorly in clay or wet soil. Do not prune since they will not sprout new growth. Take out a double leader if one forms. Intolerant of pollution, but the white firs are the most drought and heat tolerant. Z3-7. Korean firs Z5.

A. concolor 'Albospica' emerges whitish with needles fading to grey-green. The ornamental white firs keep their older branches and are more adaptable than other firs.
A. concolor 'Argentea' ('Candicans') bears long, brush-like glaucous silver needles. This extra silvery form often occurs in seedbeds. It is known as the Silver White Fir. Growth is slightly slower than the species. 3m (10ft).
A. concolor 'Swift's Silver' has recurved needles showing off the white underside. 1.2m (4ft). Z4.
A. delavayi 'Forrestii' is a slow growing form that bears dark green leaves with a very silvery reverse.
A. delavayi 'Nana' was originally found at Hillier Nursery. It bears dark green leaves with a bright silver reverse.
A. grandis 'Van Dedem's Dwarf' is a striking globose bush which often matures into a conical shape. Its dark green leaves have a silver reverse.
A. koreana 'Kohout' makes a small hummock of recurved leaves displaying their silver undersides.
A. koreana 'Nadelkissen' is slower than 'Silbermavers' but similar making a mushroom-shaped bush.
A. koreana 'Silberkugel' ('Hexenbesen Wustemeyer No.1') (1986) is a miniature dome of silver-green needles. The branches twist slightly and become flat-topped with age. A tiny plant for troughs or the rock garden. 10cm (4").
A. koreana 'Silberlocke' (Horstmann 1979) small green, recurved needles show off silver stomata giving a frosted appearance. Leaves look like they have been in the curling tongs! Grows at the Atlanta Botanic Garden where it takes the heat in just a little shade. Train into a pyramid suitable for a rock garden. A showstopper when the purple cones are evident. Plants on their own rootstock keep their colour better as they mature. Seed is said to come true and best colour is had in poor soil in full sun. 90cm (3ft). Z5.
A. koreana 'Silbermavers' makes a neat, tiny bun of silvery foliage. Extremely slow growing, tortoise move at the speed of lightning in comparison. Of German origin, but introduced by Hoey van Smith in 1898. 15x10cm (6x4").

A. koreana 'Silberperl' (1986) ('Hexenbessen Horstman') This miniature globe is suitable for a rock garden or trough, eventually forming a neat pyramid. Green needles exhibit a silver reverse. 10cm (4").
A. koreana 'Silberreif' is faster than 'Silberlocke' making a dwarf conical. Z6.
A. koreana 'Silberschmeltzer' is a slow-growing, upright, conical bush with green needles curved to show the silver undersides. May need training to encourage a leading shoot. 1.2m (4ft).
A. koreana 'Silberzwerg' shows good silver colouring on the underside, being very similar to 'Silberperl'.
A. koreana 'Silver Show' (Wittboldt-Muller) is quite a vigorous grower and very showy. Similar to 'Silberlocke'. Seed is said to come true. 1.8m (6ft).
A. lasiocarpa v arizonica 'Argentea' is typically extremely slow growing and cultivated forms are usually grafted onto speedier rootstock. Rocky Mountain Fir is the most silvered form. It appreciates moist soil; making slow growth, only a few centimetres per year, but will eventually reach 10m (30ft).
A. magnifica 'Shastensis' is known as the silver tip tree. Needles grow vertically on handsome branches on this tight little miniature. 1.2m (4ft).
A. veitchii 'Hedergott' is a flat-topped plant with curved leaves showing a silver underside. 25cm (10") in 10 years.
Cool Companion: Blue *Juniperus, Festuca, Cassiope*.
Hot Partner: Hot pink *Erica carnea*.

Abies concolor 'Argentea'

ACACIA

For all but the coldest areas, acacia brings a touch of summer to the garden with bright yellow flowers and silver-white leaves. These valuable winter colour, drought loving shrubs are superb in a conservatory in colder areas.

HOW TO GROW
Full sun is essential. Low water requirements. Sheltered spot in cool areas and a well-drained site. Young trees are very susceptible to frost. Unsuitable for clay, otherwise unfussy as to soil. Z9-11.

A. aneura is an ornamental shrub with narrow, pendulous grey leaves and yellow flowers in winter to spring. It is frost and lime tolerant and prefers a hot, dry site. 6m (20ft).
A. binervia coastal myall, is native to Australia. Happy in a range of soils, it prefers clay loam. A long-lived species whose dark, furrowed bark accentuates the glaucous, silver leaves. A large shrub or tree to 15m (45ft).
A. buxifolia is an ornamental with grey-green leaves against reddish branches and yellow globose flowers in spring. It will tolerate short periods of waterlogging. A fast growing shrub which needs protection from strong winds. 2-3m (8-12ft).
A. chinchillensis is a fast-growing, ornamental, low shrub with grey-green, bipinnate leaves and yellow ball flowers in winter to spring. Good for containers. 90cm-1.8m (3-6ft).
A. dealbata is the silver wattle, grown for its soft, feathery, fern-like, grey-green leaves on silver stems and rounded puffs of yellow flowers, which appear in January to February. Smooth grey bark when young, deeply fissured as it matures. A bushy shrub when young, needing a sheltered, sunny spot that is a must in a well-drained site. It can be pruned to maintain a compact size. 15m (50ft). Established trees can withstand temperatures to -7°C.
A. ligulata bears narrow grey leaves on a dense, large shrub. Yellow flowers are borne almost all year, but are at their most profuse in spring. Makes a fast growing screen and apparently is a favourite food of camels. 2-3m (10ft).
A. mollifolia is an attractive species known as velvet acacia for its ferny, grey-green foliage making a tall, silvery shrub or small tree. Yellow pompom flowers in winter to spring. 4-10m (16-30ft).
A. podalyriifolia is smaller. Considered to be one of the best for general cultivation. Its broad, oval silvery white foliage stands out against a darker background and is highly attractive. The Queensland silver wattle bears fragrant golden flowers in late winter and early spring. Leave it to grow to its natural, bushy shape or prune as desired. Excellent for cut flower or foliage. Fast growing to 1.8-2.2m (6-9ft)

ACHILLEA

Tolerant of dry conditions, these are an admirable, long-flowering addition to the Mediterranean-style, dry garden. Excellent for cutting and drying.

HOW TO GROW
Full sun in an open site and well-drained soil. Can grow in poor or heavy soil. Deadhead to rebloom in September.

A. ageratifolia bears narrow, deeply toothed, silver leaves beneath white flowers. 3cmx10cm (1x4").
A. 'Apfelblute' (Appleblossom) bears rosy flowers which fade with age over grey-green feathery foliage. 75cm (30").
A. argentea h. (clavennae, umbellata) has light grey-green leaves with silvery hairs. A mat-forming, trailing species with heads of attractive white flowers. This native of the Alps is an easy plant for a rock garden. A lovely ornamental variety, much favoured by Gertrude Jekyll. It is one of the most silver of the Achilleas.15cm (6"). Z5-9.
A. clypeolata has attractive grey foliage with yellow flowers. Its habit is more open than the hybrids. 50cm (20").
A. 'Hoffnung' ('Great Expectations') has finely divided grey leaves, well-matched by lovely pastel yellow-cream flowerheads. Z4. 60cm (2ft).
A. 'Huteri' bears white flowers over clumps of silver-grey leaves in early summer. 15cm (6").
A. x kellereri this sun lover bears long toothed silvered leaves and tiny, white flowers. 15x20cm (6x8").
A. 'Martina' bears large, pale yellow flower plates over the silver-green feathery foliage. 75-90cm (30-36").
A. 'Moonshine' (A. clypeolata x A. taygetea) makes a show of finely dissected grey-green leaves. Bright yellow flowers can be repeat flowering if deadheaded. Attractive, eye-catching colour for the front of the border. 60cm (2ft).
A. tomentosa bears soft, fuzzy grey-green leaves and very bright yellow flowers. The small leaves are soft and felted. 60cm (2ft).
A. tomentosa 'King Edward' the tomentose foliage of this plant gives a silvery appearance. Ferny and aromatic, it is topped by flat clusters of admirable, primrose flowers. Makes good ground cover or a rock garden plant, tolerant of heat and drought. Place this summer flowering perennial in full sun in well-drained soil. It looks beautiful on a dry bank. It will perfom in desert areas such as Phoenix, Arizona with moderate watering. 25cm (10"). Z4.
For the white garden, **A. ptarmica 'The Pearl'** is unbeatable for its white button pearls. 70cm (28").
Cool Companion: Grow *Achillea 'Moonshine'* with *Eryngium maritimum, Dianthus, Miscanthus sinensis 'Gracillimus', Artemisia.*
Hot Partner: *Euphorbia dulcis 'Chameleon'.*

Acacia dealbata

ADENANTHOS

Hardy shrubs belonging to the Protea family are suitable for the dry garden and also make a useful screen in coastal gardens. Related to *Grevillea*, their only natural habitat is confined to Western Australia.

HOW TO GROW
Full sun or partial shade in well-drained soil. Occasional deep watering once established. Tolerant of alkaline soil. Propagate by cuttings in spring, plunged into sandy soil. Hardy to -20°F.

A. drummondii is known as Woollybush for its low growing grey foliage. Pink-red flowers are inconspicuous. Makes a low screen. 90-120cm (3-4ft) height and spread.
A. sericeus is a large grey shrub or small tree with intensely silky leaves and striking bright red blossoms resembling those of *Anigozanthos*. 2-2.5m (8-10ft).

AECHMEA

Fabulous Brazilian bromeliad. Statuesque as a vase can be.

HOW TO GROW
The rosette needs to be slightly moist but well-drained. Allow to dry out a little in between watering into the urn. Bright light, but avoid direct sunlight in free-draining epiphytic soil. Fertilize from spring to summer at half strength. 20-30°C (68-86°F). It can tolerate 12°C (54°F) but do not expect flowers or much growth at this temperature. It will not tolerate frost. Z10-12.

A. fasciata is known as the silver vase plant. Impressive pink bracts and smallish blue flowers are produced at the end of summer to winter. Green-grey leaves with silver banding having small spines at the margins. After flowering, the plant dies, usually leaving offsets which can be potted up. Tolerates shade. 50-60cm (20-24").
A. fasciata 'Primera' is a smooth leaved form of the above.
A. nudicaulis 'Silver Streak' is similar, but its flowers are usually yellow.

AGAVE

Architectural succulents for dry gardens. In pots, these are best used as accent plants in the summer garden. The century plant dies after flowering, leaving offsets. It is widely cultivated in the Mediterranean. It was described by Linnaeus in 1753.

HOW TO GROW
Full sun with reflected heat and good drainage. It is tolerant of shallow soils and some shade. Drought tolerant but it responds well to a deep watering once a month in summer. Cold damage is persistent and unattractive, this plant is hardy to Z8. It will survive outdoors in London and the south coast of England in pots or in the garden. Propagate by seed or offsets. Minimal maintenance but large, dead plants are not easy to remove.
N.B. Agave juice is acidic and can burn.

A. americana bears broad leaves of a subtle silver-blue with sharp spines. A hardy evergreen capable of grabbing attention year-round. Size can be restricted when growing in pots. A mature flowering specimen of 10 years old carries its yellow flowers at the end of branches on long 5m (20ft) stems. 1.8m (6ft) with a spread of 2m (8ft).

Above left: Achillea argentea is often classified as Tanacetum
Below: The bluish green leaves of Agave americana are a wonderful complement to silver in the garden

ALKANNA

A choice alpine for a crevice in the rock garden.

HOW TO GROW
Well-drained soil in full sun. Protect against winter wet in the alpine house. Divide or sow seed in spring.

A. oreodoxa is a Turkish species with white, tomentose leaves and white flowers in summer.

ALYSSUM

Forget the one you usually see in British front gardens, here are some choice alpines to grace the rock garden and these tiny gems are much appreciated in a trough.

HOW TO GROW
Good drainage in ordinary to sandy, dry soil in full sun. Flourish in poor soil. Sow seed in spring.

A. caespitosum is a superb trough plant bearing the tiniest silver leaves topped with yellow flowers. 3x10cm (1x4").
A. cuneifolium bears tiny silver leaves and soft yellow flowers. 3x5cm (1x2").
A. lesbicum is a smaller version of **A. markgrafii** with extremely fine foliage making silver mounds covered in golden flowers. 15x25cm (6x10").
A. markgrafii fine grey leaves on upright plants with yellow flowers which cope with hard frost. 30x30cm (12x12").
A. pateri makes small mats of grey foliage with yellow flowers on 5cm (2") stems.
A. stribrnyi is one of the tiniest of plants, silver leaves in domes and soft yellow flowers to just 1x10cm (.5x4"). Offering year round interest in the xeric garden.
A. tortuosum intensely silver leaves are carried on contorted, woody stems. This outstanding trough plant bears yellow flowers in May. 10-20cm (4x8").
A. wulfenianum makes a compact mound of silver-grey foliage and soft yellow flowers. Usually long-lived. 10x20cm (4x8"). Z4.
Hot Partner: *Ajuga, Androsace, Achillea.*

ANAPHALIS

At their best in the wildflower garden, the pearly everlastings add a grey-green colouring to the palette of brighter wildflowers. Attractive to bees and butterflies.

HOW TO GROW
Grow in sun to part shade in moist but well-drained soil. Z4-8.

A. alpicola makes tiny mats of silver leaves with white, pink and black blooms on a petite alpine.
A. margaritacea is known by the name of pearly everlasting. An attractive perennial plant in early summer, but once it loses its silvery quality in leaf and turns grey-green, I do not find it attractive. White daisies with a central yellow disc make a good dried flower. Worth looking at close-up, these are extraordinarily beautiful white pearls. It can be subject to mildew.
C. nepalensis bears lanate leaves with white flowers in late summer. 15-30cm (6-12").
A. sinica 'Moon's Silver' makes neat clumps of rounded grey-white foliage with white everlasting flowers. It has a vigorous, suckering habit. 20cm (8").
A. triplinervis 'Sommerschnee' has intensely silver leaves with bunched heads of small white flowers. 75cm (30").
Cool Companion: *Plectranthus argentatus, Lavandula dentata v candicans*
Hot Partner: *Sedum 'Autumn Joy'.*

Above left: Alkanna oreodoxa
Below: Anaphalis margaritacea in October

ANDROSACE

Choice alpines, rock jasmine are sometimes challenging but always worthwhile. Usually ground hugging and handsome in both foliage and flower.

HOW TO GROW
Full sun to partial shade in well-drained soil. Often best in rocky crevices. Z3.

A. barbulata makes a slow-growing cushion of silver, woolly mats having white blooms in spring with some sporadic reblooming. Hardy and long-lived. 5x15cm (2x6").
A. chamaejasme bears small rosettes covered in silvery hairs in tight clumps. Cream flowers with a bright yellow eye which turn blood red after pollination are borne on short, hairy stems in spring and summer. Flowers are occasionally primrose yellow. When not overfed the foliage takes on the most beautiful red tones in autumn. Sweet flowered rock jasmine is a challenging species for a raised bed, scree or trough. 2x10cm (1x4").
A. dasyphylla makes low rosettes of woolly grey-green, silky foliage and white blooms with a yellow eye that turn deep rose on pollination. Similar to *A. villosa*. 8x20cm (3x8").
A. incana bears hairy, grey-green leaves forming attractive open mats with white flowers in late spring. 10cm (4").
A. lanuginosa is a choice Himalayan species. Its silvery-green shoots spread into silky mats with short, stiff stems bearing bright pink, fragrant blooms in late spring to early summer. Easy, reliable and very hardy. 8x30cm (3x12").
A. muscoidea f longiscapa has long silvery hairs on globular, silver domes. Very short stems bear white flowers. A must have Himalayan species. 5x15cm (2x6").
A. nivalis Chumstick Mountain Form bears grey foliage and large, deep pink flowers.
A. robusta v breviscapa bears dense mounds of silver hairy rosettes with a frosted appearance. It bears large white flowers with a yellow eye.
A. sarmentosa 'Sheriffii' makes soft, silver-green spreading mats. Short, stiff stems bear pale pink blooms in late spring to summer. Easy in a rock garden. 8x45cm (3x18").
A. sericea makes small silver-white, hairy cushions. Almost stemless umbels of pinkish flowers are borne on this exotic looking species from the dry alpine steppes of China. 8x20cm (3x8").
A. vandellii forms tiny cushions of tiny, silvered leaves covered with white flowers with a yellow eye on short stems. 5cm (2").
A. villosa v arachnoidea bears small rounded rosettes swathed in silken hairs in cold weather giving a silver appearance. White flowers with a yellow eye which turn pink on pollination. The foliage is often suffused pink, giving a rosy appearance to the whole plant. A choice variety from the S. Europe mountains. Easy to grow in trough, tufa or raised bed. 5x15cm (2x6").

Andryala aghardii

ANDRYALA

Another little alpine in silvery tones. Good drainage in gritty soil in full sun. Give overwinter protection. Z4.

A. aghardii makes a basal clump of silvery, narrow leaves. Yellow daises rather spoil the show for me. 15cm (6").

ANTENNARIA

Woolly leaves and pearly everlasting flowers are the attributes of the hardy, herbaceous *Antennaria*, known as pussy toes. Drought tolerant alpines suitable for edging or the rock garden. Seedheads are fluffy. Dry, light, well-drained soil in full sun. Divide in spring. Z4-7.

A. argentea is a Californian native bearing upright tufts of greyish green leaves and creamish white flowers.
A. dioica 'Pink Chenille' is a selection from Japan, notable for its bright pink flowers, soft and silky to the touch above the silvery grey mats of ground-hugging foliage.
A. margaritacea bears woolly leaves with white flowers. Naturalised in England, it was introduced in the 1600's.
A. media has felted grey foliage. A real miniature suitable for alpine scree. 5cm (2").
A. neglecta ssp gaspensis makes a superb trailer for a trough with its very silvered, tiny leaves and white flowers. 1x15cm (1x6").
A. tomentosa is one the best, a real tiny gem forming dense carpets of silver leaves to just 2cm (1").
A. triplinervis from Nepal is similar to *A. margaritacea* yet much prettier but rarer.

ANTHEMIS

A. biebersteinii bears finely divided, silver foliage with little yellow, daisy flowers. 20cm (8").
A. cretica bears silvered leaves, white daisies and is a reliable perennial that blooms almost continually.
A. cretica carpatica small white daises adorn this silvery creeper, which is handsome in a trough. 15x20cm (6x8").

Artemisia 'Powis Castle'

Artemisia absinthium

Artemisia

Artemisia 'Silver Queen'

47

ARTEMISIA

Named for the ancient Greek goddess of the moon, and highy suited to the moon garden, silver varieties shimmer. Excellent foil plants offering wonderful foliage in a variety of types including lacy. Combine these diverse, herbaceous perennials with dark foliage for a stunning effect. A must in a white garden. They are also a great foil to bright yellow and pastels. A perfect companion for bright coloured flowers and equally effective with other silver or glaucous foliage. These drought tolerant plants are suitable for xeriscaping. The tougher the plant, the more invasive so for no-overtaking, use a root barrier. Many will not set seed in cooler climates. Glorious in the right setting, though often not for smaller gardens, and not for the gardener who does not want to trim back unruly plants that outgrow their welcome every year. There are some fine cultivars suitable for perennial borders, rock gardens, containers and often found in the herb garden. Forget the flowers, these are foliage plants. Lace with staying power. Many are scented, making them an excellent subject for fresh, herbal wreaths. A great genus, with differing sizes, woody or herbaceous, clumping or rhizomatous, bushy, upright, low or groundhugging from an array of plant habits, all enjoying sun in well-drained soil.

HOW TO GROW
Low maintenance plants in dryish soils in full sun. Drainage is very important, overwatering will lead to rotting. Soils must be very free draining in winter. Deadhead. Do not overfertilize. Propagate by cuttings in late spring or early summer. At least Z4.
See also *Seriphidium*.

A. absinthium was once used to flavour alcohol, its use is now prohibited and it is better known these days as a moth repellent when leaves are dried. This plant is mentioned in the Bible. 90cm (36"). Z3-9.
A. absinthium 'Huntington' ('Huntingdon') needs shearing over in spring to remain small and neat. Deeply incised silvery grey foliage has a frilly effect. A robust wormwood with coarse foliage, larger than 'Powis Castle'. 120cm (48") but can easily be 1.8m (6ft) both ways. Z5-6.
A. absinthium 'Lambrook Giant' originated with Margery Fish as with other Lambrook cultivars. It is grown for its handsome, silver leaves. 90cm (36").
A. absinthium 'Lambrook Mist' is a good cultivar with deeply cut, lacy silver leaves. Very striking and highly useful for feathery contrast with solid leaves. 75cm (30").
A. absinthium 'Lambrook Silver' is one of the best of this bunch, both decorative and aromatic. Deeply incised silver leaves on woody stems make a handsome, neat bush of silver showers which is long-lived. Its delicate, airy appearance and good silver colouring combine excellently with red or bronze foliage. 90cm (36").

A. absinthium 'Silver Frost' is a dwarf variety that is handsome as edging, reaching just 40cm (16").
A. alba 'Canescens' this clump-forming, semi-evergreen perennial bears a cloud of silver filigree foliage almost like grey bottlebrushes. Unlike many, this is well-behaved and retains a neat shape with a dainty air. 45cm (18").
A. arborescens is a very large shrubby species, capable of reaching immense proportions. Cut off the unsightly flowers to enjoy the foliage impact. The source of many cultivars, the species has slightly larger and whiter leaves. 2m (8ft) height and spread.
A. arborescens 'Faith Raven' is a cold hardy variety, collected by John Raven in Crete. Attractive feathery leaves are elegant and evergrey. Leafy panicles of creamy yellow flowers appear in July to August. One of the few silver shrubs that perform in Sydney, Australia. 60-90cm (2-3ft).
A. arborescens 'Little Mice' has finely cut, grey-green foliage. 35cm (14").
A. arborescens 'Porquerolles' is very silver, extremely incised and compact. 60x100cm (2x3ft).
A. campestris ssp borealis v purshii makes a tufted mound of silver-blue, well cut leaves. The scented rusty orange flowers might well be worthy on this variety. From Mt. Townsend in WA State, USA. 15-20cm (6-8").
A. campestris ssp maritima v humifusa bears lovely, soft grey leaves of feathery plumes. Superb. 35cm (14").
A. caucasica (pedemontana, assoana) bears fine silver foliage on a low growing mound. It is a tufted, European alpine with white, woolly leaves which are much divided. It makes an enchanting, rhizomatous mat of ferny, silvery leaves which hug the ground. Compact and deciduous with yellow flowers in summer. It appreciates sharp drainage. 10-20cm (4-8").
A. frigida is a finely-cut, silver-leaved, N. American species with strong-smelling foliage. It is of sprawling habit, naturally found in cold, dry regions. It bears small yellow flowers. 10-40cm (4-16").
A. glacialis is a low, tufted perennial with silver-hairy leaves. Makes an attractive prostrate silver filigree mat. Resents winter wet and is usually best in an alpine house or outdoors in a trough or container. 5x30cm (2x12"). Z 3.
A. lagocephala bears grey rosettes which turn yellow and orange in autumn. 60cm (2ft).
A. ludoviciana bears lance-shaped, silver-white leaves up to 12cm (5") long which become greener with age. This hardy perennial spreads rapidly by rhizomes.
A. ludoviciana 'Silver Frost' fragrant, lance-shaped leaves on a compact plant. Pinch back stems in late spring to limit height and reduce the liability of floppy stems later in the season. Shear over to revitalise. Spreads quickly by rhizomes, though not quite as invasive as the species. Will grow in poor, dry soils. 30-45cm (12-18").
A. ludoviciana ssp mexicana v albula 'Silver King' is similar to 'Silver Queen', but has the advantage of more numerous flowers. Slender leaves are almost white.

Artemisia 'Lambrook Mist' above, A. schmidtiana below

Underground rhizomes can throw up offspring up to 6m (20ft) away from the parent. You have been warned. 60-90cm (2-3ft). Z5.

A. ludoviciana 'Silver Queen' is an upright growing herbaceous perennial with fuzzy, jagged evergreen leaves, slightly larger than the species. With sterling silver strength, this is indestructible in dry soil and spreads rapidly. More silvery from afar than 'Silver King'. 60x120cm (2x4ft).

A. ludoviciana 'Valerie Finnis' tolerates a little shade and a little more moisture than most. The finely toothed, felted leaves are almost white in this excellent, showy, compact cultivar. Vigorous, especially in sandy soils, less so in clay, with aromatic foliage that glows even on cloudy days. Cut back to keep compact. When this is done in midsummer, it will reward you and spring back with fresh, low growth. It is tolerant of heat and humidity in full sun and well-drained soil. Z4-9. 60-90cm (2-3ft).

A. ludoviciana ssp ludoviciana v latiloba is non-running with attractive white-silver leaves having a jagged edge. Shear brown flowers for the compost heap. 45cm (18").

A. manshurica is a tall airy, grey-silver plant. 60cm (24").

A. pontica although the greyest green mentioned here as opposed to the silvers; it has a definite silver sheen to its foliage making attractive ground cover.

A. 'Powis Castle' ('Brass Band')(Hancock 1978) is one of the best cultivars and perhaps the most refined. Forming dense mounds of fine, delicate filigree silvery foliage, fragrant and soft to the touch with sparse flowers. Prune to shape in spring or autumn. In just one year this can make a mound 90cm (3ft) wide and looks good in front of a sunny wall. Below Z6 grow in a pot and overwinter. In colder areas expect growth to be slower and smaller in stature. Not as unruly as *A. schmidtiana 'Nana'* and a good alternative. Although it can look rather bedraggled at this time of year, it does retain some foliage in winter. 60-90x40cm (2-3ftx16"). Z5-10.

A. pycnocephala 'David's Choice' makes a valuable contribution of soft-looking foliage especially in cool coastal gardens. A native of coastal dunes in California where it is known as sandhill sage, it makes an evergrey silver mound to 30cm (12").

A. schmidtiana 'Nana' is known as silver mound, because of its glorious habit of making a mound of lacy, felted silver leaves, quickly and easily. It is notoriously robust but can be trimmed back. It does become woody and is best replaced by one of its offspring every other year. For best effect, use it where it will not smother other plants and let it reach its enormous potential. Good drainage is essential, it copes admirably in poor rocky, dry soils however, it is not perfectly hardy and is herbaceous. 15cm (6"). Z4a-9b.

A. schmidtiana 'Silverado' is the choice for humid areas, where other *Artemisia* would succumb. 30cm (12"). Z7-8.

A. stelleriana 'Boughton Silver' (University of BC, Canada) ('Silver Brocade', 'Mori's form) is a very attractive, ground hugging perennial with brocade-like leaves, looking a little like dusty miller (*Senecio cineraria*). It will be larger in areas where it is winter hardy, making useful ground cover that is salt tolerant too. Oak-like foliage is unscented. A standby for the southern states of the U.S. especially by the coast. 15cm (6"). Z3.

A. versicolor 'Seafoam' is a froth of curly silver foliage known as curlicue sage. A vigorous groundcover in sunny, hot areas. Occasionally yellow flower spikes appear 25cm (10") above the foliage. The species itself is blue-grey, brighter silver in sun in dry soils. Combines well with blue grasses such as *Helictotrichon sempervirens* and with the blue-foliaged *Dianthus gratianopolitanus*. Z4-9.

Cool Companion: *Perovskia 'Blue Skies'*, white roses, *Eryngium giganteum*, *Malva moschata*, *Cistus*, *Convolvulus cneorum*, pink or white flowered hardy *Geranium*.

Hot Partner: *Salvia officinalis 'Purpurascens Group'*, *Anthriscus sylvestris 'Ravenswing'*, *Euphorbia dulcis 'Chameleon'*, *Sanguisorba officinalis 'Tanna'*, *Fuchsia 'Thalia'*.

Artemisia and Cosmos atrosanguineus

Artemisia borealis

Artemisia glacialis

Artemisia ludoviciana and Phlox 'Dirigo Ice'

Artemisia pontica above, A. 'Boughton Silver' both below

51

ASTELIA

New Zealand evergreen plants with impressive, bold architectural foliage similar to *Phormium* and just as good for a striking foliage display. They make a bold statement planted either side of a doorway or down a long drive. Dynamic in floral art. Tolerant and undemanding.

HOW TO GROW

Astelia appreciate a cool position in semi-shade in free-draining, humus-rich soil on the dry side. Need protection from harsh frosts and also from the hottest midday sun. An open position ensures the best leaf colour. They tolerate dry conditions but will appreciate a good mulch. Kept in such conditions they may survive lower temperatures than many *Phormium*. Divide mature clumps in spring or winter. Z9.

A. banksii (below) has silver colouring with thinner leaves, often sold as frost hardy but I would protect. Not the most dramatic, but a welcome addition to a pot forming a weeping clump. Tolerates dry conditions and salt winds. 1m (3ft).

A. chathamica 'Silver Spear' (left) bears striking silver, sword-like foliage. The silver satin sheen on the strappy leaves can easily be rubbed off, so handle with care. Excellent in a pot on the patio or in the border. Individual leaves can be 10cm (4") across and as much as 2m (8ft) long. White flowers can appear, rarely in cultivation, in October and November followed by a crop of orange berries, often buried amongst the foliage in late summer on female plants. Tolerant of dry conditions once established. 1.2m tall and wide (4ft).

A. nervosa has silver lance-shaped leaves up to 1m long (3ft), but not as good as *A. chathamica 'Silver Spear'*. This is a good companion plant for tree ferns in moist soil in sun or part shade.

Hot Partner: Oustanding with dark *Phormium* such as *P. 'Platt's Black'*, *Cordyline 'Red Star'*, *Heuchera 'Silver Scrolls'*.

Cool Companion: *Hebe*, grasses, *Bacopa 'Blizzard'*, *Caryopteris 'Dark Knight'*.

ATRIPLEX

Interesting, fast-growing annuals add unusual colour and are useful in decoration. A good choice for salt soils and drought. Annual orach can be eaten like spinach.

HOW TO GROW
Appreciate good drainage and as little water as possible. Killed by frost. 9b.

A. argentea is known as silverscale. Its grey leaves are covered in silver hairs. The branched, rounded bush bears inconspicuous yellow-green flowers. It grows in alkaline clay soils in native prairie.
A. californica is a grey perennial, an attractive little shrub tolerating full sun, salt and sand. It makes good groundcover and bears yellow flowers.
A. canescens has edible, grey leaves and is very drought tolerant once established. Tiny, whitish flowers are followed by four-winged seeds. Salt tolerant and excellent to prevent erosion. 1.5m (5ft).
A. cinerea the grey saltbush is normally found in parts of Australia. A silvery white subshrub which layers from adventitious roots. 1.5m (5ft).
A. halimus bears satiny, silver leaves clothing an evergreen bush. Use in the mixed border or as a windbreak. Prefers a well-drained, sunny site. 120cm (4ft).
A. hymenelytra is known as the desert or silver holly, a native of Utah and California. From thickened, gnarled woody bases this makes a compact plant with greenish flowers borne in spikes and followed by flattened fruits. Tolerates extreme drought but often defoliates.
A. lentiformis bears silvery white flowers against green leaves. An evergreen shrub for a drought site in full sun. It has been used by native American Indians to flavour food owing to its salty taste. 90cm-1.8m (3-6ft).
A. leucophylla makes flat, grey groundcover. Tiny whitish grey flowers nestle amongst the grey foliage.
A. polycarpa known as cattle spinach is similar to *A. lentiformis*. Found in very dry lakes and a favourite with desert tortoises. 1.8m (6ft).

BALLOTA

Handsome leaves for the drought garden, fascinating and easy. Thriving on neglect these hardy perennials cloak the garden in silvery leaves.

HOW TO GROW
Full sun in a sheltered site, little water and well-drained soil. Will tolerate semi-shade. Sow seed in spring or take semi-ripe cuttings in summer. Cut hard back in spring to encourage lush growth. Divide perennials in spring. Take cuttings from subshrubs in spring or early summer. Z9-10.

B. acetabulosa forms low bushes of soft, grey-green with whitish backs making an attractive evergreen display. Small purple to pink flowers are insignificant but there are highly desirable, persistent green calyces reminiscent of Bells of Ireland (*Molucella laevis*). Easy even in dry shade but greener than *B. pseudodictamnus*. 75cm (30").
B. africana is a common feature in the Cape, where it is the only species found in South Africa. It is easily identified by its aromatic, crinkled and felted grey foliage. Stems are felted too. Pink to purple flowers are carried in whorls. Up to 1.2m (4ft).
B. cretica is worth getting to know, especially if you have a scree. This dainty, silver white foliage shrub appreciates an open site in full sun. Average to poor soil. 30cm (12").
B. nigra 'Archer's Variegated' is a knock your socks off variety with white variegation and pink-purple flowers in June. It is more or less evergreen. Z6. 35cm (14").
B. nigra 'Zanzibar' is white mottled in its variegation and a taller plant than *'Archer's Variegated'* at 1m (39").
B. pseudodictamnus is known as silver horehound. This hardy perennial looks like it is under a blanket of snow with its fuzzy, round leaves on greenish white stems. White or pale pink, lipped flowers with pale green calyces in midsummer. It is attractive at the front of the silver border or admirable for flower arranging with white stems and white dusted leaves. Up to 90cm (3ft).
Cool Companion: *Lavandula, Salvia officinalis Purpurascens Group, Nicotiana 'Lime Green'*.

Ballota acetabulosa

Ballota pseudodictamnus

Begonia 'Two Face'

BEGONIA

Begonia 'Bella'

No foliage lover can live without rhizomatous begonia. If I had to choose only one type of plant I could have, this would probably be it. Foliage types come in abundance, are astounding, easy to grow and very rewarding. The darkest are described in my book 'Black Magic And Purple Passion', the silvers are just as wonderful. These plants enthrall me; leaves can be different on one plant, especially young and older leaves. The silver begonia hailed from India. Unrivalled as house plants, great for the conservatory and those lucky Zone 10 dwellers can have begonia outside in the border in light shade. In cooler zones, they will enjoy a summer holiday outdoors.

Begonia 'Connee Boswell'

HOW TO GROW
Barely moist, well-drained soil in bright shade. Warmth and humidity are favoured and judicious watering, never overwater. A slow-release fertiliser is ideal in the growing season. A minimum 10°C (50°F) night temperature is necessary. An east facing window is ideal.

B. 'Abel Carriere' (Svahn) is a beautiful silver-green form with green veins, very handsome small heart-shaped leaves, 15cm (6") long. This is one of the oldest rex cultivars, an upright grower, dating from 1878. It makes a good hanging basket begonia. I hope I age so well!

B. annulata is an Asian species with silver leaves having an intriguing dark centre and a neat dark edge. I obtained this as *B. griffithii*, but by any name it is quite captivating, but then one begonia and I'm anybody's!

B. 'Bella' is a sultry beauty in pewter with lilac veins and a lilac edging. Not to be confused with the Bella series semperflorens begonia.

B. 'Brianna McCain' (Worley) bears silver-green leaves with a silver centre, lots of curls.

B. 'Connee Boswell' (Johnson) is admirable for its silver rhizomatous, erect growth with a pink cast giving a pewtered look. Nice pinkish purple edging to the palmate leaf with a lacy effect. Makes an outstanding easy specimen which does well on a windowsill. Named after the jazz singer. 45cm (16").

B. 'Contessa de Rosea' is a delightful silvered pink confection. Makes me think of pink silk accompanied by pink boa, definitely Countess blood here, a real aristocrat of large silver leaves with deep veins, a little twist and a maiden's pink blush.

B. 'Coral Sands' TM bears silver pustulate leaves with a pink blush on a super rex hybrid.

B. 'Curly Silversweet' is an erect growing rex type with purple stems supporting silver leaves which curl back on themselves to reveal seductive crimson undersides. An easier rex that does not defoliate in heat. Large pink flowers are produced in winter making this a must for any foliage collection.

Begonia 'Contessa de Rosea'

55

Begonia 'Coral Sands' above

Begonia 'Dewdrop' above, B. 'Fireworks' below

Begonia 'Flamingo Shoals'

Begonia 'Green Gold' above, B. griffithii below

56

B. 'Deja Thorus' (Worley) bears pearly silver, medium leaves. A spiralled and ruffled rhizomatous variety.

B. 'Del Ray Silver' bears handsome cut leaves astonishingly silvered with a very dark heart and wavy edge. The underside is almost as attractive.

B. 'Dewdrop' (Lewis 1947) simply shimmers and glistens in silver. Central veins have a pinkish tinge. This rex cultivar is one of the best solid silvers but can suffer from leaf spot although my four year old plant never has yet.

B. 'Don Miller' is a mallet type bearing smallish green leaves, densely spotted with silvery white and contrasting pink flowers.

B. 'Emerald Giant' (1981) this rex hyrid is a green and silver duet. The central veins and edge are dark green, the rest is silver with silver dots entering the green margin. Goes dormant for me in winter.

B. 'Evergreen' (Wepper 1935) is a rex type with handsome silver leaves and prominent green veining.

B. 'Fireworks' (Kartuz) is an astonishing combination of a dark maroon centre veining into silver, edged with a pink border. The silvering comes as the leaves mature. Large pink flowers on this rex cross. Majestic specimen, be prepared to fall in love. 30cm (12").

B. 'Flamboyant' (Yorke) bears bronzy green leaves covered in silver patches or wholly silvered, similar to 'Silver Slipper'. Dark pink flowers can appear anytime in the growing season on this easy rhizomatous variety.

B. 'Flamingo Shoals' reminds me of the pointillist painters. Leaves are so heavily dotted in whitish silver as to be solid. The pinkish hue when young remains on older leaves as a neat edging on this rex hybrid.

B. 'Frosty' bears richly silver-dotted angel wing leaves with a rose underside and a pebbly appearance on brilliant red, upright, short stems. Constant humidity needed for success with this one.

B. 'Gay Paree' (Lowe) bears medium to large leaves with a silver coating. Rhizomatous.

B. 'Grey Feather' makes a dramatic basket subject with its pointed, wavy, slender leaves of green etched with grey veins. A medium to low growing cane type which is an easy to grow variety.

B. 'Gypsy Maid' is an attractive metallic silver form with hints of a purple blush and green veins. This is not the cane form 'Gypsy Maiden'.

B. 'Hallelujah' (Mounger) a blend of green, soft purple and metallic silver and grey which works well on the spiralled leaves of this rex hybrid.

B. hatacoa 'Silver Leaf' (1971) is probably the king of narrow leaved, silvered begonia. Pointed narrow, lance-like leaves are silver with a greenish cast. Makes a lovely, erect pot plant or in a basket where the pinkish-red reverse is on view. 60cm (2ft).

B. 'Hurricane Bay' is a beautiful silver-leaved rex hybrid with a green edge and darker heart. Perfect spiralled leaves make this a very elegant plant.

Begonia haticoa silver leaf above, B. 'Hurricane Bay' below

57

Begonia 'Green Gold' and Ophiopogon
planiscapus 'Nigrescens' in the author's garden

B. 'Ironstone' is a beautiful silver variety with a dark stitched edge. A very elegant rex hybrid.

B. 'Kismet' bears juvenile pinkish leaves which mature to silver with broad conspicuous green veining on a compact angel's wings. This small leaved miniature needs high humidity. 20cm (8").

B. 'Lalomie' is an outstanding rex and one of the easiest to grow, withstanding the heat of summer and short winter days. Lush, deep green veins and a pink blush edging that bleeds into the silver ruffled leaves. Remarkable .

B. 'L'Escargot' (PPAF) is a certain winner with its combination of silver and dark green bands on a large swirled leaf, much more handsome than a snail! The 30cm (1ft) leaves are borne on red hairy stems. 25-40cm (10-16").

B. 'Little Brother Montgomery' (Johnson) displays a very dark centre which contrasts well with the silver surround edged in a dark margin. Palmate leaves make a very attractive specimen plant. Rhizomatous shrub-like growth, one of its parents is thought to be *B. palmata*. It bears attractive pink flowers from red buds.

B. 'Looking Glass' (Worley 1981) is a good, upright grower with very shiny, silver leaves and olive green central veins. Makes a spectacular leafy specimen with reddish undersides. Look no further for a silver reflection. I have noticed that sometimes the green veins are narrow, sometimes broad on this variety. Pink flowers are borne in winter on this cane-like variety. 30-90cm (1-3ft) in a container in partial sun.

B. 'Mad Hatter' (Logee's) silver leaves and a grey border with a twist like *B. 'Cathedral'*. Small white flowers is the description at Glasshouse Works of this plant. The plant I have seen differs its leaves are silver, very metallic, very pustulate, the backs even more interesting in red with green veins.

B. 'Martin Johnson' (Corwin) has to be one of the most striking silver rex begonias, which scores a ten out of ten from me, I have been growing it for three years. First the leaf shape grabs your attention, a maple leaf with a central spiral, but your eye is held by the colouring, a swirl of black centre, silver and pink which blends into the picotee edge.

B. 'Mikado' is outstandingly elegant with its grey-plum edge, wide silvered band and deep near black centre. A very beautiful rex hybrid.

B. 'Millie Thompson' starts off dark green with a silver sheen and matures to stunning silver with near black veins and edging.

B. 'Mirage' (Worley 1987) bears silver-green leaves dappled with pinkish tones when young with a red reverse. The more light this gets, the more pink comes through the surface. White to light pink flowers are borne in late winter. A vigorous and sturdy rhizomatous variety.

B. 'Namur' is an attractive cultivar with spiral leaves, a tiny green heart and greenish silver leaves having a thin green edge to finish off.

Begonia 'Ironstone' above,
B. 'Little Brother Montgomery' below

59

Begonia 'Looking Glass'

B. 'Nano' is a silvered variety, with medium-sized leaves and pink undersides.

B. 'November Frost' (Woodriff) bears small to medium, silver-frosted leaves with a grey edge and a double curl at the sinus. White flowers can appear throughout the growing season. A very attractive and distinctive rhizomatous variety.

B. 'Olympic Queen' (Anderson) small, pointed white leaves are the feature of this begonia. Despite its unusual colour, this makes good growth. White flowers can appear at any time.

B. 'Pearl Ripple' bears green leaves pebbled with silver.

B. 'Pink Champagne' is a pink-silver creation worthy of drinking to, raise your glass. The pointed leaves are edged in dark contrasting perfectly with the silver band which blends to pink against the dark centre. Leaves up to 15cm (6") long. A rex hybrid which is not difficult and has class.

B. 'Pink Nacre' (Lowe) large silver leaves with dark green edges on an easy rhizomatous variety producing good specimen plants.

B. 'Pink Surprise' makes a good terrarium plant with its silver leaves and white flowers on a rhizomatous variety.

B. 'President' has green central veins fading out half way on the silver leaves neatly stitched in green at the margins.

B. pustulata 'Argentea' is an attractive silver-leaved variety with a stitched green margin. Silver leaves are well marked in green on this neat and classy species.

B. 'Queen Olympus' (Bishop) the sharply pointed leaves have a dark green margin and are otherwise completely silver and slightly hirsute. A compact grower bearing many light pink flowers from February to May.

B. 'Raspberry Crush' what better to follow *B. 'Pink Champagne'* than a raspberry dessert? Double spiralled leaves with a pinkish blush and a pewter overlay are highlighted by a dark centre and a raspberry margin on this scrumptious rex hybrid.

B. rex (Putzey) the King of the kings. The plant that started the *rex* hybrids came from India. A large leaf with a dark heart enhanced by a shimmering silver band is finished off by a dark green band.

Begonia maculata

Begonia 'Martin Johnson'

Begonia metallica

Begonia 'Purple Stardust'

Begonia pustulata argentea

Begonia 'Queen Olympus'

61

B. 'Rocheart' is pebbled in silver on green leaves with a dark heart.

B. rubro-venia is a silver-spotted, green pointed-leaved species. *B. rubro-venia silver* is the same as *B. haticoa*.

B. 'Shari' is well worth adding to your collection. Dark veining goes from plum to green against a silver background which is blushed pink towards the centre.

B. 'Silver Cloud' (Bishop) bears pistachio green leaves covered in a mass of silver spots almost giving the appearance of solid silver on this *rex* with green veins.

B. 'Silver Greenheart' (Woodriff 1981) silver leaves with a delicate, stitched green outline. Nicely textured, very silver.

B. 'Silver Jewel' (Horton 1955) bears green leaves streaked with silver. Handsome, pustulate leaves having a green stiched velvety edge on this easy rhizomatous variety.

B. 'Silver King' is a silver beautifully veined in green. Nice red underside. A real classic.

B. 'Silver Lace' is a real favourite of mine. The dark green filigree edge contrasts nicely with the silver veined in green. Dark red undersides and often shows a pink blush to the leaves.

B. 'Silver Mist' is a solid silver.

B. 'Sierra Mist' (Bishop) stardust sprinkled on a dark leaf. A quite dramatic cane-like begonia with pink flowers.

B. 'Sierra Silver Mist' is a palmate type with silvered leaves and slate veins and lovely white-pink flowers.

B. 'Sierra Silver Moon' (Bishop) bears pearly, silver spiralled leaves that are red-backed. Light pink flowers on this cane begonia.

B. 'Silver Peridot' (Cole 1978) bears large, silver-patterned leaves. This *rex* hybrid will not tolerate low humidity but is excellent in a terrarium.

B. 'Silver Queen' has very silvered leaves with a green 'star' centre and a green margin. The reddish undersides make a nice *rex* specimen.

B. 'Silver Sands' is a small leaved *rex* with silver foliage having green veining.

B. 'Silver Shadows' (Anderson) is a dazzler that would make any shade shine. Star-shaped silver leaves are veined in green combined with pink flowers.

B. 'Silver Star' has a star-shaped, silver overlay on olive leaves, edged in a dark slate. Reddish tones predominate on the reverse. White flowers in winter on this old rhizomatous variety.

B. 'Silver Sweet' is another of the very old rex cultivars, an easy-to-grow variety with silver leaves and green veins. 30-45cm (12-18").

S. 'Sinbad' is so silver as to appear almost white. Lovely mallet angel wing form with pale green veining. Pink flowers are produced all summer. Prefers dryish shade and can suffer from mildew and overall is not an easy plant. 35cm (14").

B. 'Sir Percy' (Zug 1952) metallic silver leaves have a definite pink flush and some bronze hints on this rhizomatous variety.

Begonia 'Silver Cloud' above,
B. 'Silver Greenheart' below

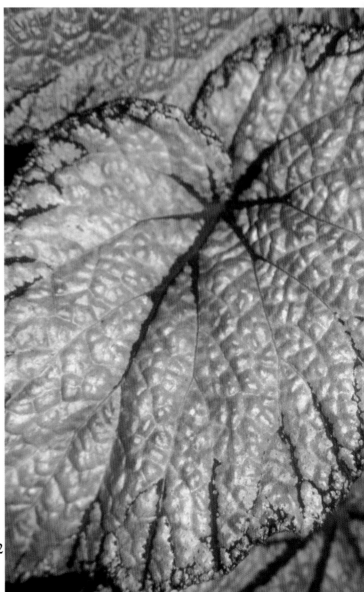

Begonia 'Silver Jewel' above,
B. 'Silver Lace' below

Begonia 'Snow Queen' above,
B. 'Solid Silver' below

63

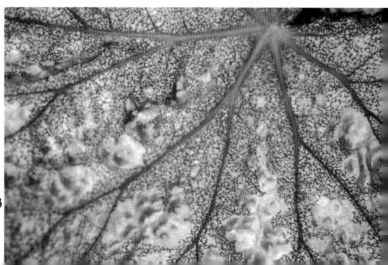

B. 'Snow Queen' bears dark green leaves sprinkled in snow-like dots.

B. 'Solid Silver' has large, textured leaves, puckered and extremely metallic.

B. species from Siam bears pointed leaves with a silver overlay and deep green veining.

B. 'Tropical Breeze' bears medium green leaves with silver blotches on a *rex* hybrid.

B. 'Two Face' (Woodriff 1979) took a long time to settle in, but is worth the trouble for its incredible leaves with silver, pink and green hues which change colour when you turn the plant. Absolutely amazing with the light behind when the red underside shows through. A scandent or trailing variety. Can suffer leaf spot. 30cm (12").

B. venosa is a rare and wonderful species with whitish leaves afforded by the power of powder. Small white flowers are carried above the foliage. 60cm (2ft).

B. 'Wanda' is a tremendous variety with pustulate silver leaves and green veins covered in red plush. A very handsome rhizomatous variety with pink flowers for a terrarium.

Of the cane-like varieties that are well spotted, 'Alamo Snow' is silver on bright green; 'Russian Sabers' silver on very dark green near black, stunning; 'Olei Silver Spot' is worth growing just for the tremendous pink flowers let alone the silver-spotted, green foliage; 'Sylvan Triumph' is indeed a triumph in silver. Its leaves are so densely covered with silver spots as to be almost solid and 'White Ice' is outstanding for its snow covered silver spots and pink flowers.

Hot Partner: silver and dark *Begonia* such as *'Fireworks'* go well with *Ipomoea 'Black Heart'* and *Helichrysum 'Icicles'*.

Begonia 'Silver Sands'

Begonia 'Tropical Breeze' above,
B. venosa below photographed in friend , Camilla Shivarg's
garden in London

Two Begonia species, one from Java above,
and from Thailand below

BRACHYGLOTTIS

Suitable for the coast and for Mediterranean gardens, *Brachyglottis 'Dunedin'* is one of the most planted shrubs, unfortunately. It used to be known as *Senecio*. I find it hard to recommend these usually untidy shrubs with their large daisies. It has its uses as a hedge in coastal gardens.

HOW TO GROW
Moist but well-drained soil in sun.

B. buchanannii 'Silver Shadow', 'Frosty' and **'Silver Waves'** are all cultivars in circulation. All are grey-green leaved and bear yellow daisy flowers.
B. compacta is desirable for its compact form and wavy leaves suffused soft grey-silver accompanied by yellow daisies through summer. A low maintenance, hardy shrub, suitable for coastal areas, which is easy to keep, just trim once a year. 75cmx1m (30x39").
B. greyi the coastal daisy is hardy in dry sites. Yellow flowers, soft grey foliage and rounded form are the attributes of this shrub. Trim yearly to shape. It is often *'Dunedin'* that is sold under this name. 1.5x1m (5x3ft).
B. repanda x greyi bears silver leaves, soft hairy on the upper surface. Yellow daisies are borne in summer on this spreading shrub from New Zealand. 1.75m height and spread. (6ft).
B. 'Silver Dormouse' is probably the most silver-leaved of its kind though older leaves are still green.

CALCEOLARIA

A half hardy perennial from Chile displaying excellent colour contrast.

HOW TO GROW
Slightly humus soil in an alpine house. Sun or part shade in loam. Needs protection from wet.

C. arachnoidea bears white-felted, narrow leaves in a crowded rosette, against which the maroon-purple pocket flowers really stand out on long stems in June to July. Hailing from South American and Andes grasslands this is a fairly easy alpine and flowers the first year. In high altitude gardens, this will grow outdoors. 15-23cm (6-9").

CEDRUS

Favourite conifers, these paler forms, approaching white make useful contrasts amongst darker plants.

HOW TO GROW

C. atlantica 'Sahara Frost' has new spring growth which is icy white, it then becomes variegated in summer. Come autumn and winter, it is greyish with white tips. A relatively fast growing form that becomes a very unusual tree. Introduced by Bill Janssen of Collector's Nursery in Washington, USA. 60cm (2ft). Z6.
C. atlantica 'Sahara Ice' is from the same stable and similar in all but its much slower growth rate, becoming a large shrub or small tree. 60cm (2ft). Z6.
C. atlantica 'Silberspitz' (Silver Sprite) is an upright, narrow form with white new growth tips. Colour is best in shade. Found and introduced by Horstmann Nursery, Germany. 2x1m (8x4ft). Z6.
C. deodora 'Deep Cove' makes a compact, conical shape with snow-white foliage in spring when it looks truly stunning. Its pale foliage makes it susceptible to sun burn. In the summer months, the foliage mellows to a greyish green with white tips. Introduced by William Goddard of Floravista Gardens, Victoria, BC. Z6.
C. deodora 'Silver Mist' also from William Goddard comes this delightful form making a mounded bush of whitish cream foliage. One of the best White Himalayan Cedars which takes shade and responds to pruning to keep it dwarf. 90x60cm (3x2ft). Z6.
C. deodora 'Snow Sprite' like freshly fallen snow, this is a bright mound of whitish foliage from William Goddard. Slightly smaller than the above. 90x60cm (3x2ft). Z6.
C. deodora 'White Imp' from the same stable, being very similar, this making the smallest mound of whitish foliage over a green base. Shimmering silver. It can be sheared to keep dwarf, best in partial shade. 90x60cm (3x2ft). Z6.

Cedrus deodora 'Silver Mist'

*Cedrus, the blue cedars make a nice solid fixture and
contrasting silvery blue in the silver garden*

CELMISIA

Known to be difficult and tricky, these native New Zealanders adapt quite well to the British and similar climates if one pampers to their cultural requirements. Lovely dwarf silvered alpines with white daisies. The best I have found is a hybrid dwarf shrub with broadish leaves and large daisies. They make excellent subjects for pots.

HOW TO GROW
They prefer scree and free-draining soil with added grit. They dislike thin chalk soils, but otherwise are not too fussy, having a preference for neutral to slightly acidic soil and a fair quantity of sun. Water during drought in summer but bear in mind that waterlogging kills these frost hardy plants which are common in snow-tussock grassland in their native habitat.

C. angustifolia silver form may be a hybrid originating from the garden of Alex Dugid of Ballater, Aberdeenshire. A free- flowering form with large white daisies in summer over silver foliage. A choice plant. 15x100cm (6"x39").
C. argentea has silver-haired, tufted mounds topped by white daisies in summer. A fine alpine. 10cm (4").
C. bonplandii is a strong, low growing silver green mat bearing the usual white daisies. 10cm (4").
C. brevifolia is a dwarf shrub with silver green foliage. 20cm (8").
C. 'David Shackleton' is probably the most silvered variety.
C. densiflora silver leaved forms a dense cushion with pale mauve flowers.
C. hectorii bears silver rosettes in a neat, spreading mound with white daisies in summer. 15cm (6").
C. incana bears compact silver foliage, completely covered in white hairs giving insulation against the cold mountain air. White daisies with yellow centres in spring to summer. It has broader, shorter leaves than many and is known as mountain musk. 15cm (6").
C. Inshriach hybrids bear small, silver leaves. Almost like a mini *C. semicordata*.
C. insignis bears very silver, narrow leaves.
C. major is an excellent choice for coastal areas with its silver-green leaves. 20cm (8").
C. ramulosa the plant usually sold under this name makes a neat tuft of slender, silver foliage with white daisies in summer. 10cm (4"). However, the true *C. ramulosa* makes a small shrub to 30cm (12").
C. ramulosa v tuberculata has silver stiff leaves on stems on a shrubby variety. 25cm (10").
C. semicordata has large silver-green leaves. This robust, herbaceous plant forms large clumps. The stiff, leathery leaves to 30cm (12") long and up to 10cm (4") wide are white on the underside. One of the most attractive with rosettes up to 1m (39") in diameter. 50cm (20").

C. semicordata ssp stricta has the largest silver leaves of the bunch, a very handsome foliage plant. Leaves are narrower than the type and have heavily rolled margins.
C. semicordata ssp semicordata has silver-green leaves on the upper surface, more white-silver beneath.
C. sessiliflora makes a small cushion of neat, silver foliage. Dislikes hot, sunny sites. 10cm (4").
C. spectabilis 'Eggleston Silver' at Eggleston Hall they are very proud of this, a hardy, beautiful silver form with three layered pure white daisy petals to 7cm (3") across.
C. spedenii bears silver, needle-like leaves making small tufts, a sweet little gem with outstanding silver colouring. 10cm (4").
C. walkerii bears bright silver foliage on a dwarf shrub. 25cm (10").

Top: Celmisia insignis
Below: C. semicordata.

CENTAUREA

Quite distinct from the usual cornflowers we grow, these are, for the main part, choice alpines.

HOW TO GROW
Moderate water. Best in lean and mean sites. Z7-10.

C. akamantis comes from the endangered Akamas peninsula in Cyprus. It is unlike any other I have seen, a fine filigree of silver wiry stems.

C. argentea has elegant, silvery fern-like leaves. Plunge in pots and partly starve to bring out its whiteness. Yellow flowers to 1cm across are borne in summer. Likes sunny, dry crevices.

C. cineraria (candidissima h.) is known as pink dusty miller. The grey-green foliage is handsomely divided. Bears mauve-pink cornflowers. One of the few grey shrubs that goes wild in shade and this plant needs careful siting and a little effort to keep it from swallowing other plants. It can reach 3m (10ft) across.

C. cineraria 'Colchester White' is a fine cultivar, leaves are much more divided and colour is much whiter than the species. Fine and airy yet tough.

C. cineraria 'Magic Silver' bears bright silver-white, slightly undulating leaves. Good as an edging annual. An unusual alternative these days to *Senecio cineraria*, has better bright yellow cornflowers than the latter's feeble daisies. 15-30cm (6-12").

C. clementei is a handsome grey-foliaged plant. Pick off the golden flowers and enjoy the foliage alone. The jagged leaves of this Spanish native are found growing on cliffs.

C. epirotica growing in scree in its natural habitat in Greece, this alpine makes felted, silver rosettes with almost stemless pinkish purple cornflowers. Sun and good drainage in the rock garden.

C. fischeri hails from the Russian Caucasus and features densely tomentose, grey-green foliage in low mounds with white cornflowers in early summer. 25x25cm (10"). Z3.

C. 'Hoar Frost' has greyish-green foliage with narrow blades, but is really set off by the clean white flowers with purplish tints at the centre. Upright growth to 30cm (12").

C. pindicola bears rosettes of undulating grey leaves with stemless white cornflowers. This alpine spreads by underground runners.

C. pulcherrima has silver-grey leaves and stiff stems bearing pink cornflowers in summer. 45cm (18").

C. triumfettii ssp stricta bears attractive silver foliage on a perennial cornflower, which has complementary violet-blue flowers from May to July. Well-drained soil in a sunny position. It is happy on chalk. 45cm (18").

CEPHALOCEREUS

Furry white cactus, but not strokeable, beware the almost hidden spines. Mature specimens are very architectural, looking like hairy sculptures.

HOW TO GROW
Full sun, dry soil. Easy in hot zones, in areas of Tucson and Phoenix it likes some afternoon shade. Does not withstand frost. Z9b-11.

C. palmeri has white wool in rows down the length of the column. Almost looks like a cotton wool cactus. Bears pinkish flowers.
C. senilis the old man cactus needs a comb and mirror to keep his silver-grey hair tidy. Hairs at the top of the barrel appear to stick up like a mad professor. Soft, silky hairy appearance. When mature 6-15m (18-24ft). Will tolerate -4°C (25°F) briefly if kept dry.

CERASTIUM

C. tomentosum is the most over-used plant along with *Aubrieta* in mockeries of rockeries in English front gardens. A humble carpeter that makes a silver mat topped with white daisies in late spring to summer.

HOW TO GROW
Full sun in average well-drained soil. Prefers poor soil. Shear over after flowering. Z3-10

C. alpinum v lanatum bears white flowers and densely hairy foliage. Forming a tight cushion, this needs extra good drainage. It is not as silver as *C. tomentosum*. 8cm (3").
C. candidissimum is similar to *C. tomentosum* below, the whitish leaves and snowy white flowers make a superb eding plant.
C. tomentosum is an easy-care perennial, its silvered leaves are covered in white blossoms in June giving rise to the common name of snow-in-summer. It is wonderful as a massed edging plant in very well-drained soil. Use its ability to spread to best effect tumbling down a wall. Very susceptible to aphids.
C. tomentosum 'Silberteppich' ('Silver Carpet') bears frosty foliage to creep over the ground, very similar to the species. An easy groundcover in dry sites with easy maintenance and no fertilizer. 15-30cm (6-12").

Cephalocereus senilis

70

Centaurea clementei

Centaurea akamantis

Celmisia Inschriach hybrids above
C. spedenii below

Cerastium candidissimum
Opuntia microdasys below

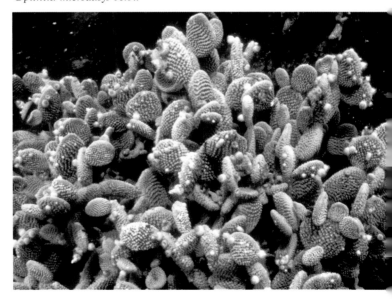

CISTUS

Extremely drought tolerant, shrubby Mediterranean species suitable for low water gardening. Many of the white flowered species or hybrids are eminently suitable for the white garden.

C. albidus is known as the white-leaved rockrose. Greyish white, tomentose leaves adorn the compact bush and fabulous pink, crinkled flowers. 90cm (3ft). There is also a white form which is highly desirable, **C. albidus f albus**.
C. x argenteus 'Silver Ghost' is a sport from *'Silver Pink'* with grey-green leaves and handsome white flowers having a prominent central boss of yellow stamens.
C. x canescens f albus bears attractive white flowers over grey-green foliage.
C. x cyprius v ellipticus f bicolor 'Elma' is another white-flowered variety with leaden grey foliage in cooler weather.
C. symphytifolius ssp leucophyllus bears grey-green leaves that are paler on the reverse. Large, pink flowers have a boss of yellow stamens. 90cm (3ft).
C. osbeckiifolius bears large, hairy silky leaves in grey-green. Largish pink flowers. Prefers acid soils. 90cm (3ft).
C. x pulverulentus bears pink-purple flowers over greyish green foliage. 1m (40").
Hot Partner: late season species *Salvia*.
Cool Companion: *Ceanothus*.

CLEISTOCACTUS

Flowers are typically closed in this genus of South American cactus. These columnar forms are quite vigorous as cactus go.

HOW TO GROW
Need space for their roots and are best potted on every year. Temperatures above 8°C (45°F). Z10-12.

C. baumannii makes columnar clumps of grey woolly cactus fingers. One of the easiest to grow bearing red flowers in summer.
C. baumannii 'Bruneispinus' makes columns covered in white spines. 1.8m (6ft). Z9b-11.
C. brookei is a shrubby cactus with unbranched, sprawling stems. 5cm (2") thick stems are covered generously in silver grey hairs.
C. hyalacanthus bears grey furry stems with pinkish flowers. 1m (4ft).
C. straussii has short grey fur with a neat, clipped appearance. Grows in groups of slender columns with pink flowers. Its very silky silvery look has earned it the name of Silver Torch cactus. Prone to root rot if wet in winter. 2m (8ft).
C. tarijensis bears erect slender stems to 12cm (5"). It is covered in grey hairs and grows in clumps.

CONSOLIDA

Tall, stately annuals like their cousins, the perennial Dephiniums. A most unusual and Gothic addition to the garden in metal grey.

HOW TO GROW
Sow in situ from March to April or in August to September to flower the following year. Easy in full sun.

C. 'Earl Grey' named after my favourite tea, this beauty is steely grey in flower, a most unusual colour in the garden and one which would sit well with purer than pure whites and pearly grey foliage. Double slate-grey to gunmetal blooms, but it can be variable. 1.2m (4ft).

CONVOLVULUS
Superb choice for dry gardens or the Mediterranean look.

HOW TO GROW
Sunny site with poor to moderately fertile, deep, well-drained soil.

C. althaeoides has deeply incised, grey-green leaves covered in hairs making a cushion. Bright violet morning-glory blooms are borne in summer to autumn.
C. althaeoides ssp tenuissimus bears finely dissected, silvery green leaves on a vigorous trailing plant which can also be used as a climber. Pink trumpet flowers are borne in summer. 1.8m (6ft).
C. boisseri v boisseri has low spreading silver cushions of overlapping leaves of a silky appearance which are deeply veined. Large, stemless pink buds swirl open like a flamenco dancer's skirt to reveal pearly white morning glory blooms in late spring and summer. A Spanish species for sun and dry sites. Completely hardy. 8x20cm (3x8").
C. cneorum is one of the most attractive small shrubs, the best of the bunch. Silvery, super silky, soft foliage, reminiscent of olive leaves in shape. Great texture, great look. White flowers are attractive too and have a maidenly pink blush.
C. incanus is a trailing variety with silver leaves and bluish white flowers in summer.
Cool Companion: *Cistus, Dianthus, Festuca glauca*.

Convolvulus boisseri

Convolvulus cneorum and Salvia argentea

Cotyledon orbiculata above,
C. undulata below

COROKIA

Versatile New Zealand natives with interesting twisted branches. These tender shrubs which keep their leaves all year are amply evoked by the common name of wire netting bush.

HOW TO GROW

Open, sunny position or a little shade. Wind tolerant. Best grown against a wall in moist soil.

C. x virgata 'Silver Ghost' has angled branches and small silver-white leaves. Tiny flowers in spring are followed by berries attractive to birds. Leave this evergreen to grow its own way, or clip to shape. Hardy and easy. 1m (3ft). Z8.

COTYLEDON

From mountainous regions of Africa, here is one ice-cool succulent.

HOW TO GROW

Avoid afternoon sun in hot climates. Sun to light shade. Need little water, allow to dry out between waterings. Protect from frost. Z9-11.

C. orbiculata bears green leaves totally covered in white powder enhanced by a dark maroon edging. Thick succulent leaves arise from the base like a lunar landing model. Incredible and superb. This succulent often has a dark red edge to its rounded leaves. In summer clusters of orange, bell-shaped, drooping flowers are borne on long stems. Known by the not so cool name of pig's ear. In cultivation it reaches 1.2m (4ft). **'Silver Waves'** is a good silver form.
C. 'Stagshorn' is a most unusual succulent with grey-green, elongated leaves. Place it in the warmest spot in the garden and protect from frost.
C. undulata has silvery leaves and wavy edges, best colour is produced in cool conditions.

73

Crassula 'Morgan's Pink'

CRASSULA

Fantastic succulents exhibiting some of the most interesting shapes and colours in the plant world.

HOW TO GROW
Shade to part shade, avoid exposure to extreme heat with protection from frost. Well-drained soil. Feed every third watering, water moderately, very little in winter. Z10-12.

C. alstonii from Namaqualand has green-white leaves almost in a textured ball shape, pressed together in a spherical rosette. Small pink flowers appear in clusters.

C. atropurpurea v arborescens is known as the silver dollar plant. Rounded green-grey leaves are finished with a soft whitish bloom and a purple edge. A neat succulent shrub to 3m (10ft) in its natural habitat, but less in cultivation.

C. dubia has spectacular grey-green leaves combined with white flowers in summer. Evergreen when protected from frost. 45cm (18").

C. grisea makes angular rosettes with silvered leaves having a pink-brown cast. 15cm (6").

C. 'Ivory Pagoda' is recommended for its grey rosettes.

C. 'Morgan's Beauty' is no false claim for this near white succulent looks like a sculpture of flat silver-grey pebbles, neatly and artistically arranged. Bunches of salmon-pink flowers adorn this plant in summer. Protect from frost. 15cm (6").

C. obliqua the grey-green leaves of the jade plant are edged in maroon with little dots. This evergreen might survive in a warm, sheltered spot but does need frost protection. A large specimen in flower is quite something. 80cm (32").

C. perforata makes a small shrub with branches to 60cm (2ft) long. Tiny greyish-green leaves are stacked one on top of the other like buttons. Whitish flowers are borne in late summer. This only needs to be kept in a small 10cm (4") pot. 60cm (2ft).

Crassula obliqua

Cynara cardunculus

CYNARA

Fabulously large, fabulously architectural, fabulously silvery, just fabulous. This has to be the best of the large silver plants. Gigantic in proportion and makes quite a statement in the garden or the vegetable patch. Lovely with purples and pinks. Add a theatrical air with flair. Native to the Mediterranean, it has become invasive in some areas of the U.S., particularly in California and also in some parts of Australia.

HOW TO GROW
Well-drained light, moist soil in full sun. Divide in March to May. Sow seed in March to May.

C. cardunculus produces leaves to 30cm (12") long with spikes of artichoke flowers. The statuesque proportions of the hardy, perennial cardoon or artichoke thistle are not intended for a small space, but where space is no problem, the cardoon gives fabulous colour, texture and stature to the border. Its tremendous, basal deep-lobed leaves arch gracefully to 1.2m (4ft) in length. They are eye-catching, so too the colour and the height. It is a giant in all respects. The purple thistles in April to July which attract bees, give the perfect contrasting colours which can be used in companion plantings. The Victorians used to blanch the stems and use like celery, but nowadays it is grown more for its ornamental value which can extend well into winter if the seedheads are left on the plant. 2x1.2m (8x4ft).
Cool Companion: *Allium cristophii, Stachys byzantina, Phalaris arundinacea 'Feesey'.*

DICHONDRA

A silver annual trailer that can make stunning baskets or be used as groundcover. Enjoy the silver shimmer.

HOW TO GROW
Grown from seed. Best in moist but well-drained soil in full sun.

D. micrantha 'Silver Falls' bears small, silvered leaves which make a handsome trailing plant. As groundcover it smothers out weeds. Use it to advantage in hanging baskets, it cascades to 90cm (3ft).
Perfect Companion: Other seed-raised goodies such as *Solenostemon* and purple, shrubby *Alternanthera*.

Dichondra micrantha 'Silver Falls' above, Dicliptera below

DICLIPTERA

An ornamental from Uruguay with good foliage and flowers. Known as Hummingbird plant or King's Crown. I have also seen it referred to as silver acanthus, it is a member of the acanthaceae family.

HOW TO GROW
Heat in light shade to full sun and tolerates drought. Prefers a moist soil which is very well-drained. Z8b-11.

D. suberecta (Justicia, Jacobinia suberecta) this evergreen perennial has felted grey leaves and this beauty is topped off with terminal clusters of hot tubular red-orange flowers from late spring to early autumn. Foliage dies off around 5°C, roots are hardy to -12°C. 50x100cm (20"x39").
Perfect Companion: *Artemisia*.

Digitalis purpurea ssp heywoodii below

DIGITALIS

Stalwarts of the cottage garden, foxgloves are elegant with their large tubular bells. A British native with towering stems of beautiful flowers to watch over the garden.

HOW TO GROW
Well-drained garden soil in sun or light shade. Tend to seed prolifically. Most are biennial. Z4-8.

D. dubia bears silver-grey, hairy leaves with attractive pink flowers. This perennial foxglove is a Spanish native and enjoys a sunny site. 38cm (15").
D. purpurea ssp heywoodii bears downy foliage with a measurable silver effect. Whitish flowers. Known as the silver foxglove; this delightful form is excellent in full sun in a well-drained site. 45cm (18").
D. purpurea ssp heywoodii 'Silver Fox' bears silver foliage with angel pink and cream spotted flowers. Claimed to be 99% true from seed. Flowers are quite showy and deter attention from the foliage.

76

Draba longisiliqua

DINTERANTHUS

From the northern Cape, these unusual succulents are definitely a talking point, similar to Lithops (living stones).

HOW TO GROW
Will not tolerate overwatering, they need a summer rest. Minimum temperature 5°C.

D. pole-evansi is an amazing - 'that cannot be a plant!' - it is a stone look-alike. Solitary or clumping rounded 'stones' of light grey are slightly mottled. Needs to rest in summer. Yellow flowers.
D. vanzylii has irregular brown markings.

DRABA

Neat little silver cushions are on offer with these alpines for rocky crevices and rock gardens. When in bloom, they are smothered with flowers which cover the little cushions. One of the first to bloom in spring.

HOW TO GROW
Lots of sun, otherwise lean and mean conditions for best growth. Z3.

D. acaulis makes a tiny, tight silver cushion almost smothered in bright yellow flowers in early spring. Young plants may be loose, but these slow-growing alpines from Turkey eventually form dense cushions on maturity. 5x8cm (2x3").
D. cappadocica makes tight, velvety grey buns becoming a yellow mound in flower in spring. One of the elite. Take especial care when watering or we shall be talking a load of old rot!
D. longisiliqua makes low mounded cushions of silver rosettes made up of tiny, rounded leaves. The foliage is finely woolly. An excellent choice for the rock garden. 5x10cm (2x4").
D. mollissima will take a little shade and tolerate some wet which is surprising given its soft silver wool. This is the wooliest of the Drabas. Short-stemmed yellow blooms are borne in spring. Takes a long time to reach 5x15cm (2x6").
D. aff. tomentosa from Tibet comes this plant making small cushions of white tomentose leaves. White blooms are borne on short stems in spring. It is best in a crevice. 5x8cm (2x3").

Dudleya pulverulenta

DUDLEYA

A striking, Californian native that makes an almost hardy xeriscaping plant.

HOW TO GROW
Tolerates full or part sun and sand. Good drainage is essential and it is best to plant at an angle so that rain drains away. Likes to be dry in summer. Z8-10.

D. farinosa is an attractive succulent making low-growing rosettes of narrow, pointed, grey-silver leaves, which look almost white. The floury (farinose) coating repels water. Panicles of yellow flowers in summer adorn this great summer container plant. 10cm (4").
D. pulverulenta known as chalk *Dudleya* is a whitish evergreen succulent, a bit like a very large *sempervivum*. Older leaves appear green. The basal rosette is 60cm (2ft) and usually solitary, being very slow to clump. The leafy flower spikes bear pink flowers not to be missed. The centre of the rosette is almost like sugar candy icing.
Perfect Companion: Grow with other succulents for a stunning display.

DYCKIA

These native bromeliads of Brazil and South America are found in rocky places. A relative of the pineapple which is easy to grow.

HOW TO GROW
Full sun in cactus soil. They appreciate being well-watered. Bear in mind the large root system when choosing a pot. -7°C (20°F). Z9-12.

D. fosteriana makes striking clumps of spiky metal grey foliage which looks best in full sun.
D. marnier-lapostollei is even more silver, very silver, with its broad, spiny foliage and somewhat more handsome too. With too much sun, the leaf tips turn brown. 30cm (12") mature rosette. Z10-12.

ECHEVERIA

Use wide, shallow containers to show these succulents off to best advantage. Tender, but make good summer patio subjects or sink into the ground in the border.

HOW TO GROW
Easy in full sun in well-drained, gritty soil. Although drought tolerant, these succulents enjoy a deep watering and fertilization throughout the growing season. Avoid splashing water on the leaves. Keep frost free.

E. 'Crug Ice' makes neat pale green rosettes covered in a white bloom. The slender stem bears bright orange, knock-out flowers.
E. derenbergii (Graptoveria) has palish green-silver rosettes with evergreen leaves tightly packed together forming attractive, low-growing rosettes. In late winter racemes of bell-shaped yellow flowers are borne.
E. elegans has fleshy, silvered green leaves in a neat rosette with pink flowers in summer. This is a hardy evergreen. 15cm (6") high and twice as wide.
E. laui makes almost white rosettes, ghostly and glowing. Great luminescent contrast to darker or just green succulents. The icing on the cake. Flowers rise on pinkish stems.
E. lilacina makes handsome rosettes of a pearly grey.
E. 'Los Reynos' is outstanding for its silver, spoon-shaped leaves have a distinct peak very similar to my favourite succulent *Aeonium 'Zwartkop'*. Here the leaves form a tight rosette. Protect from frost. 15cm (6") and more than twice as wide.
E. 'Perle d'Azur' makes pearly grey and deep pink rosettes of pointed succulent leaves with pale yellow flowers in August to December. Protect from frost. 20cm (8").
E. pulvinata and the cultivar **'Frosty'** are very silvery.
E. shaviana what a beautiful plant this is, the silvery leaves are very wavy at the edge. Pink flowers match the pink edges of the leaves. 20cm (8") and twice as wide.
E. 'Topsy Turvy' has greyish green leaves that twist and curve to form rosettes that will certainly catch attention. Protect from frost. 15cm (6").
E. 'Van Breen' makes delightful silver rosettes of paddle-shaped leaves when protected from frost. 15cm (6").

ELAEAGNUS

A quick growing, deciduous shrub or small tree offering fragrance and colour in the garden. A tolerant shrub for difficult situations. Adaptable for hedging, edible landscaping and for attracting wildlife.

HOW TO GROW
Well-drained moist, light, acidic or alkaline soil in full sun. Withstands drought. Z3.

E. commutata (argentea) is known as silverberry. Its leaves are dusted with mealy silver. The silver coloured berries are sweet and edible. A slender, open form with reddish brown stems. 1.8-3m (6-10ft). Z2.
E. multiflora this wide-spreading shrub bears dark green leaves with silvery undersides and fragrant silvery blooms in late spring that are followed by reddish brown fruits. 3m (10ft). Z5.
E. 'Quicksilver' is grown for its attractive, narrow silver leaves and more besides. It has sweetly fragrant, small cream-yellow flowers in summer followed by small yellow oval fruits. Suitable for shallow chalk and enjoys a well-drained sandy soil. Found in England as a chance seedling and named by Roy Lancaster. Prune to several inches to encourage basal sideshoots. Can provide light shade for underplanting. Up to 6m (20ft).
E. umbellata is a wide spreading shrub with silvery young leaves, yellow flowers and small scarlet-red berries.
Cool Companion: *Cistus, Eucalyptus, Euphorbia.*
Hot Partner: *Euphorbia griffithii 'Fireglow', Clematis viticella* cultivars.

Left: Eriogonum acaule
Below: Elaeagnus 'Quicksilver'

ERIOGONUM

Ground hugging alpines or wildflowers in silver tones. Silver buckwheats have attractive foliage. Bob and Rebecca Skowron have a fine selection of these at Rocky Mountain Rare Plants.

HOW TO GROW
Normally found in rock crevices in full sun, they require well-drained soil.

E. acaule makes a silver dome of the tiniest leaves with little yellow flowers nestled into the tiny finger foliage. It grows in chalky soil.

E. cespitosum has small whitish leaves and yellow flowers.

E. crocatum bears silver-white, felted leaves and stems and yellow flowers. It is known as Conejo or Saffron Buckwheat. 20-25cm (8-10"). Z9-10.

E. kennedyi makes compact silver mounds with pink flowers on short stems.

E. ovalifolium is a white mound of tiny leaves in rosettes.

E. ovalifolium v depressum is similar and bears pink flowers on lax stems.

E. ovalifolium v nivale bears slightly looser white rosettes with deep pink flowers on short stems.

E. ovalifolium v ovalifolium bears yellow flowers above the white foliage.

E. ovalifolium v pauciflorum bears sparse tiny white flowers on short stems above looser grey-green, elongated, slender foliage.

E. pauciflorum and many of its cultivars are silver-leaved. All make tiny mats of grey foliage.

E. shickleyi bears ground hugging grey-green foliage with flowers nested or on very short stems.

E. umbellatum v polyanthum is silver-leaved with white flowers which mature to fawn.

E. wrightii v scaposum bears grey-green rosettes of tiny leaves and pinkish flowers on short stems. It is a sweet little ground-hugging alpine.

Eriogonum ovalifolium v depressum above
Eriogonum crocatum below left

ERIOPHYLLUM

The woolly sunflower I would grow for the leaves alone.

HOW TO GROW
In dryish soils in full to part sun.

E. lanatum is the woolly sunflower, a native of California. Bright yellow sunflowers are held in loose clusters atop stems in late spring. A delight in themselves but the winner for me is the foliage. Grey-green on top and silver woolly below, it is beautifully cut and fragrant. Bushy plants are 60-90cm (2-3ft).

ERITRICHIUM

Ground hugging, doming alpines in silver tones. These woolly leaved alpines are often tricky to grow. They are desirable for their stunning, forget-me-not blue flowers.

HOW TO GROW
Best in pots and need protection from too much rain. For trough or tufa in sharply drained, gritty soil in full sun.

E. howardii bears tiny silvery grey leaves in a dome topped with clear blue forget-me-not flowers. Easier in cultivation than *E. nanum*.

E. nanum (E. aretoides) bears tiny rosettes of green leaves well cloaked in silver hairs. The most outstanding feature of this plant is its clear blue, forget-me-not flowers in early summer. A real dainty beauty. This is the official plant of Grand Teton National Park in the U.S. It is a challenge to grow but known as the ultimate alpine and Glory of the Alpine Flora. 5-8cm (2-3").

80

Eriophyllum lanatum above, Eritrichium centre

ESPELETIA

An alpine from the Andes which is something to talk about! It is a tree-like species of the *Asteraceae* family with a large rosette of leaves. A little known and unusual relative of the sunflower.

E. pycnophylla is one huge rosette of felted, silvery leaves. 150 living leaves can be had on the end of one of the tree-like trunks. Dead leaves tend to line the trunk, offering protection and heat insulation against cold in the high altitude areas where this grows naturally.

ESPOSTOA

These woolly, columnar South American cacti are excellent for a warm, shady patio, this species cannot take full sun. Flowers are uncommon in cultivation and only occur after 10-30 years in their natural habitat.

HOW TO GROW
In their natural habitat they are found in very rocky soil. In cultivation, grow in any well-drained soil. They are rot prone if wet in winter, and do not tolerate frost. Never overwater.

E. lanata is a woolly cactus indeed. Knit a sweater from this one! 10cm (4") thick stems can eventually branch in their natural habitat to make a tree-like plant 4m (16ft) tall.
E. melanostele is similar but shorter and thicker stemmed. 2m (8ft).

Espeletia pycnophylla below

Eucalyptus gunnii

81

EUCALYPTUS

Fast growing Australian trees offering interesting foliage and sometimes outstanding bark. Keep the juvenile foliage by choosing varieties which coppice well.

HOW TO GROW
Occasional deep watering in full sun. Recommended Z8b-10, but some survive much lower temperatures. Essential to plant when young. Height given is in its natural habitat, expect much smaller proportions in the average garden but these long-lived trees often reach 10m (30ft) so site accordingly.

E. alba is the white gum, for its smooth bark becomes powdery white with age. It is a semi-deciduous gum that is both drought and frost tender. Sydney Parkinson was one of the artists employed by Sir Joseph Banks on James Cooks' first voyage to the Pacific, where he made a sketch of E. alba. 20m (60ft).
E. albens is known as white box for its slate-grey to bluish leaves. Its large canopy provides dense shade. 25m (78ft).
E. caesia is stunning, its grey foliage combines with powder-white branches to encapture the raptured. A pendulous, sprawling habit similar to flowering weeping cherry sports showy, creamy white flowers. A drought resistant and cold tolerant tree known as Silver Princess has larger flowers. 6m (20ft). Z9.
E. campaspe known as silver topped gimlet is an attractive, greyish-white leaved tree with a track record of being cold hardy and drought tolerant. It needs excellent drainage. 7.5m (30ft). Z9.
E. citriodora is a clean looking tree with a straight whitish grey bark and a sparse, open canopy. The long, narrow green leaves smell pleasantly of lemon when crushed. Popular under glass in colder areas, not for outdoors in the U.K. 15-25m (60-100ft). Z9.
E. coccifera is the Tasmanian snow gum, a spreading tree with peeling white bark. The long grey-green leaves are peppermint-scented. Wind and salt tolerant. 9m (35ft).
E. conspicua is the silver-leaved stringybark, very similar to E. cinerea (Silver Dollar) with attractive, rounded silver leaves often used in floral arrangements. Hardy and can be grown outdoors in Z7. 12m (40ft) in warm areas.
E. cordata is the heart-leaved silver gum, a variable tree with very upright growth in cultivation with attractive silver-white juvenile leaves which keep their form even as the tree gets very tall. Longer, adult leaves are only seen at the very top of mature leaves. The smooth bark is predominantly white. Excellent for coastal planting in moist soil. Outstanding as a shelter tree and tolerates a little frost but not drought. 4.5-20m (18-80ft). Z8.
E. crenulata has silver leaves, distinguished by crenulated margins. Useful in cold, wet areas, even in waterlogged soils. Very shade tolerant. 10m (30ft). Z9.

E. dalrympeana has beautiful white bark which sheds to reveal pinkish patches. Foliage can be variable but good silvery blues are to be had. Hardy to 3°F. 50m (150ft). Z8.
E. dunnii is a tall spreading tree which sheds its bark in strips to reveal a smooth white bark often with a scaly or corky trunk base. It grows quickly in rich soils with high rainfall. Hardy to 9°F.
E. erythrocorys is worthy for its grey to white peeling trunk. An excellent container plant, handsome in leaf and in its greenish to yellow flowers. 3m-6m (10-20ft). Z9.
E. grandis is noble with its smooth white to bluish bark and white flowers on a large tree to 60m (180ft). It can make growth of 1.8m (6ft) a year. Z9.
E. gunnii ssp divaricata is more silvery white than the species with pointed leaves. It coppices well. Vigorous, fast growth and hardy. 30m (90ft).
E. gunnii 'Silverdrop' is quite hardy and attractive in its silvery leaves.
E. laevopinea is known as silvertop stringybark, its crown has a silvery cast. One of the hardiest yielding good quality wood and good for the essential oil. Put a few drops in a bowl of water and inhale when you have a cold, it works wonders. 30m (120ft). Z9.
E. melanophloia bears silver leaves with rough, grey ironbark. It normally retains its juvenile leaves. White flowers are borne in summer. Moderately drought and frost tolerant. 10m (30ft). Z8.
E. nitens can have silvery bark. Nice blue leaves and red stems on a tall, fast growing tree. 15m (60ft) at least. Z8.
E. papuana is a shade tree with presence. Effective at night for its smooth white bark. Drought tolerant and cold hardy. One of the species called ghost gum. 10m (40ft).
E. pauciflora ssp niphophila bears beautiful adult whitish bark which peels to reveal undertones. Blue-green leaves and reddish stems. The snowy gum makes fast growth occuring in spring. Good drainage is essential. 30m (90ft).
E. pulverulenta is the silver-leaved mountain gum, threatened in its native habitat but widely available commercially. Its smooth bark shreds and it bears white flowers. It is similar to E. cinerea but more cold hardy. Its silvery grey juvenile foliage is the one usually on offer in the florist's shop. Not very hardy and a bit of a gangly tree. 3-10m (10-30ft). Z8.
E. 'Silver Dollar' makes a great specimen plant and is suitable in a container. Cut back for larger silver-grey, glaucous rounded leaves. Bark is grey and fissured when mature. It bears clusters of small white flowers in summer. The overall effect is silver rendering it superb for floral arrangements. Tolerates heat well in the Southeast U.S. 15m (60ft) often smaller in cultivation.
E. 'Silver Princess' has pink flowers.
E. tenuiramis is known as the Silver Peppermint from Tasmania. Smooth cream-coloured bark with grey patches is coupled with pendulous, shiny, silver-green leaves and white flowers. Requires good drainage. 15m (60ft). Z9.

GERANIUM

Handsome in leaf and flower, species *Geranium* are well worth growing. Cranesbills are hardy geraniums not to be confused with bedding geraniums.

HOW TO GROW
Alpines are not usually too tricky if attention is paid to drainage. Others are suitable in any reasonable soil.

G. x antipodeum 'Stanhoe' has silvered leaves and light pink flowers. This makes attractive ground cover with careful attention to drainage to just 7cm (3") high with a spread of 75cm (30").

G. argenteum is for those who like a challenge as this is not the easiest alpine geranium to grow. Admirable, nevertheless for its attractive silvery leaves (often used as a parent for this reason) and nicely cupped and veined clear pink flowers. A sumptuous but difficult little number. Appreciates a sunny position in rock crevices with protection from winter wet. 20cm (8").

G. incanum bears much divided, soft textured, grey-green leaves beneath a mass of purplish flowers. Spreading into a dense carpet with flowers almost all season long, this is an ideal garden plant. Looks pretty when used to soften the edge of a path. Equally at home in pots or hanging baskets. A South African native which is best in full sun, where it forms tight carpets, but will tolerate semi-shade. Hardy on the Californian coast, if cut back by frost, it regenerates in spring and normally self-seeds anyway. 25cm (10"). Z9b-12.

Geranium macrorhizum 'Variegata' is handsome in its white-streaked, green foliage making attractive groundcover on which pink tints appear in autumn. Lavender flowers bloom in abundance. It is tolerant of dry periods once established. Z5-8.

G. phaeum 'Variegatum' has burgundy flowers almost outmatched by the irregularly white edge and speckled green foliage. 45cm (18"). Z5-8.

G. sanguineum 'Variegatum' has deeply notched leaves displaying a white border beneath the lavender-pink flowers. 25cm (10"). Z5-9.

G. Silver Cloak Group the cut silvery foliage of this *G. incanum x robustum* cross has the perfect companion in its pinky-mauve flowers from May to July. 45cm (18").

G. 'Silver Shadow' is a seed variety with serrated silvery leaves and deep pink blossoms.

G. 'Silver Sugar Plum' bears filigree grey-blue foliage with striking violet-pink blooms in full sun. Z7-9.

G. yoshinoi 'Confetti' is an outstanding variety with marbled green and white foliage displaying pink tints in cooler weather. Pink flowers appear in May and June on this low spreader which makes some of the most handsome groundcover available. 20cm (8") tall and a spread of 90cm (36"). Z6-9.

Geranium 'Pink Spice' above
G. argenteum below

GNAPHALIUM

A choice but rare alpine. Plants in the same genus are found in the wild flora of Oregon and California.

HOW TO GROW
Rock garden conditions.

G. mackayi is a beautiful foliage plant forming low, flat mounds having small yellow flowers nestled amongst the silver foliage. Silver puff seedheads. Choice, hardy alpine member of the Aster family from the South Island of New Zealand. 5x20cm (2x8").

GRAPTOPETALUM

Known as mother of pearl plant, this is a silvery succulent which can make a useful patio plant in cooler climates as an outdoor display in summer.

HOW TO GROW
Full sun to light shade in well-drained soil with added horticultural sand. Allow to dry out before watering. Fertilize monthly. During winter, water only enough to keep the plants from shrivelling. Easily propagated by leaf or stem cuttings. Z9a-11.

G. 'Ghostly' is an apt name for this whitish, blue-tinted pink cultivar. Very pretty, it trails nicely from a basket.
G. paraguayense known as ghost plant is a charming succulent native of Mexico. Rosettes of grey leaves have a pinkish cast. Individual rosettes are up to 15cm (6") across and are best not handled as they can drop from the plant. In spring white flowers appear. In desert areas this will take morning sun only. In cool areas it is ideal as a houseplant. 30cm (12").

HAASTIA

These alpines, endemic to New Zealand are quite curious. The large cushion-forming species look like sheep from a distance which has earned them the common name of vegetable sheep. An excellent addition to the alpine house. Very much like sponges covered in cotton wool! Specimen plants are usually to be seen at alpine society shows.

HOW TO GROW
A reputation for not being easy makes this genus a challenge to grow. Avoid winter rain, give summer ventilation and pray the gods smile upon your efforts. Sow seed and grow in a deep, high gravel mix with coarse sand.

H. pulvinaris makes large cushions in the wild amongst rock and scree, but is a difficult plant in cultivation, as its small, hairy, grey rosettes are prone to botrytis. Its tightly rolled leaves are sheep-like from a distance. A good plant rarely reaches more than 20cm (8") before succumbing. Inconspicuous flowers are borne in summer.
H. pulvinaris v minor makes large grey cushions with age, up to 2m (8ft) across.
H. sinclairii bears greyish white, hirsute leaves.
H. sinclairii v fulvida is an attractive grey rosette forming variety. Grown at 1800m in its native habitat.

HALIMIUM

Very similar to and often confused with *Cistus* in the horticultural trade.

HOW TO GROW
As for *Cistus*.

H. halimifolium bears grey leaves combined with sunshine yellow flowers. 1m (39").
H. lasianthum has silver leaves and yellow flowers. Its loose habit spreads to 2m (8ft). 1m (39") tall. **'Hannay Silver'** is much larger and more vigorous with silvery, hairy leaves.

Graptopetalum paraguayense

84

Haastia pulvinaris

HEBE

The silver *Hebes* are so good for gravel, seaside or coastal gardens. Handsome foliage offering a foil for other colours and textures. Good in the border or containers.

HOW TO GROW
Unfussy as to soil. Easy and low maintenance.

H. albicans is a compact New Zealand native with white flowers from pinkish buds in summer. This very hardy evergreen makes a bushy, much-branched mound of smokey-grey leaves. An excellent border shrub and good in a container too. 60cm (2ft).
H. albicans 'Snow Cover' silvery green leaves and lavender flowers on a trailing variety which is very handsome tumbling from a container.
H. albicans 'Sussex Carpet' is a hardy, low spreading form with silver leaves and beautiful white flowers in June and July. 20cm (8") high and 40cm (16") wide.
H. 'Pewter Dome' makes a hardy, rounded dome of grey-green leaves on a much-branched shrub. Leaves are smaller than *H. albicans*. Short, dense, pointed spikes of white flowers appear in May to June from pink buds in light shade or sun. Raised at Jackman's Nursery, Woking, Surrey before 1972. 30-45cm (12-18").
H. pimeloides is a small, upright grower with grey leaves and mauvish flowers in summer. 30cm (12").
H. pimeloides 'Quicksilver' semi-prostrate, open, arching black stems bear silvery blue small leaves. Small, pale blue flowers are borne in June to July. Raised by Graham Hutchins of County Park Nursery in 1965 and selected for its grey foliage. 40x60cm (16x24").
H. pinguifolia 'Pagei' is the most commonly planted of the silver-leaved ones, a mainstay of large rock gardens. An attractive grey-green foil of tiny, numerous leaves with white flowers in May. This hardy evergreen makes a good front of border plant. 30cm (1ft).
H. pinguifolia 'Silver Beads' bears tiny silver foliage lending interest season long. 45cm (18").
H. pinguifolia 'Sutherlandii' makes a compact, rounded dwarf bush with a more upright, dense habit than *'Pagei'*. White flowers adorn the dome in May. It is one of the hardiest hebes. 15cm (6").
H. recurva 'Aoira' bears grey, pointed leaves, but I would grow this for the white flowers in July to August. It is a beautiful New Zealand form.
H. recurva 'Boughton Silver' makes a compact, evergreen, silvery shrub with occasional white flowers. 60cm (2ft).
H. 'Silver Dollar' is silver-green variegated with a red edge, but more creamy yellow in spring. Shoot tips are stunning burgundy in winter. 45cm (18").
Cool Companion: *Artemisia ludoviciana 'Valerie Finnis'*.
Hot Partner: *Ajuga reptans 'Atropurpurea'*.

HECHTIA

Sharp-toothed plants from tropical America and Mexico. One of an attractive number of bromeliads.

HOW TO GROW
Frost free, though will survive 26-28°F for short periods.

H. argentea is often seen as *Dyckia* and it does resemble this genus. Rosettes of thin, arching leaves with sharp spines with clusters of small white flowers. One foot long silver leaves are striking.

Hechtia argentea

Hebe pinguifolia

Hebe albicans 'Silver Edge' above, H.'Red Edge' below

HELIANTHEMUM

The versatile, shrubby rock roses are perfect for a hot, sunny border. Make it Mediterranean style. Summer blooms, long, tall glasses of cooling drinks, and rose and peachy blossoms to match. Evergreen in most areas and drought tolerant.

HOW TO GROW
Need very good drainage, especially in winter. Trim lightly after blooming. Z4.

H. 'Cheviot' a perfect peach of a colour against the foil of grey leaves. A superb companion to *Euphorbia 'Dixter'*. 25x45cm (10x18").
H. 'Henfield Brilliant' has bright orange-red flowers, brilliant in their intensity, but ever more so against the backdrop of silver-grey foliage. 25x45cm (10x18").
H. 'Raspberry Ripple' an ice-cream name and you want this one when it gets hot. Its hot pink flowers sizzle against the cooling silvery foliage. 15cm (6").
H. 'Rhodanthe carneum' ('Wisley Pink') is a study in pink and grey as the delicious, large rose-pink blooms sit amongst the mound of very silvery foliage. Its soft, alluring colouring goes well with *Eryngium variifolium*. 30cmx60cm (12x24").

Helichrysum ambiguum

HELICHRYSUM

From alpine everlastings to annuals for hanging baskets, this is a genus as varied as its habitats. Cushion alpines from Crete, Turkey, Yemen, Australia and South Africa. Superb drought-tolerant plants for the water-wise garden.

HOW TO GROW
Full sun and very well-drained soil. Appreciate good air circulation. Low humidity is preferred. Too much water will cause rotting and death and care must be taken where wet winters are the norm. Propagation is by seed and cuttings. Rock garden types are unlikely to be hardy even with protection and appreciate lean and mean treatment. See also **Ozothamnus**.

H. adenocarpum from South Africa bears silvery lanate leaves in rosettes with yellow flowers. Appreciates a slightly humus, sunny site. 30-45cm (12-18").
H. albo-brunneum makes large tufts with its crowded, silky satin grey rosettes like ribbons with wavy margins. White everlasting straw flowers have burgundy phyllaries. A hardy South African alpine which is worthy and grows well in dry landscapes. 25cm (10").
H. ambiguum bears clear grey basal, spathulate to oblong leaves with yellow to white flowers on long stalks in spring and summer. Makes delightful hummocks of rock hugging mats. In its natural habitat it is found amongst chalky rocks in Spain and the Balearic Islands. 15cm (6").
H. amorginum is a Greek species with basal, intensely silver leaves. Short, narrow stems bear 5 flowers in a flat flowerhead. Makes tufts in rocky crevices. 15-30cm (6-12").
H. appendiculatum from South Africa this makes a fine display of lanceolate, basal grey leaves to 8cm (3"). Clusters of yellow, sometimes pink daisy flowers are borne in summer in deep, well-drained soil. 30-60cm (12-24").
H. arenarium bears dense, lanceolate leaves of intense silver-white which are hirsute. Clusters of orange, red or yellow flowers in summer on short stems. A good subject for the alpine house. Found in dry grassland in its natural habitat. 20-30cm (8-12").
H. argentissimum from grasslands and rocky areas of South Africa makes basal rosettes of silver-grey leaves. Maroon backed white flowers have large bracts. Makes a favourable carpet. 10-15cm (4-6").
H. argyrophyllum is a grey-leaved plant from South Africa which looks nothing short of fantastic on a dry slope. It appreciates a rock garden site or sandy soil in an open position. An adaptable plant which grows well in both summer and winter rainfall regions. A low growing groundcover with canary flowers having a dark centre which remain on the plant for two months and are everlasting when cut within a week of opening. Dislikes fertilizer but an organic feed will promote season-long growth. Try it cascading from containers. 10cm (4").

Helichrysum appendiculatum
Helichrysum arwae

Helichrysum meyeri-johannis
Helichrysum sibthorpii

Helichrysum italicum

89

H. arwae is a little known variety from the Yemen, excellent for the rock garden. Crowded, lanceolate silver leaves with pink buds open to white flowers in summer. This shrubby, loose cushion is superb in a trough, raised bed or alpine house in poor, dry soil. Similar to varieties from South Africa's Drakensberg Mountains. 10cm (4").

H. 'Ashley Forest' makes silver groundcover to 70cm (28").

H. aureum ssp scopulosum is a dazzling South African variety, alluring with its silken foliage in grey rosettes with large yellow paperflowers in summer. Showy yet easy.

H. basalticum has rosettes of densely white hirsute leaves to 4cm (2") long. Flattened heads of yellow flowers, 20 at a time are borne in summer. This handsome mat-forming species possesses a sweet curry scent. 8cm (3").

H. bellidoides from screes in New Zealand this alpine with soft, silvery lanceolate leaves particularly to the underside, bears white flowers. Appreciates gravelly humus and is suited to the rock garden. 10cm (4").

H. caespititum has narrow silver, hirsute leaves with pink or white flowers. A South African native making carpets of neat foliage. 5cm (2").

H. cephaloideum makes grey lanate rosettes with broadly lanceolate basal leaves. Yellow flowers are borne in compact flowerheads on short stems. 30-40cm (12-16").

H. chionophilum makes a low spreading mat of silver-white foliage looking neat and attractive winter long when kept on the dry side. Linear leaves are 10cm (4") long topped by yellow flowers. A plant from rocky scree in Turkey. 10-15cm (4-6").

H. chionosphaerum is a trailing plant with silver-white leaves in rosettes. Branching stems carry white or yellow flowers with a yellow disc. 5-20cm (2-8").

H. compactum is a fine Turkish species forming basal clumps of grey, woolly foliage. Hairy, upright stems bear yellow daisies. Grow in hot, sunny, rocky sites. Best habit and colour is had by growing lean and mean. 8cm (3"). Z3.

H. depressum makes a low, small dark grey-green tuft, looking superb in a scree. 40cm

H. 'Drakensberg' hailing from that famous region so bedecked with wonderful plants in South Africa. Small, felted grey leaves with short stems and yellow flowers in July on an excellent performer.

H. filicaule bears greyish lanceolate leaves and grey stems with greyish white flowers. 10cm (4").

H. frigidum makes tiny tufts of prostrate silver stems and leaves. Terminal single, silvery white everlasting flowers appear all summer. From Corsica, this is ideal for a trough or raised bed. 10cm (4").

H. glaciale bears silvery leaves making small carpets. This South African native bears white flowers.

H. 'Graeme Paterson' makes silvery carpets to 70cm (28") wide. A prostrate form suitable for containers naturally occurring in alpine areas of New Zealand. Adorned with white papery flowers in summer. It needs good drainage and sun.

H. heldreichii is one of the best silver plants which is hardy in England. Remove the yellow flowers and simply enjoy the linear foliage which looks lavender-like. A Mediterranean native it is similar to *H. rupestre*, making tufts. 60-90cm (2-3ft).

H. 'Helping Hand' was developed by the National Botanic Gardens of Canberra as the floral emblem for the International Year of Volunteers. Best in full sun or semi-shade in well-drained soil, it is also suitable for pot cultivation. Its silvery grey leaves are set off by the pure white flowers with a yellow centre.

H. herbaceum bears alternate silver leaves with large yellow-orange solitary flowers. 15cm (6").

H. 'Icicles Silver' bears fine, narrow intensely silver leaves making an elegant addition to a dry border. Velvety to the touch. A compact seed variety which needs no pinching out. Z5.

H. italicum is more grey-green, but still very capable of giving a silver haze when planted against darker green or purple foliage. This well-known plant is noted for its unusual scent. Hardy in full sun, well-drained soil and excellent for the beginner. Small, everlasting yellow daises can be removed with pruning to keep the plant compact. 60cm (2ft).

H. italicum ssp serotinum bears silver, linear foliage with a curry aroma combined with yellow daisy flowers in summer. 1m (3ft).

H. meyeri-johannis found on rocky slopes of East Africa, this subalpine displays grey hirsute, broadly lanceolate leaves with red flowers on the outer petals and pink on the inside in summer to autumn.

H. milfordiae makes low, tight silver rosettes in mats of beautiful felted, silken foliage. From crimson buds everlasting flowers to 2.5cm (1") make their appearance in sunny, well-drained sites. A pleasant effect of two-tone buds and open flowers. A good, gravelly hardy scree plant needing little attention. Alpine house protection is needed in winter in England and it does well in tufa. A superb, hardy plant from South Africa. A favourite alpine variety with me for foliage alone. 5x20cm (2x8"). Z4.

H. mimetes has grey-white, oval leaves to 2.5cm (1") long. Many small lemon-yellow flowerheads appear in summer. An upright shrub which prefers humus soil. 20-50cm (8-20").

H. montanum bears densely white, lanate, narrow leaves and yellow flowers in clusters. The soft silver leaves make an attractive, shrubby carpet. 30cm (12").

H. obconicum bears beautiful, silver-green, oblong pointed leaves. This shrubby species is grown at Sollyer Botanic Garden in Mallorca, Balearic Islands. Stems are felted, and flowers are everlasting. It was seen by Joseph Banks in Madeira in 1768.

H. oreophilum bears white tomentose, lanceolate leaves to 8cm (3"). Lemon yellow flowers are borne on compact flowerheads on erect stems. 20-30cm (8-12").

Helichrysum 'Icicles'

H. orientale bears broad silvery, tomentose, dense basal leaves. Unopened buds are covered with silvery bracts which open to lustrous, creamy yellow in July to August. Flowers are scented. Excellent in a sunny scree or alpine house. An attractive evergreen native of Crete and southern Europe. 15-30cm (6-12"). Z7.

H. pagophilum has densely grey-white hirsute leaves in tiny rosettes forming neat cushions with straw yellow flowers in spring to summer. A highly ornamental alpine.10cm (4").

H. sp. aff pagophilum JJH is a high alpine from Halda forming dense cushions of silver foliage with yellow stemless flowers making a great trough specimen.

H. petiolare bears long silver-grey stems which can be used to weave amongst other plants or to great advantage in hanging baskets. The aromatic, silvery grey licorice plant is two-tone, one side grey, one side silver. This excellent filler on low growing, long stems can snake through other perennials. An excellent cooler for hot combinations and perfect in baskets and containers as a trailer. It is a gentle beauty, soft in colour, soft to touch, with a graceful habit. It can be used as an annual or perennial. This is on the exotic pest plant list in California. 90cm (3ft). Z9-10.

H. petiolare 'Goring Silver' is a less vigorous variety.

H. plicatum bears very silver foliage with bright yellow, papery flowers. This Turkish species does well on hot, stony gravel. Soft silver leaves make attractive spreading mounds which are highly decorative. 10cm (4"). Z3.

H. plumeum makes a compact, dwarf shrub bearing gnarled and twisted silvery, upright stems superb in the alpine house. Recorded at low and high levels of the Hunter Hills Conservation area in New Zealand. 40cm (16").

H. populifolium is an unusual shrub with grey leaves from South Africa, restricted to sandstone areas. Large, soft poplar-like leaves to 13cm (5"+) are round to heart-shaped. The white felted underside is most striking, accompanied by greener upper surfaces covered in grey felting as are the stems. Tiny flowers are borne in abundance in clusters in a large, terminal inflorescence. A great plant for textural interest, which can be pruned lightly in spring to keep in shape. Plants offered in cultivation are often *H. hypoleucum*. 1.2m (4ft) although appears to reach half that in England.

H. 'Ruby Cluster' is one of the best I have encountered. Small grey leaves and clusters of ruby red flowers in bud, open to straw yellow nestling amongst the foliage.

H. 'Schweffellicht' (Sulphur Light) bears silver-grey foliage with sulphur-orange, tawny flowers which pale as they age from July to August. This clump-forming perennial has woolly stems too. Can withstand heavy frost. 35cm (14").

H. sessilioides makes a wonderful cushion of silvery green, slightly hairy foliage. Typical everlasting flowers snuggle into the foliage with white bracts and a yellow eye. A hardy plant from Natal which is excellent in a trough.

H. sibthorpii has attractive felted hairy, silver leaves. This Greek native bears delightful salmon-pink buds which open to yellow. 10cm (4").

H. 'Silver Dome' is a low growing compact mound of silver foliage. Ideal in the rock garden or pots. It is very attractive. 15x30cm (6-12").

H. 'Silver Mist' with its finely textured silver leaves and stems, it makes a perfect companion plant in the border. It shines in full sun. A seed variety which is self-branching. 15-20cm (6-8").

H. 'Silver Spike' bears almost white-silver, fine leaves, eye-catching in the border where it makes a fast growing mound. Possibly the same as *'Icicles Silver'*. 25-30cm (10-12"). Z8-10.

H. splendidum is a feathery, silver shrub topped by a mass of tiny, yellow everlasting flowers in summer. Flowers have a slight sweet scent and when cut last well in water. Stems are woolly and felted on this fast-growing shrub. Slender leaves point heavenwards with leaf margins rolled, making leaves appear narrower. A camphor aroma is evident when leaves are crushed or bruised. 1.5x1m (5x3ft) in 2 years. This South African native is found on rocky slopes, forest margins and stream gullies as well as mountain tops. The plant has been used to treat rheumatism. Give the plant a little room so that it does not smother neighbours.

H. stoechas bears white hirsute, narrowly linear leaves to 2cm (1"). It has variable flowerheads in summer. Has been burned in houses to purify the air and was used by the Romans to adorn statues. 20-50cm (8-20").

H. stoechas 'Silverlover' is remarkable for its shining silver leaves. Z8.

H. thianschanicum (lanatum) is found wild in Australia. It is a highly decorative, shrubby species with small leaves covered in silver fuzz. 30cm (12").

Hot Partner: *H. petiolare* is an excellent basket plant associating well with purple, red and pink plants such as *Lobelia, Scaevola, Verbena, Petunia*.

Helichrysum sessilioides

HELLEBORUS

The stinking hellebore, *H. foetidus*, what a misnomer and unfair representation of a common name this plant has. A fine foliage plant which is handsome in flower too. It is in this species that most silvery leaved forms occur. Tough, undemanding and handsome.

HOW TO GROW
Part sun to light shade in humus rich soil. *H. foetidus* usually self seeds. Z7-8.

H. argutifolius Janet Starnes Strain is a variegated form with evergreen leaves well splashed and speckled in white. The elegant leaves are coupled with handsome large greenish to white flowers in winter. Full sun in this case would probably lead to some leaf burn, so provide midday shade in sharply drained soil. It appears to be more vigorous than the similar *'Pacific Frost'*. There is also a form in which the flowers have a brilliant touch of red, known as *'Sparkling Red Eye'*. 60cm (2ft). Z6-9.

H. argutifolius 'Silver Lace' (PBR) is simply breathtaking. Stunning in shape, stunning in colour, stunning in venation. Pewtered spiky, toothed foliage possesses a delicate tracery of veins. Light green flowers in spring. A nice, year- round foliage spectacle that is best in semi-shade or shade. A superb perennial from Lynda Windsor and Rodney Davey of RD Plants, Devon, England. 45-90cm (18-36").

H. foetidus 'Frenchy' discovered in the French Alps bears silvery, narrow foliage with red hints and some red flushes on floral sheaths.

H. foetidus 'Red Silver' is a seedling strain from two of the nicest people in horticulture, Ernie and Marietta O' Byrne of Northwest Garden Nursery in Oregon. Silver-grey leaves with superb red petioles, tepal base and stems coupled with immensely attractive green flowers. An absolute staple in light woodland. Prefers a little more sun and very sharply draining soil. Z5.

H. foetidus 'Silvertooth' should not disappoint with its dramatic silver leaves and fantastic toothed margins. A spontaneous selection from Barry Glick of Sunshine Farms in the U.S. It is a real silver spear for the woodland or shade garden.

H. foetidus 'Sopron' selected by Hellebore collector and specialist, Will McLewin of England, this has dark metallic foliage, larger and more robust than the species. Blooms are quite open rather than cup-shaped with a paler flower. Makes a nice big specimen.

H. foetidus 'Wester Flisk' is probably the oldest selected grey leaved form. Red at the main stem often reaching into the petioles with pendent green flowers. Choice if you can obtain one close to the original which came from Scotland. Sadly, this appears to be variable in cultivation nowadays.

H. lividus is noteworthy for its silver marbled leaves. Not absolutely hardy.

H. sternii 'Boughton Beauty' has the veining from its parent *H. lividus*, and the hardiness of its other parent *H. argutifolius*. Unfortunately this attractive cultivar named by Valerie Finnis of the U.K. has become quite variable in cultivation. The greyish leaves are nicely veined.

H. sternii 'Rachel' from New Zealand's John Dudley comes this hellebore with superb aqua-green toothed leaves decorated with silver veins. Greenish pink flowers in spring. Slightly more winter hardy than *H. lividus*, one of its parents. 30cm (12").

H. 'Sunmarble' from Sunshine Farms also bears intricate marbling on leathery, evergreen leaves. White, sterile flowers to 12cm (5") last for months. Hardy.

HEMIGRAPHIS

Tropical foliage often used as an aquatic. Also suitable as groundcover.

HOW TO GROW
Well-drained soil, bright light and night temperatures of 60°C (16°F).

H. alternata has a silver overlay on its oval leaves.

H. coloratus 'Silver Waffle' makes superb silver-pewter groundcover. Handsome veined leaves on purplish stems. Full sun darkens the foliage to deep purple making this a great companion for the purple waffle plant, *H. repanda*. White flowers contrast perfectly. A great basket plant.

Hemigraphis alternata

94

HEUCHERA

Who could ask for better foliage? Versatile, the best cultivars are evergreen and have good flowers too, the only reason coral bells were once grown, now often secondary to the shimmering, chameleon-like foliage.

HOW TO GROW
Full sun to part shade with good drainage. Lift and replant every three to four years. Z4.

H. 'Autumn Haze' (TN) the silver base of this compact form is adorned with cinnamon and purple. 20cm (8").
H. 'Can Can' (TN) the silvery leaves with a ruffled edge might well have you dancing, especially when the delicate flowers on tall stems start to sway.
H. 'Crown Jewel' has green-veined, silvery leaves. The round to heart-shaped ruffled leaves are maroon on the underside. One of the jewels in its crown is its ability to sail through torrid torrents or sizzle in the heat and still send up coral bells. Compact. 90cm (36"). Z4-8.
H. 'Frosty' bears white and variegated frosted foliage, topped by coral flower spikes. It appreciates excellent drainage.
H. 'Geisha's Fan' (TN PPAF) bears dark leaves with a silvery veining on attractive wide, fan-shaped foliage. Pink flowers.
H. 'Gypsy Dancer' (TN 2004) light pink flowers lead the eye down to dark metallic foliage which is superbly veined. Unlike most, this does not need long cold treatment to bloom and is expected to perform well in warmer climates such as California.
H. 'Jade Gloss' bears silvered leaves with large, prominent green veins and a brilliant red underside, topped by pink flowers.
H. 'Mint Frost' (TN) minted frost, nothing comes cooler than this hybrid. Red petioles and a red blush in autumn add pizzazz to this spectacular form. In winter, the foliage turns purple and the veins silver. Captivating.
H. 'Monet' has whitish leaves splashed with green topped with contrasting red flower spikes on this vigorous form.
H. 'Petite Pearl Fairy' has small, bronzed leaves marbled elegantly with silver. A floriferous little gem, its pink flowers on 25cm (10") stems are eye-catching against the small mound of metallic foliage. Appreciates rich soil and full sun.
H. 'Pewter Moon' bears silver-grey leaves with pewter veining and delicious maroon undersides. Showy, ice pink flowers in late spring. Not evergreen. 60-75cm (24-30").
H. 'Pewter Veil' (TN) offers stunning silver-pewter leaves with intricate veining in bronze and green. A copper-pink blush adorns the plant in spring. Sprays of creamy flowers appear in June.
H. 'Prince of Silver' bears silver leaves overlaid with purple. 30cm (12").

H. 'Ruby Veil' (TN) bears large leaves up to 20cm (8") across with metallic grey venation over ruby red. Sun tolerant and a reliable performer.
H. 'Silver Indiana' (PBR) is evergreen, its misty foliage is covered in silver. Off white flowers are displayed on straight stems. 35cm (14").
H. 'Silver Lode' (Oliver PPAF) is dark, matt silver with dark green veining. The underside of the leaves is reddish purple. White flowers come from pink buds on burgundy stems. One of the new breed for winter show power, tolerant of dry summer shade and a prolific flowerer into July. Up to 1m (3ft).
H. 'Silver Maps' is a dwarf form of *'Silver Scrolls'* having smaller leaves with the same colouring and pattern.
H. 'Silver Scrolls' (Oliver PPAF) is a miracle of wide, scalloped silver foliage having a plum overlay and veins with white coral bells on purple stems in June to July. It is best in shade but does tolerate morning sun. 60cm (24").
H. 'Silver Shadows' (TN 1994) shimmering metallic pewter leaves with a rose overlay in spring on a compact mound with amazing 15cm (6") leaves.
H. 'Snow Angel' has strong white patterning on green leaves matched with bright pink flower spikes.
H. 'Strawberry Candy' has green foliage marbled with silver and outstanding coral bells. Plant this for flower and foliage.
H. 'Venus' has leaves of metallic silver with a slight trace of green here and there and dark veins. Good foliage with a nice sheen, nearly white flowers are second best. Part of the *'Planet Collection'* from Holland, very similar to Oliver's *'Silver Scrolls'*. 30-40cm (12-16"). Z4.
Cool Companion: *Blue Hosta, Brunnera macrophylla 'Looking Glass', Lychnis coronaria, Echinacea 'White Swan'.*
Hot Partner: *Athyrium niponicum v pictum, Berberis thunbergii 'Atropurpurea Nana'.*

Heuchera 'Amethyst Myst'

Heuchera 'Cancan' above, H. 'Geisha Fan' below　　　*Heuchera 'Silver Shadows', H. 'Gypsy Dancer' below*

Heuchera 'Green Spice' below　　　*Heuchera 'Pewter Veil' below*

96

Juniperus

x HEUCHERELLA

Combining the attractive foliage of *Heuchera* with the pretty bells of *Tiarella*, you are on to a winner. These are great shade plants, tolerant of overhead trees such as apples, beech or maples.

HOW TO GROW
Full sun or light shade in fertile, moist but well-drained, neutral soil. Z4-9.

x H. 'Quicksilver' (Oliver) has metallic leaves with a rich, red-purple reverse. From 45cm (18") stems, soft pink buds open to white starry flowers in May and June for 9 weeks. Winter leaves take on darker hues and a purple flush appears in spring before the silver overlay delights. Unlike most, this is bred with a different *Heuchera* parent, offering drought tolerance and toughness.
x H. 'Silver Streak' another of Dan Heims' great achievements. Palmate leaves have overlays of platinum and purple. White flowers with a hint of lavender are carried on sturdy stems from April to July. A second flush of flowers is possible in late season. 30cm (12").
x H. 'Viking Ship' maple like silver-mottled leaves develop little babies separated from the tips. Pink flowers.
Hot Partner: *Geranium phaeum*.
Cool Companion: *Carex nigra, Athyrium niponicum v pictum*.

HIPPOPHAE

H. rhamnoides bears silvery leaves but is usually employed as an ornamental for its display of bright orange fruits in autumn. Plants of both sexes are needed for fruiting. 10m (30ft). Z3.

HYPTIS

This is a selection from a wildflower I found during my research, unknown to me beforehand. An interesting evergreen useful for attracting bees.

HOW TO GROW
Best in sun in well-drained soil, needing no extra water in cool coastal climates. Try it in a hot, sunny wildflower garden. Z8.

H. emoryi 'Silver Lining' is a shrubby member of the mint family known as desert lavender. The rounded, grey leaves of this Californian native remind me of *Ballota*. Foliage is scented sage-lavender and quite delicious combined with lavender flowers. It is drought tolerant, but does respond to watering in some hot climates or to increase the growth rate. May need shearing to maintain compact form. Hardy to 20°F. Up to 1.8m (6ft) and 90cm (3ft) wide.

JUNIPERUS

The silvery junipers make a superb foil in the garden whether in the border or amongst other conifers and are especially handsome in winter.

HOW TO GROW
Full sun to partial shade. Unfussy as to soil.

J. communis 'Berkshire' is a small, globose plant with silver-green leaves which display purple hints in winter. Superb for the rock garden or trough. Enjoys being in the sun. 30cm (1ft) high and twice as wide in 20 years. Z4.
J. communis 'Kenwith Castle' makes a neat mat of silvery green leaves.
J. communis 'Sentinel' has silvery green leaves which make a slim column.
J. scopulorum 'Moonglow' is probably the most silver of the junipers with a hint of powdery blue. This dense growing upright, conical plant makes a fine subject for topiary. 1.5-3m (5-10ft).

KALANCHOE

Known as panda plant or pussy ears although the leaves can become more horizontal with age. Good for rock gardens in arid regions.

HOW TO GROW
Best in full sun to light shade or bright, indirect light indoors with little water. Good drainage essential. Fertilize once during the growing season with half strength fertilizer. Water once a month. In winter, water enough to prevent shrinking only. Enemy number one-overwater to kill! Propagate by stem or leaf cuttings. Z9-12.

K. beharensis in this form is silvery leaved and quite enormous. Absolutely amazing, I love this silver giant.
K. pumila is a wonderful pearl of a plant. Low growing, silver succulent foliage and pure pink flowers from mid spring to summer in full sun. A stunning container evergreen with protection from frost. 20cm (8").
K. tomentosa has to be a favourite succulent. It reminds me of one of those 1970's nodding dogs for the back of a car that were covered in a felted material. Both upright leaves to 7cm (3") and stems are velvety. Its grey-white felted leaves are edged and spotted in brown. Bears yellow-green flowers with red glandular hairs, often not seen in cultivation. From Madagascar, this makes a nice houseplant in cooler regions such as the U.K. A dense, leafy perennial shrub which branches from the base to 50cm (20"). If growing outdoors in Z10-12, give midday shade. Takes some time but can reach 1.5m (5ft)

Kalanchoe tomentosa above,
K. beharensis top left,
K. pumila below

Lavandula 'Blue Ice'

Lavandula 'Goodwin Creek Grey'

Lavandula 'Blue Mountain White'

Lavandula lanata

Lavandula dentata

Lavandula stoechas 'White Madrid'

LAVANDULA

Needing no introduction, the silvered lavenders are the most sought-after and probably some of the most attractive and superb mainstays of the dry garden. The scent is exquisite on a warm summer's day, the epitome of relaxation. Dependable, drought tolerant and handsome in flower with a heady aroma, particularly from *angustifolia* varieties. Think fragrant edging, think perfumed laundry, think relaxing oil. The pleasures of lavender are many in the home and garden where it deserves to be used en masse. Perennial queen of the dry landscape. Most lavenders bloom for around five weeks.

HOW TO GROW
They appreciate really good drainage and a site out of humid, wet soil which causes rot. Lots of sun in lean soil; they relish neutral soil. Good air circulation deters fungal diseases prevalent in wet areas. Trim to keep compact, but never cut back into old wood. Many cultivars trimmed in June will offer a second flush of flowers. They do cross-pollinate, so if you wish to collect seed, grow plants in isolation and bear in mind that some of the best cultivars are sterile. Seed is a slow process and it also has short viability. Cultivars must be grown from vegetative cuttings, seed-raised plants should never be sold under the cultivar name. In Zone 8 and above expect your plants to flower earlier and to get bigger. Z5-9.

L. x allardii is a French hybrid bearing broad, silver, toothed leaves and performing well in hot, humid areas. Light lavender flowers. A tall yet quite compact hybrid not rangy like the French types at 120-150cm (4-5'). Z9-10.

L. 'Ana Luisa' is as pretty as its name, there is so much down that it appears white. Shimmering leaves with bluish lavender flowers in June to August give a luminous cast. Foliage similar to its parent *L. lanata*; it remains handsome into winter. 60cm (2ft). Z6.

L. angustifolia has the best fragrance for oil production and if you want to know how to keep your bronze statues glowing, rub them with this as they do in the Metropolitan Museum of Modern Art. Known as English lavender, it is actually a Mediterranean native. Often found mislabelled as *spica, officinalis* and *vera*. The hardiest of all lavenders cultivated since 1568.

L. angustifolia 'Blue Ice' include this new introduction for its ghostly pale blue flower and calyx. It is an exquisite complement to the darker cultivars. 60cm (2ft).

L. angustifolia 'Blue Mountain White' a beautiful rare form, valued for its white flowers. Introduced from New Zealand. 60cm (2ft).

L. angustifolia 'Bowles Early' sometimes seen as *'Bowles Grey'* bears dense, fine silvery foliage with a scent to be relished. Flowers in late summer. 60cm (2ft).

L. angustifolia 'Folgate' bears grey-green leaves with abundant purple-blue flowers. Easy. 40-50cm (16-20").

L. angustifolia 'Graves' has the distinction of possessing the longest, upright grey-green leaves of this species. Tantalising green buds tinged purple open to dark violet blooms in June to July. 90cm (3ft). Z5.

L. angustifolia 'Hidcote' is a well-known and popular dwarf variety, an old mainstay and safe choice. Dark, midnight violet flowers over grey foliage. Admirable in a cool climate. Z5-7.

L. angustifolia 'Imperial Gem' makes a grey-green bush topped by rich, vibrant violet petals with darker calyces. This selection from *'Hidcote'* is a good performer and a neat grower that is impressive en masse. 60cm. Z5.

L. angustifolia 'Loddon Pink' aromatic light pink flowers will grab the attention swaying above the compact, silver-grey foliage. *'Jean Davis'* is similar, thought to be the same at RHS trials, but more research is being done. I believe it is a smaller variety. Mountain Valley Growers in the U.S. say the difference is in the taste! 50cm (20").

L. angustifolia 'Martha Roderick' is exceptional for its fragrance, performance and light lavender colour combined with silver-grey leaves. A reliable, slow-growing U.S. variety, superb for a low hedge with its compact, rounded growth and season-long bloom through summer. Crush and sniff. 45cm (18"). Z5.

L. angustifolia 'Miss Katherine' (Norfolk Lavender) is an excellent cultivar for those who crave pink lavender. Deep pink flowers with distinctive silver calyces top a shapely mound of grey-green, toothed foliage. Your pink prayers are answered in fragrant allure. 60cm. Z5.

L. angustifolia 'Miss Muffet' (1999 PBR) bears lilac-blue flowers over diminutive silvery foliage. Not to be hidden away on the tuffet, this Miss Muffet deserves pride of place. 30cm (12").

L. angustifolia 'Mitcham Gray' has deep purple flowers over fragrant grey foliage. Long flowering stems and a quick grower make this a nice anchor. Z5-10.

L. angustifolia 'Twickel Purple' is a handsome but variable variety. The National Collection has had three different varieties all under this name. Will the real *'Twickel Purple'* stand up? Silvery, aromatic foliage can blush purple in winter. Deep lavender-blue flowers are nicely shaped, dense and fragrant on long spikes from mid to late summer. Vigorous, strong grower. 50cm (20").

L. buchii is not a species you will find everywhere, especially not under this, the correct name, it is often found as a subspecies of *pinnata*, yet *buchii* has shorter bracts and is a much taller plant. Endemic to Tenerife, it is worth seeking. The distinguished, silver fern-leaf has aromatic, rubbery foliage and bears light blue to lavender flowers, darker at the base on long, thin stems and blooms almost all year. Flowers are held on a trident. Compact in growth, it is best grown from seed, which is produced abundantly, easy to raise and comes true. Z8-10.

Lavandula 'Richard Grey'

L. x christiana bears architectural silvery foliage, long-stemmed and finely cut, trident flowerheads hold blue flowers. Good container subject, which needs protection from frost. 40cm (16").

L. dentata is slightly delicate but well worth the effort for its deeply toothed, aromatic leaves and pale flowers. More green than silver. 90cm (30").

L. dentata 'Silver Queen' appreciates a warm, sheltered spot. Handsome indoors in northern areas with its compact habit. Z7-10.

L. dentata v candicans bears soft, grey, furry, dentate aromatic leaves paired with pale blue-mauve flowers with showy, terminal purple bracts in June and July, although capable of blooming almost year round in the right conditions. Greyer than the species. Protect from frost but it is more robust than the species. Native of North Africa, Madeira and the Cape Verde Islands. 50cm (20"). Z7-10.

L. 'England' is a miniature gem of silver foliage. Light violet-blue flowers are as dainty as the foliage in summer. Excellent for a tiny garden space. 30cm (12"). Z6.

L. 'Goodwin Creek Grey' from the nursery of the same name in Oregon, U.S. is an accidental cross between *L. heterophylla* and *L. lanata* from Jim Becker blooming throughout the year in warm climates with its deeply toothed, white-silver foliage looking excellent in large tubs. Long spikes of small, soft lavender-blue flowers. One to try in the southern U.S. states as it will take some heat and humidity. In fact, one to try anywhere, grow it in the border or as edging. Vigorous yet compact, sturdy, elegant and fragrant, a glorious cultivar but only half-hardy. Z7-9.

L. x intermedia is slightly later flowering than *angustifolia*. Used nowadays for oil production, but the oil is of inferior quality to *angustifolia*. A good choice for hedging, line your path with these varieties. The long leaves are twice the size of *angustifolia*.

L. x intermedia 'Alba' bears pure white flowers over silver foliage.

L. x intermedia 'Arabian Night' good grey leaves take on purple tints in winter. Very fragrant, mid-blue to violet flowers from June to July. Nicely aromatic bushy shrub, which is great in the border. 60cm (2ft).

L. x intermedia Dutch Group is a name that refers to many beautiful silver foliage plants.

L. x intermedia 'Fragrant Memories' (1994) makes a fine, handsome silver foliage, bushy mound with broad leaves. Long pale purple flowerheads flowering in mid to late July. 80cm (32").

L. x intermedia 'Fred Boutin' is one of the most silver, looking good in winter. Long, slender spikes of pale violet flowers in summer. If you are looking for a paler contrast to a darker *'Hidcote'* or *'Imperial Gem'*, this is it. Dense, rounded habit and fragrance make it a good ornamental in mixed beds. Found as a seedling at Huntington Botanic Gardens, U.S. 45cm (18").

L. x intermedia 'Futura' is a compact, aromatic silver-grey leaved variety. Light blue flowers appear from June to July. 80cm (32").

L. x intermedia 'Grappenhall' combines aromatic silver leaves with large pale mauve, fragrant flowers. Purplish hints to the foliage in winter. One of the largest varieties making a good specimen with tall bloom spikes superb for cutting. 80cm (32"). Z5.

L. x intermedia 'Grosso' (1972) makes an attractive mound of grey-green foliage topped by fat flowers (7-15cm, 3-6" long and 2cm, 1" wide) in dark purple tones which are very fragrant having a scent between that of lavender and rosemary. Easy to overwinter in dry soils. A good choice for all round use and grown worldwide commercially for oil. Make your lavender wands from this. 60cm (2ft). Z6.

L. x intermedia 'Maillette' is worth planting for its winter foliage effect. Grey leaves with lavender-violet flowers and darker calyces from June to July. Used commercially in oil production for its superb scent. 35cm (14").

L. x intermedia 'Provence' one of the top commercial oil producers, slate-grey leaved with excellent, powerful and sweet scent and lanceolate foliage. Lavender-blue flowers can appear from summer to autumn. 60cm (2ft) although it makes a much larger specimen with time.

L. x intermedia 'Seal' aromatic flowers on long stems, florally lavender-purple, foliar grey-silver. A tall growing variety, an old one, but still worthy for its strong scent. 60cm-80cm (24-32"). Z5.

L. x intermedia 'Silver Dwarf' a tiny, silver gem.

L. x intermedia 'Walberton Silver Edge' a variegated type with green leaves having a silvery cream edge. Light blue fragrant flowers. I prefer straight silver foliage to this variegated version. 40cm (16").

L. x intermedia 'White Spikes' with its pleasantly fragrant white flowers and soft grey foliage is like driven snow. Subtle sage green buds evoke a relaxed mood. Flowers from June to October and is a good choice for cut flowers. An old variety, known before 1880. 60cm (2ft). Z6.

L. lanata is tougher than you might expect. The woolly, white-leaved lavender comes into flower when other lavenders are waning. Deep purple corollas and dark blue flowers. Appreciates a warm, sheltered site as it will not survive frosts but it is usually water-logging that kills the plant. 60-90cm (2-3ft). Z8-10.

L. lanata x angustifolia 'Gorgeous' (2003 Downderry Nursery) is a real dark beauty. Deep flowers over silvered foliage is a winning combination. 70cm (28").

L. lanata 'Lambikins' is a fuzzy leaved, fat toothed variety with soft grey leaves and light lavender flowers with a subtle scent. 45cm (18"). Z8-10.

L. lanata 'Silver Leaf' has soft near white foliage with small dark violet flowerheads.

L. lanata 'Silver Frost' the fabulous silver winter foliage is complemented in summer with dark purple calyces and lavender flowers.

L. latifolia has broad grey-green leaves. Lavender blooms appear in late summer.

L. 'Lisa Marie' was introduced by Ken Montgomery of Anderson Valley Nursery, a cross between *L. angustifolia* 'Martha Roderick' and *L. dentata*, which exhibits the best characteristics of its parents. Superb silvery foliage in compact mounds with frosted grey buds opening into blue-violet in June to September. An exquisite charmer. 45-60cm (18-24"). Z6.

L. minutolli is an architectural gem from the Gran Canaria. The green-grey, felted foliage has a delectable sweet scent. Incised, felted arrowhead leaves are topped by blue-purple flowers. Responds well to severe pruning. Tender, a good choice for a conservatory. 60cm (24").

L. 'Moroccan' is a *lanata x angustifolia* cross bearing the best attributes of its parents, hardiness from the latter and bright silver foliage from the former. Profuse dark blue flowers on slender stems give yet another reason for rendering this a good choice. 60cm. (2ft).

L. pinnata is an outstanding species for its aromatic silver, dentate foliage which is ferny paired with its blue flowers on triple stems, intricately veined, which spiral along the flowerhead. Makes a good specimen container plant. Protect from frost.

L. 'Richard Grey' (1980's) is a soft, woolly felted hybrid with very silvery foliage appearing almost white, compact growth and bright purple corollas. Close to 'Sawyers'. It is hardy given very good drainage in a sheltered spot. 60cm (2ft). Z5.

L. 'Sawyers' bears exceptional, bright silver-grey foliage coupled with pointed, fragrant, violet flowers with darker calyces in June to August. A form well suited to hedging for its spherical shape. Not easy to overwinter unless it is kept exceptionally dry. 60cm Z6.

L. 'Silver Frost' is one of the most silver lavenders with silvery blue calyces and deep purple corollas. Forms a shimmering cushion of woolly foliage with abundant flowers. 60cm (2ft). Z6-9.

L. stoechas 'Kew Red' is a different colour break, not an easy one to grow, and I am not enamoured. Pale pink bracts and violet-red blooms on a long flowering variety with grey-green foliage. For flowers, *stoechas* has long been my favourite but this colour does nothing for me at all. 60cm. Z8. Many *stoechas* cultivars have grey-green foliage. For the white garden, **L. stoechas 'White Madrid'** is admirable. The bunny ears are white.

Hot Partner: *Heuchera 'Silver Scrolls', Cotinus 'Grace'.*

Cool Companion: *Agastache foeniculum, Perovskia atriplicifolia, Salvia officinalis Purpurascens Group*, white *Cistus, Ceanothus.*

Tender lavenders look great in containers with a cloud of airy *Gypsophila elegans* and the innocence of *Ompahlodes linifolia*, add white trailing *Lobelia* to soften the sides of the container with *Sutera* and *Verbena*.

LEONTOPODIUM

A hardy perennial often grown as a biennial. Edelweiss is the well-known, national flower of Switzerland. it is now endangered in the Alps owing to over collection.

HOW TO GROW
Full sun in well-drained, gritty soil, alpine conditions. Needs good care. Z4-9.

L. alpinum is forever associated with 'The Sound of Music' in my mind. It is a symbol of eternal love. Starfish-shaped woolly leaves surround the small flowers on this dainty alpine, much loved for its white blooms in summer. One of the sweetest members of the Aster family. 15cm (6").

L. kurilense linear leaves are felted on the underside and make small clumps in rock crevices with white flowers.

LEPTOSPERMUM

Make good hedges or standards. Most are tolerant of light frosts and extended dry periods. A superb choice for coastal areas as they are salt tolerant and make a good windbreak in exposed sites.

HOW TO GROW
Full sun or partial shade in well-drained soil. Z8.

L. laevigatum bears grey-green foliage and white flowers in spring and summer. Gnarled trunks develop on mature plants and this is a good choice for the small garden. 3-6m (10-20ft).

L. lanigerum is the woolly tea-tree. Tolerant of hard frosts once established. An attractive medium shrub with fine, grey-green leaves and slightly scented white flowers in spring to summer. 2-3m (8-12ft).

L. 'Silver Fantasy' *scoparium* has numerous cultivars, some with silver foliage. This one bears pretty, clear pink flowers on a large shrub with some frost tolerance. It will perform in partial shade. 2-3m tall (4-8ft).

L. myrtifolium 'Silver Sheen' is not as silver. This small shrub has a silver sheen to the dark green leaves covered in deep pink blooms in April to June. Frost hardy. 1.5cm (5ft).

Cool Companion: *Ceanothus 'Snow Flurry', Lavandula 'Sawyers'.*

LEUCADENDRON

These members of the Protea family make beautiful, silver trees, which have a relatively short life span, around twenty years. As a cut leaf, *L. argenteum* stems last a week.

HOW TO GROW
A sunny position with excellent drainage, good air circulation and adequate water. Dig in plenty of humus before planting. Keep well-watered for two years until well established. Mulch deeply. Z8.

L. album is the linear leaf conebush. Whitish bracts surround a central cone. This South African shrub is not threatened. It thrives on well-drained, sandstone slopes. 2m (8ft).
L. argenteum is one fantastic South African small tree known as silver tree. Found on Table Mountain and growing in large stands up above Kirstenbosch, this is one of nature's loveliest sights. Its natural habitat is being eroded by urban development. It has a delightful upright, symmetrical form. The lance-shaped, grey-green leaves are covered in silver hairs which reflect light and give a soft, shimmering look to the plant. A good choice for coastal gardens. Male and female flowers are borne on separate plants. Silver trees are very resentful of root disturbance. For me this pure silver, large leaved variety is the best. 3m (10ft).
L. 'Cloudbank Jenny' is a beautiful, medium sized, male shrub with grey-green leaves having red tips. Bright red cones are formed in spring and the surrounding foliage turns yellow.
L. discolor has grey-green leaves maintaining a bushy, erect habit if pruned when young. Creamy bracts surround the red central cone.
L. galpinii bears narrow, twisted, silver leaves with silver cones in winter to summer. Scented male flower cones are smaller than the females.
L. linifolia is grey-green although more green. It is an unusual form with a conifer look about it. Silver cones appear in spring. This makes a handsome, large container plant to 1.5m height and spread (5ft).
L. uliginosum makes a slender, silver-grey shrub with creamy yellow bracts in spring. 1.8m (6ft).

LEUCOGENES

A perennial herb which closely resembles *Edelweiss* but hails from the southern hemisphere, namely New Zealand, so please don't burst into that chorus of The Sound of Music again. Ideal for trough, rock garden or scree.

HOW TO GROW
Well-drained, gritty, acid soil in full sun. Take cuttings in late summer.

L. grandiceps is known as the South Island Edelweiss. It bears tiny silver leaves in tiny, ascending rosettes with comparatively large white flowers. 12cm (5").
L. leontopodium bears grey foliage all year round on compact ground cover. Good drainage is essential. This is known as the North Island Edelweiss and bears Edelweiss type flowers on short stems. 15cm (6").
L. tarahaoa makes a distinct cushion of tightly packed rosettes of small, pointed silver-grey leaves.

LEUCOPHYTA

Superb for beach gardens, these Australian natives provide good foliage contrast in the garden. Easy and low maintenance forming good weed-defying groundcover. Often labelled under the synonym *Calocephalus*.

HOW TO GROW
A sunny position in well-drained soil. Never overwater. They dislike humid areas and appreciate good airflow. Tolerant of wind, coastal conditions and light frost. Give a light feed in autumn and an occasional trim. Z9.

L. brownii makes a dwarf bush grown for its handsome silver foliage aptly known as the cushion bush. Fine branches are densely covered in silver hairs. 1x1.5m (3-5ft).
L. 'Silver Nugget' is a tiny mound of silver leaves excellent in a pot in well-drained soil. This compact form from Tasmania makes a mound with bright yellow button flowers borne in spring and summer. 30cm (12").
Cool Companion: *Astelia 'Silver Spear'*, *Beschorneria yuccoides*, *Lavandula*.
Hot Partner: *Thuja occidentalis 'Heatherbun'*.

Leucadendron argenteum

Leucophyta brownii

Mammillaria bombycina

Lychnis coronaria

Mammillaria compressa

LYCHNIS

Yet another silver leaved plant with the common name of dusty miller. Rebloom is encourged by deadheading. This is an easy to grow short-lived perennial.

HOW TO GROW
Full sun in well-drained soil. Will perform in poor soil and bright shade. Z3-10.

L. coronaria has bright eye-catching magenta blossoms in June to August atop silvery foliage. Large, woolly basal leaves in winter give rise to furry stems with bright rose-pink blossoms. An excellent cottage garden plant in well-drained soil. Stunning en-masse and much used in combinations with other hot colours. One that shouts and self-seeds profusely. 90cm (3ft).
L. coronaria 'Alba' is the variety for the white garden having the same foliage paired with white flowers. It is refined and elegant.
L. coronaria 'Angel's Blush' again has the typical silver foliage, soft to the touch, with white flowers, blushed pink with deeper pink striations.
L. coronaria 'Blushing Bride' bears the typical foliage but with blushing pink flowers fading to white petal edges. Very maidenly. I believe this to be the same as the *L. coronaria 'Oculata'*.
L. coronaria 'Gardeners' World' is a sterile form with white, woolly foliage beneath fully double, rich red flowers. Excellent hot colour from June onwards. Deadhead for continuous bloom. 60cm (24"). Z5-9.
L. coronaria Oculata Group bears the same foliage but with bright white flowers with a pink eye to 2cm (1") across. 60cm (2ft).
Cool Companion: Blue *Delphinium* or *Consolida* (annual larkspur), *Cosmos 'Sonata White'*.
Hot Partner: *Cosmos atrosanguineus, Nicotiana 'Domino Red'*.

MAMMILLARIA

Well known barrel type cacti can have soft white hairs or white spines.

HOW TO GROW
Sandy soil, well-drained in warm conditions. Fairly easy in four to five hours of bright light. Z9b-11.

M. candida looks like a spider has woven a neat grey-silver web around its paunch. The solitary, wide stems can cluster with age. The dense white spines cover the stem most effectively when grown in bright light. Pink flowers are borne in spring. -7°C (20°F) for short periods.
M. compressa makes small columnar growth with whitish tops and spines.
M. gemminispina almost looks like it has a crocheted top, which is near white with dark pink flowers in spring. -7°C (20°F).
M. hahniana has grey hair, the length and thickness of which varies. Dark pink flowers are borne at the tip of the rounded stems. -4°C (25°F).
M. nejapensis is a little green barrel with dense white spines.
M. plumosa is like a cotton wool brain. 5cm (2") wide stems form dense white mounds up to 30cm (12") wide. Small yellow flowers poke through in spring; these are not showy, but have a powerful sweet aroma. It is rot prone if water is trapped in the spines. -10°C (15°F).
M. supertexta has super texture in its fine white spines which completely cover the single, 5cm (2") across stems when grown in bright light with a minimum of water and fertilizer. Tiny, deep red flowers circle the stem in spring. It tolerates some frost.

Mammillaria

Cleistocactus straussii

Mammillaria

Mammillaria bocasawa

Marrubium incanum

MARRUBIUM

A Mediterranean perennial herb known as silver horehound from the rocky slopes of Italy, Europe and the East Mediterranean.

HOW TO GROW
A sunny spot in a dry garden, it is good for xeriscaping. Needs protection from winter wet. Z3-10.

M. incanum (M. candidissimum) bears whitish stems and grey-green foliage, densely felted on the underside. Near white flowers in summer. Similar to *Ballota*. 50cm (20").

MELIANTHUS

This shrub is a honey, one of the most architectural plants with such handsome foliage that it deserves to be in all gardens. It is one of those large shrubs that you can cut back hard and it will still make a quick show.

HOW TO GROW
In a warm, sunny position with good drainage. Although adaptable, it flourishes best in deep, rich soil with a good dose of water. Cut back hard to encourage new growth. Can survive frost, sending new growth up from the base. Easily propagated from seed or cuttings. Z7-8.

M. major is known as the honeybush for the sweet smelling flowers which attract birds to their nectar. It is a South African native, which bears large, bluish grey-green, pinnate leaves with a sawtooth edge. Leaves can be up to 45cm (18") long and cascade slightly. They are most attractive but have an unpleasant smell when bruised. In late spring to midsummer spiked racemes of brownish red flowers are borne on long stems. It makes quick growth and looks particularly handsome in spring. A very choice and worthy shrub. 2.5m (10ft), smaller in cool climates. It survives outdoors in South Yorkshire, England.

MENTHA

There is one word that always needs to be adhered to when growing mint - contain. You can leave pots free-standing or sink into the border. Grown in paths, foot traffic releases the scent. Described as the hospitality herb by Ovid, there is always enough mint to go around. It could win the Olympic gold medal for running! Only let it loose if you want a mint-only garden! Mint, delicious in flavour, knows no boundaries.

HOW TO GROW
Sun to part shade in rich, moist, well-drained soil. In the hottest zones, protection from hot afternoon sun is preferable. Divide every other year. Cut back flowering tops to keep a steady flush of new leaves. Sink containers in the ground, or create barriers with slate.

M. longifolia is known as silver or Himalayan mint. A vigorous, fragrant ornamental plant whose young, pointed leaves are silvery. Bears clusters of lavender flowers in late summer which have given rise to yet another common name of buddleia mint. Its strong spearmint flavour makes it a good choice for tea and it can also be used for mint sauce. It will attract bees to the garden but can be invasive in rich, moist soil in sun or part shade. Grow it with the darker mints and purple basils. 60cm (2ft).
M. suaveolens 'Variegata' is known as apple or pineapple mint. Its green and white variegated leaves are richly scented and combine with blue flowers in July to September. 35cm (14").
Hot Partner: Dark red roses.
Cool Companion: White or silver roses.

The new green leaves of Melianthus major soon turn bluish. The jagged-edged leaves shimmer in the border, making a handsome backdrop for silver foliage.

Origanum rotundifolium

METROSIDEROS

A great feature plant and suitable for a hedge to create privacy. These are popular evergreens for coastal areas.

HOW TO GROW
Full sun or part shade in well-drained soil. It tolerates coastal conditions. Protect young plants from frost. Cut back and feed with a slow-release fertilizer after frosts.

M. excelsa (tomentosa) is the New Zealand Xmas tree. At first a bushy shrub, it forms a stout leader with a large canopy. Deep green, oblong leaves are silver on the underside. In summer red flowers are borne.
M. 'Moon Maiden' is a compact, rounded tree with grey-green, glossy leaves and many clear yellow flowers reminiscent of bottlebrushes in early summer. Hardy in coastal areas. 5mx3m (20x12ft).

ONOPORDUM

An architectural beauty. Scotch thistles are thought to have been introduced from Europe in the 1800's as an ornamental. Capable of producing 20,000 seeds per flowerhead with long viability. It is a restricted noxious weed in much of the U.S. and Australia. I am partial to thistles, I like the shape of the flowers, they are one of the first plants I was ever attracted to; found growing beyond the fence of my primary school, I was intrigued by what I thought was a beautiful flower. Scotland's national flower was first used in the 15th century as a symbol of defence.

O. acanthium the cotton thistle has large, grey-green leaves to 45cm (18") long. In summer its spiny, silver stem shoots up to flower. It can be invasive if allowed to seed but is quite a stunning accent with its purple-mauve thistle flowers. Hardy Biennial. 3m (10ft).

OREOCEREUS

Old man of the Andes cactus typically have long grey hair with stout yellow spines.

HOW TO GROW
Bright light is needed for the spines to be covered in hair, but this species will not tolerate high temperatures. Keep dry in winter. -7°C (20°F).

O. celsianus is not as densely hairy as others, but has the thickest stems up to 10cm (4") wide. 2m (8ft).
O. espostoa looks like a mummy with hairy bandages wrapped around finger columns.
O. henricksenianus v densilanatus bears slimmish stems to 8cm (3") and dark red flowers in early summer.
O. trollii makes hairy, white columns.

ORIGANUM

A silver beauty indeed. These tiny rosettes are like sugar icing on a wedding cake.

HOW TO GROW
Appreciates well-drained soil in sun. Keep water away from the base of the plant.

O. dictamnus known as Dittany of Crete forms neat rosettes of greyish leaves.
O. rotundifolium has greenish white flowers and the little rounded leaves have silvery veins.

OROSTACHYS

Little known members of the *Crassulaceae* family are akin to *Sedum* and have been classified under *Cotyledon*. Known as Dunce Caps for the way the flowers are borne in ascending clusters. They make interesting groundcover.

HOW TO GROW
Full sun, in poor, well-drained soil. Not fully hardy and an alpine house is best over winter as they dislike winter wet. Propagate by seed or by detaching rosettes. Z6-10.

O. furusei bears smooth, pearly grey to blue rosettes to 5-10cm (2-4") across that are most handsome. Beige flowers are borne in spikes in summer. Plantlets are borne on runners. It is found amongst rocks in East Asia and Japan.
O. iwarenge is a low growing succulent forming rosettes of grey foliage and huge pyramids of white flowers in autumn. Leaves are thin and lax to 7cm (3"). It is monocarpic and is suitable for a rock garden. In Japan you will find it growing on roof tops.
O. malacophylla has sweet, neat grey rosettes with greenish white flowers in summer.

Origanum dictamnus

OZOTHAMNUS

Many of these were once found under *Helichrysum* and they are very similar to all but the botanists eye.

HOW TO GROW
Full sun, low water needs in a well-drained site.

O. coralloides is a hardy, evergreen New Zealand native with grey foliage and bright yellow daisy flowers. 30x40cm (12x16").
H. 'County Park Silver' silky, silver miniature 'whipcord' foliage forms dense, overlapping mounds making flat carpets. Rarely flowers, but when it does, blooms are cream. 8x20cm (3x8"). Z6.
O. rosmarinifolius 'Silver Jubilee' is a celebration of silver grey, needle-like leaves with scented, whitish grey, flat flowerheads from pink buds in July to August. This slow-growing eversilver shrub is dense and compact. Superb with the pink buds against the foliage but just as sweet when the buds open. Appreciates a sheltered position. A good coastal plant from South East Australia. 1.5m (5ft).
O. selago bears compact grey foliage. Highly attractive and abundant in flower. Tiny yellow daisies smother the foliage. This small New Zealand alpine is often found growing in rocky places. 30x40cm (12x16").
O. 'Sussex Silver' bears fine, erect branchlets of small, silver leaves. Frost hardy. 1.5m (5ft).

PACHYPHYTUM

Related to *Echeveria*, these succulents usually withstand cooler temperatures. The silvery types are covered in a powdery white bloom, a thumbprint leaves its mark by removing this bloom. They appear like little sugared almonds and are just as sweet to look at. Excellent in rock gardens and for use in non-hardy succulent wreaths.

HOW TO GROW
In light shade to part sun. Moderate water in summer, little water in winter. They are best kept on the dry side. Grow from seed or cuttings. Z9-12.

P. bracteosum bears fat, spoon shaped, succulent leaves of a silver appearance blushed pink at the end.
P. compactum bears small, cylindrical grey-green leaves with stunning red flowers in summer. Newest foliage is greyest, older foliage is green. 10cm (4"). -7°C (20°F).
P. glutinicaule is very similar but without the green.
P. oviferum is also very similar and is known as Moonstones. The greyish silver succulent leaves remind me of sugared almonds. *Pachyphytum* are usually said to have insignificant flowers but this bears absolutely gorgeous green flowers in winter.

Pachyphytum oviferum

PEPEROMIA

The daintiest of the *Arum* family. Their leathery leaves in metallic shades make splendid houseplants. Remarkable succulent foliage can be used indoors in cool areas in dishes, baskets or terrariums.

HOW TO GROW
Can be sensitive to chill, so watch for fluctuating temperatures. Brighter light will bring out the silver. Moderate humidity and high temperatures of 23-29°C. Allow to dry between waterings as they are prone to stem rot. Easily propagated from stem cuttings. Z10-12.

P. argyreia the watermelon *Peperomia* bears rosettes of heart-shaped, leathery, glossy deep green leaves, striped in silver. Fetching in striped pyjamas against red stems!
P. campylotropa has waxy, pewter leaves nicely dimpled. A dwarf for the terrarium.
P. griseoargentea is the ivy-leaf *Peperomia*, which has almost rounded leaves on long petioles forming rosettes with silvery grey leaves and coppery edges. Slightly sunken, darker veins.
P. incana is known as the felted *Peperomia*. A stiff and semi-erect succulent when young, later spreading. Broadly ovate, grey-green leaves and stems are covered in white, woolly hairs. An easily grown species from Brazil tolerant of low humidity as long as it has very bright light.
P. marmorata is the sweetheart *Peperomia*, dull to bluish green leaves are striped silvery grey with indented veins on this rosette forming species.
P. metallica makes erect, bushy growth. Elliptical, dark red leaves have a broad silver central band.
P. orba 'Princess Astrid' is erect and shrubby with ovate, spoon-shaped, softly hairy, grey-green leaves having a broad, central silver stripe. Dwarf stature making multiple crowns; it is excellent for terrariums.
P. repii is known as the Purple Cloud Plant having low, much-branched purple stems covered with glossy, purple leaves with a midrib flare of silver. It makes rapid growth.
P. 'Silver Bandit' has reclining stems holding elegant, dimpled leaves with a central silver band. This Andean species is a challenge to grow, needing a coolish location to display the colours to best advantage.
P. 'Silver Heart' bears heart-shaped leaves of pale green with a central silver stripe.
P. 'Silver Ripple' is a silver-green variegated foliage plant with ripples and bumps and lumps, all in the right places.

PEROVSKIA

A nice filler plant in the border with an airy, see-through quality. An easy beginner plant.

HOW TO GROW
Performs best in full sun and well-drained soil. Tolerats dry soil and will grow on chalk. Best to cut back to several inches in spring. Z3-9.

P. atriplicifolia 'Blue Spire' bears silvery green, aromatic foliage and is coupled with the best of colour combinations, blue flowers. Known as Russian sage these woody based plants have slender, upright stems and panicles of blue-violet flowers. Growth can be lax. They have a blue, hazy effect in the border. White stems are attractive in winter. 1m (39") with a spread of 90cm (3ft).
P. atriplicifolia 'Filigran' is an introduction from Ernst Pagels with finely divided foliage giving a lacier effect. Growth is more upright and flowering time is extended. A wow plant. 90cm (3ft).
P. atriplicifoia 'Little Spire' is a shorter, more compact version. 60cm (2ft).
Cool Companion: *Salvia officinalis Purpurascens Group, Cerinthe major 'Purpurascens'*.

Perovskia 'Blue Spires'

PICEA

Spruces are hardy evergreens of a most attractive persuasion.

HOW TO GROW
They are susceptible to frost when young. They do best on soils which do not dry out but are well-drained in partial sun. Plant in early spring. Z4.

P. glauca 'J. W. Daisy's White' bears new foliage of cream-white, fading in autumn to grey-white on a neat, conical plant which makes a nice accent.
P. mariana 'Austria Broom' makes a small, slow spreading plant with short, grey needles.
P. mariana 'Nana' is a lovely, silvery blue which combines well in grey plant schemes.
P. omorika 'Frohnleiten' is the most silver of the dwarf *omorika* forms. It makes a small, bushy, flat-topped plant.
P. omorika 'Shcneverdingen' is a globular dwarf with lovely silvery colouring.

Above right: Picea mariana 'Nana'
Below: Picea 'J.W. Daisy's White'

PINUS

Love those needles. Although many pines make stately landscape plants, many of the silvery blues are dwarfs often used in bonsai. These dwarf types are slow-growing unlike the wild type.

HOW TO GROW
Best in sun in light, sandy to medium loam in poor soil with average moisture but well-drained. Cuttings are best taken from young specimens. Z5.

P. koraiensis 'Silvergrey' is an upright pine with long, thick, silver-grey leaves.
P. parviflora 'Arakawa' this dwarf pine bears silver-grey, twisted leaves. Removing the lower branches will reveal the interesting, pebble-like marks on the bark.
P. parviflora 'Brevifolia Baasch's Form' bears dark blue needles with a silver reverse. A conical plant having many side branches.
P. parviflora 'Fukuju' bears short, twisted and recurved silver-grey leaves on a short, conical plant.
P. parviflora 'Gyokuei' is a slow growing cone with curved leaves of silver-green.
P. parviflora 'Kiyomatsu' makes a small cushion of dark green, silvered leaves on matchstick sized stems. A tiny plant for trough or rock garden. 12cm (5") in 10 years.
P. parviflora 'Sai-da-jin' makes a short bush with upright stems and grey-green twisted needles.
P. parviflora 'Tani-mano-uki' has creamy white leaves and is best in shelter. Orange-red buds and stems in spring add interest to this slow-growing plant.
P. peuce 'Horstmann Dwarf' is a slow-growing, short conical pine with incurving, grey-silver leaves.
P. strobus 'Elf' has dark grey-green leaves on a very slow-growing conical plant.
P. strobus 'Elkin's Dwarf' makes a cushion plant with short, silver leaves.
P. strobus 'Mary Butler' is distinguished by its very long leaves, which have a silver reverse.
P. strobus 'Northway Broom' is a dwarf, flat-topped bush with dark grey-green needles.
P. strobus 'Sea Urchin' is distinctly silver making a tiny dome. 15cm (6") in 10 years.

Plectranthus argentatus

Pinus

PLANTAGO

A silver rock garden plantain. This is a beautiful, silky addition to an alpine garden.

HOW TO GROW
For sunny, rocky sites.

P. nivalis is a well-behaved plantain which does not sucker much. The ground hugging, basal rosette is silvery hairy and it needs protection against low temperatures. Briefly in flower, small white flowers, it is coveted for its leaves. Found growing in its native Sierra Nevada in southern Spain at high altitude. It is a symbol of eternal love and known as star of the snow (*estrella de las nieves*), it certainly is a star in the plantain family. 10cm (4").

Plantago nivalis below, Plectranthus hirtellus variegated right

PLECTRANTHUS

Grow a little moonshine for light shade in the shape of fabulous foliage from sunny South Africa and Australia. Superb in the border, shining stars in containers. One of my favourite foliage plants in shining, refined silver with a velvet quality.

HOW TO GROW
Morning sun and afternoon shade is perfect for these *Solenostemon* (Coleus) relatives. In warmest and desert regions bright shade is perfect. Cut back every year to prevent plants becoming woody. Feed container plants well. They can be wintered indoors or under cover. Protect from frost. Z10.

P. argentatus has superb soft, velvety grey leaves like a silver sea. This is a great choice for shade. It can even be used under oak trees and will bring a flash of lightning to any dark corners. Usually considered tender but it can come back after frost has cut it to the ground. Unlike coleus, it possesses interesting flower spikes on purplish stems which do not have to be pinched off to encourage leaf growth but are best deadheaded. 90cm (3ft) and a spread of 1.8m (6ft).
P. argentatus 'Hill House' is named after the nursery where it was discovered as a sport in Devon. Its creamy edged, silvery leaves are very attractive. Up to 60cm (2ft).
P. forsteri 'Marginatus' (P. coleoides 'White Surf') upright, large green leaves are variegated with a white edging and slightly pointed. 60cm-1.5m (2-5ft).
P. hadiensis v tomentosus has grey-green leaves covered in silvery hairs. A great choice for baskets. Up to 60cm (2ft).
P. hirtellus variegated is the most attractive of the variegated forms to my eye. Green leaves are neatly edged in clear white on this stunning plant. Up to 60cm (2ft).
P. oertendahlii 'Silver Star' launched at the Dutch flower auction in 2000 has still to catch on in England. It should do so at a fast rate from now on. It is coveted for its silver-topped leaves which are purple on the reverse. They release a pleasant scent when crushed. The star is the purple flowers, downy like the foliage. Use it indoors or on the patio to make a splendid show.
Hot Partner: *Solenostemon* (Coleus) in hot shades such as *'Merlot', Tradescantia pallida 'Purpurea'.*

Plectranthus hadienis above, P. argentatus 'Hill House' below left, P. fosteri 'Marginatus' below right

POTENTILLA

Shrubby potentillas are attractive in the border or rock garden. These are welcome for flower and foliage.

HOW TO GROW
Sun or light shade in well-drained soil.

P. anserina is considered invasive, which is such a pity as it has the loveliest silver foliage of all potentillas. It spreads by runners. Silverweed does well in sun.

P. argentea has nicely divided green leaves with a silver reverse and yellow flowers. Known as silver cinquefoil, this perennial is found in dry, gravelly areas, introduced into the U.S. and Canada from Europe. 15-30cm (6-12").

P. atrosanguinea v argyrophylla has silver undersides to its green leaves. An attractive variety in flower having orange and yellow flowers with a red eye.

P. beesii is a bushy, dense subject with silvered foliage and golden yellow flowers. Raised by Bees from seed collected in China. This form does not produce seed.

P. fruticosa 'Grace Darling' I include as its dark green leaves have a slight silver sheen. The salmon-pink flowers appear slightly darker in sun and have a pale yellow-cream reverse. A tough, hardy, small-leaved variety. Raised by Jack Drake of Inshriach Nursery.

P. fruticosa 'Hopley's Pink' is a bushy form with broadish, silvery leaves which performs well in sun. White flushed pink flowers have a white reverse.

P. fruticosa 'Maanelys' (Moonlight) is a tall, erect variety suitable for hedging. Pale primrose flowers with a darker centre fade as they age against large silver foliage. Raised in Denmark by Axel Olsen.

P. fruticosa 'Primrose Beauty' bears silvery foliage with pale primrose flowers having a darker centre making a show from early summer to early autumn. Similar to *'Wessex Silver'* but more open and with slightly larger flowers, this cultivar was raised by Cannegieter in Holland in the 1950's.

P. fruticosa 'Vilmoriniana' bears well-silvered, broad foliage. Stems are very hairy, holding cream flowers with pale yellow centres and a pale reverse. Upright in habit, this form was raised from seed sent from China in 1905.

P. fruticosa 'Wessex Silver' makes large, bushy plants with hairy stems. Pale yellow flowers and creamy reverses are perfect against the silvery foliage. A seedling of *'Primrose Beauty'* raised by Wilf Sims in 1986. It has smaller flowers than its parent but has better resistance to mildew.

P. hyparctica nana is a mat-forming arctic alpine with tight, silver-felted leaves and almost stemless, large yellow flowers. This is good in tufa rock. 5cm (2").

P. 'Pastel Pink' bears grey-green to silver, small foliage on a small plant suitable for the rock garden. Thickish stems bear white flowers with just an angel's breath of pink, sometimes hardly visible, and a white reverse.

P. 'Silver Schilling' bears very silver foliage on a bushy, vigorous plant. Golden yellow flowers shine bright on this foliage beauty. Raised by Tony Schilling from seed collected in Nepal in 1983.

P. 'Teesdale Silver' was selected from 'Teesdale' by Wilf Sims in 1996 for its silvery-blue, large, long leaflets. It bears golden flowers.

Potentilla anserina

Pulmonaria come in numerous spotted forms

PULMONARIA

These small perennials make ideal carpets in light woodland. Their foliage goes on and on, usually through winter here in Sheffield even though their best time is spring. Pulmonaria are not just foliage plants, they have great little flowers too, and when the low spring sun shines through the petals, they are exquisite.

U.S. breeder Dan Heims, has been producing varieties which are mildew resistant in the Pacific Northwest, and should prove so here in the U.K. *P. longifolia* and its hybrids have the greatest resistance to mildew. I am talking silver here, not spotted, there are numerous varieties with silver spots too. Much work to clarify names within this genus has been carried out by English nurserywoman, Vanessa Cook, to clear up the confusing number of varities sold under different names. My first *Pulmonaria* was given to me by my father-in-law, and I have grown them ever since. They are easy hybridisers in the garden.

HOW TO GROW
These are shade lovers, but will take a little sun in moist ground. Plant in soil that never dries out. Z4-9.

P. 'Apple Frost' (TN) bears bright apple-green leaves overlaid with silver almost obliterating the green. Blue flowers turn pink. Mildew resistant.
P. 'Berries & Cream' (TN) slightly rippled shimmering silver foliage and raspberry pink flowers make this a very attractive cultivar. Mildew resistant. 20cm (8").
P. 'Botanic Hybrid' bears a profusion of those funnel-shaped flowers of pale-blue to pink on lax stems from March to May over pointed silver leaves. 30cm (12").
P. 'British Sterling' has magenta flowers that open blue. Silvery foliage shimmers.
P. 'Cotton Cool' bears narrow silver leaves, mostly upright growing, topped by pink flowers which quickly turn cobalt-blue. Leaves to 30cm (12") long emerge spotted soon turning completely to silver. A deservedly popular U.K. cultivar. Mildew resistant. 40cm (16").
P. 'Diana Clare' has lovely silvered leaves and violet-blue flowers striped purple in February to May. An excellent, vigorous *longifolia* hybrid.
P. 'Excalibur' (TN) is a shining silver gem, with a little green margin surrounding the outstanding silver leaves. Mildew resistant. Raved about by many, an excellent new introduction. 30cm (12").
P. 'High Contrast' (PBR) is an excellent choice for warmer areas where its mildew resistant, silvered foliage performs well. Large pink flowers fade to blue.
P. longifolia 'Ankum' bears narrow, very silvery leaves with bright blue flowers.
P. longifolia ssp cevennensis has very long silvered leaves to almost 60cm (2ft). Accompanied by dark blue flowers.

Pulmonaria 'Cotton Cool' above, 'Diana Clare' below

Pulmonaria 'Excaliber' below

Pulmonaria 'Majeste' above, P. 'Moonshine' below

P. longifolia 'Dordogne' has long silvered leaves with violet-blue flowers.

P. 'Majeste' (1986) is a French cultivar from La Ferme Fleurie, unfortunately suffering mildew even in cool areas. Slow growing but tough. Pink and blue flowers. Admired by many.

P. 'Mary Mottram' has delightful frosted, elliptical silver leaves with a narrow green margin and blue-mauve flowers. Semi-evergreen. 30cm (12").

P. 'Moonshine' (TN, PBR) has rounded silver foliage with a dark green edge and small blue flowers. Mildew resistant. 30cm (12").

P. 'Northern Lights' (PBR) has very silver foliage with purple and rose-red flowers. Mildew resistant. 30cm (12").

P. 'Opal' (PBR) bears spotted or often wholly silvered leaves and very large, beautiful pale blue flowers which open palest pink. Makes tight clumps of perennial foliage. 50cm (20").

P. 'Pewter' the name says it, grow it for the outstanding pewter foliage. Long funnel pale blue flowers turn dark blue for weeks in spring. 45cm (18").

P. rubra 'David Ward' is distinguished by its cream margin to green leaves. Handsome and desirable, selected by Beth Chatto and named for her head gardener. Pink-red flowers are borne in January to April. Keep out of wind and sun. 30cm (12").

P. saccharata 'Silverado' (Luc Klinkhamer PBR) is one I have grown and admired for its well-silvered foliage. A fine cultivar with almost wholly silver leaves, with a tiny green spotted margin.

P. 'Samurai' is a cross between P. 'Majeste' and P. cevennensis which is considered to be an improvement on the former with long, pure silver leaves having a pronounced dark green edge and blue flowers. Good sun tolerance. 30cm (12"). Z4-8.

P. 'Silver Lance' bears long, narrow, pure silver foliage with beautiful coral-red flowers.

P. 'Silver Maid' ('Margaret Owen') bears silvery leaves.

P. 'Silver Shimmers' (TN) has to be the best of the silver-leaved lungworts. Like molten metal, its narrow leaves are wonderfully silver-plated with a well-ruffled edge. Almost white with contrasting pink and steel-blue flowers.

P. 'Silver Streamers' (TN, PBR) has nicely ruffled edges to the silver, lanceolate leaves to 30cm (12") long with a mass of blue to rose-pink flowers. Mildew resistant.

P. 'Silver Surprise' has longifolia in its blood or should I say sap. Long, silver leaves sit handsomely beneath typical flowers of blue and pink in February to April. 25cm (10").

P. 'Spilled Milk' (TN) is a low growing compact form with smallish, well-silvered and blotched leaves and blue flowers fading to pink. Extremely mildew resist. 20cm (8").

P. 'Tim's Silver' bears solid silver leaves with a green margin and mid-blue flowers. 30-40cm (12-16").

P. 'Weetwood Blue' bears exceptionally clear blue flowers and silver spotted foliage.

Pulmonaria 'Silver Streamers' above, P. 'Silver Shimmers' below

PYRUS

Used as a specimen in the garden, this is a lovely focal point. Standing sentinel in a white garden, this is a lovely sight. A shimmering, silver sparkler for the garden.

HOW TO GROW
Grows best in sun, but is adaptable. Dislikes extremely wet, dry or alkaline soils, but is tolerant of poor infertile soils. Susceptible to fireblight. Z4-7.

P. salicifolia is the willowleaf pear tree, with beautiful silvery, narrow foliage. Showy, white flowers are borne in mid-May. 6m (20ft).
P. salicifolia 'Pendula' is a spreading tree with drooping branches. A graceful native of Iran and Turkey. 4.5m (15ft).
P. salicifolia 'Pendula Silfrozam' ('Silver Frost') has a weeping habit similar to the other cultivars. A floriferous form with white flower clusters.
P. salicifolia 'Silver Cascade' has a pendulous habit and similar silver colouring.
Cool Companion: *Euphorbia characias ssp wulfenii, Iris foetidissima 'Variegata'*.

RAOULIA

New Zealand alpine plants best suited to scree where they make interesting ground-hugging mats of silver foliage. Cushion plants with class.

HOW TO GROW
Require excellent drainage but not a sun-baked site. Add gravel to humus-rich soil in part shade. Plant in scree or alpine house to protect against winter wet. In pots 60% sharp grit and 40% ericaceous compost makes a good growing media. Pot on every year. Can be overwintered in an unheated greenhouse. Z7-9 or Z6 with protection.

R. apice-nigra forms a mat of silver foliage.
R. australis bears flat mats of tiny, silver hairy rosettes with profuse, fluffy yellow flowers appearing like little specks amongst the foliage in June. An abundant native plant known as scabweed found in open, stony places. This is not reliably hardy in the U.K. Plants sold under this name are often *R. hookeri*. 5cm (2").
R. beauvardii makes ground hugging, flat mats of silver foliage, hairy on both surfaces.
R. buchananii is found on the wetter mountains of the South Island in New Zealand.
R. bryoides bears grey leaves with red flowers in summer.
R. eximia is almost indistinguishable from the grey rocks of its natural habitat. It forms tight, grey-white mounds up to 60cm (2ft) high and 1.5m (5ft) across. The tiny leaves are covered in hairs to trap moisure. The tiny flowerheads are nestled amongst the leaves.
R. grandiflora bears grey leaves, densely silvery hirsute with white-yellow flowers in late spring making good groundcover. Found on the highest mountains on both the South and North Islands of New Zealand.
R. hectori bears silver-grey lanceolate leaves with golden margins. Tiny white flowers are borne in summer.
R. hookeri makes flat mats of thickish, felted pale grey leaves which are almost white with yellow flowers borne in summer. Grow in poor, free-draining rocky soil. 3cm (1").
R. x leucogenes (Leucoraoulia) forms spreading carpets of silvery rosettes looking splendid over a rock.
R. x loganii (Leucoraoulia) makes a tight silver cushion.
R. mammilaris is similar to *R. eximia* but bears larger red flowers over grey leaves.
R. monroi bears very small grey leaves on a ground hugger with distinctive form.
R. petriensis bears silvery leaves on open groundcover.
R. x petrimia 'Margaret Pringle' makes a cushion with silvery green leaves that is best in an alpine house.
R. tenuicaulis makes silvery green groundcover on slender stems with white flowers. 3cm (1").
R. youngii appears white with its densely hairy, lanate leaves to 7cm (3"). White flowers to 15cm (6") across are borne in summer. 3cm (1"+).

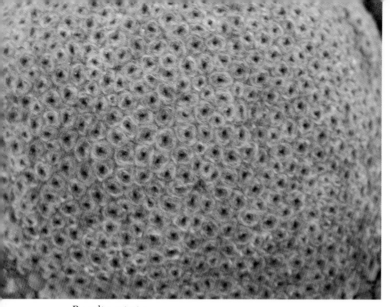

Raoulia eximia

RHODANTHEMUM

Big white daisies with yellow centres. The plant stays the same but it has been known under many names.

HOW TO GROW
Easy to grow in sun, with average watering, does not mind short, dry periods.

R. hosmariense bears beautiful silver filigree foliage and large, open-faced daisies throughout spring and summer. This Moroccan evergreen species is for the border in warmer climes or the container in cooler areas. It can be in flower almost all year round. Unopened buds are fascinating with each silver bract neatly margined with a black fringe. 20x30cm (8x12"). Z5.

RUBUS

Mainly used for their ornamental, silvery white stems or the undersides of leaves, there is one plant offering a silver shimmer. Many are suited to the woodland border.

HOW TO GROW
Easy, often too vigorous in light shade. Divide in spring.

R. biflorus is grown mainly for the effect of its thorny, silver stems in winter. Cut back to the ground each spring. Stems are not as upright as *R. thibetanus* 'Silver Fern'. 1.8m (6ft). Z5.

R. cockburnianus bears white-bloomed stems but is notoriously invasive and best not planted in the garden unless you are wild.

R. henryi v bambusarum eat your heart out bramble lovers! An evergreen, climbing shrub, and its scandent habit shows off the white felted undersides to perfection. Narrow, leathery, bamboo-like leaves are trilobed. Pink flowers in slender racemes are followed by black fruit. Appreciates good soil in any aspect.

R. lineatus I spotted at the Chinese Garden in Portland, I was staying with my friend, Kathy Chretien, at the time, and this was also planted in her garden and much commented upon. It looks Oriental, and is highly attractive with its five pleated, pointed leaflets, handsomely mid green atop and silky silver beneath. This semi-evergreen shrub bears small white flowers followed by red fruits. Moist, well-drained soil out of cold winds.

R. pectinellus trilobus I first set eyes on this at the Harrogate Flower Show, the attractive leaves are blushed with silver with a darker green heart. Found in its natural habitat creeping along the forest floor in Taiwan and rooting at the nodes, this is an excellent semi-evergreen for the woodland border in well-drained shade; it is usually too vigorous for the border. White flowers are followed by red berries. 32°C (0°F). 10cm (4").

R. thibetanus 'Silver Fern' is eye-catching for its white stems sited against a darker background. An ornamental bramble with distinctive shape, semi-erect, displaying the white stems to perfection, which rise like water jets from a fountain. Stems are improved by severe pruning in spring. Fern-like, silver-grey foliage adds that little bit extra and small purplish flowers followed by black or red fruits are another feature. This is a star winter performer. Z6.

R. tricolor is a creeping evergreen with the underside to the green leaves, nicely silvered.

Perfect Companion: the obvious choice for whitish stems is *Ophiopogon planiscapus* 'Nigrescens'.

Rubus pectinellus trilobus

RUMEX

Distinguished by its silver colour and unusual leaf shape, grow this as front of the border groundcover whether you wish to eat it or not.

HOW TO GROW
Cut back hard in June. In hot climates this will appreciate some shade. Easy. Z6-8.

R. scutatus 'Silver Shield' is a decorative edible with shiny, rounded evergreen, silver leaves making a striking small mound. The tart leaves can be used in salads. My friend, Camilla Shivarg who has a glorious garden, alerted me to this. 25cm (10").

Salix lanata

SALIX

The willows, often so gentle in their foliage yet so formidable in their roots; bear this in mind when planting. Willows can offer fantastic foliage, winter bark and spectacular catkins. Many are fast growing, moisture loving shrubs. They resent dry soils and need to be planted well away from drains and buildings.

HOW TO GROW
Moist soils in sun. Dwarf and prostrate types are best with protection from afternoon sun in hot areas. Restrict growth by cutting back. Z4.

S. alba is a fast-growing, native British tree with narrow, silver-backed leaves sparkling in the sunlight and shimmering in the breeze. Long, yellow catkins are borne in May. A good choice for coastal regions helping to prevent erosion. 7.5x5.5m (25x18ft). in 20 years.
S. alba v sericea (S. alba f argentea) known as the silver-leaved willow, this quick grower makes a good hedge in exposed conditions well away from buildings and drains. If pruned hard each spring it will make a handsome clump of silver leaves, otherwise it will make a medium-sized tree.
S. arctica has greyish, oval pointed leaves with silky white hairs and brown catkins making a prostrate shrub.
S. 'Boydii' is an upright growing British native shrub with silver leaves.
S. candida has young leaves which are an incredible bright white. The sage willow makes a large shrub.
S. caprea the goat willow is a British native with grey leaves coming after the showy catkins in March. Cut back to the ground every few years to restrict size. 5.5x4.5m (18x15ft) in 20 years.
S. chaenomeloides the Japanese willow displays silver, purple to pink buds opening to silvery catkins. New leaves are reddish brown maturing to deep bue-green and are pubescent on the underside. It makes a large, rounded shrub. 4.5m (15ft). Z6.
S. cinerea has silver-grey on the undersides of the leaves. A large native British shrub with broad leaves which are greyish on the upper surface and intensely grey beneath with contrasting red veins. Abundant yellow catkins on bare, pubescent grey-green branches. 3m (10ft) in 20 years.
S. elaeagnos bears narrow, silvery leaves to 10cm (4") long on a short, bushy tree which makes an excellent choice for the smaller garden. 4.5m (15ft). Z4.
S. exigua has handsome silver-grey foliage on a medium-sized tree or large shrub with slender greyish-green branches. Pruned back each spring to 15cm (6"), it produces arching stems covered in silky, silver leaves which shimmer in the breeze. Small, pale yellow catkins appear at the same time as the foliage. Needs moisture when establishing, but will then tolerate drier conditions than most. 4m (13ft) if pruned, otherwise 6m (20ft).

S. hastata 'Wehrhahnii' is a semi-dwarf willow with grey foliage. Catkins are white at first, turning yellow in February to March.

S. helvetica bears soft, silvery foliage coupled with grey-white catkins. An excellent small shrub in sun on the rock garden or scree.

S. interior forms thickets and is of most use for bank stabilisation on moist or wet sites. Its narrow, silvery leaves are carried on smooth reddish brown branches. 1-4.5m (3-15ft). Z2.

S. lanata is a fine rare shrub that never fails to catch the eye. Woolly, silvery almost rounded leaves and silvery catkins in early spring. This slow-growing, hardy British native is best in sun. I first found this at Barnsdale and was captured. This extremely hardy willow can be found growing in Iceland.

S. nakamurana v yezoalpina has large leaves to 7cm (3") with a silver-grey tomentum and large silvery catkins on short fat stems. Its arching form makes small mounds perfect for the rock garden. 30x90cm (1x3ft) in 5 years.

S. 'Onusta' is quite rare. Grow it for its pink-grey catkins, exhibited over a long period in spring.

S. repens 'Nitida' has branches laden with silver leaves making quick groundcover. It bears silver catkins in spring.
Cool Companion: Stachys byzantina, Plectranthus argentatus, Fuchsia 'Thalia'.
Hot Partner: Aster 'Lady in Black'.

Salvia argentea

SALVIA

Some of the species are delicious in flower, but the ones I have selected here have been chosen for their foliage.

HOW TO GROW
Full sun and very well-drained soil. Overhead watering will often lead to rot. Zone depends on species.

S. aethiopsis has silver leaves with fine-toothed leaf margins. A cold-hardy sage with white flowers that can die after seed set unless drainage is excellent. Z7.

S. apiana is known as white sage for the colour of its wonderfully aromatic foliage, often noticeable before the plant itself is seen. White flowers appear in spring to autumn. A shrubby, Californian species occurring in dry, rocky exposed sites. Expect bees to buzz around this plant. Capable of self-seeding; it needs excellent drainage and will survive in a dry scree. Drought and frost tolerant to -2°C. 90-120cm or larger (3-4ft). Z8.

S. argentea is one of the loveliest silver plants, distinguished by its handsome basal leaves. Densely covered in hairs; the effect is of white-silver leaves. Like pieces of teddy bear fur, this bears rosettes of pointed leaves worthy of a place at the front of the border where it can be easily admired. White to pink parrot beak flowers. Usually biennial if allowed to seed, but can be a short-lived perennial if prevented from seeding. An outstanding ornamental for its foliage rather than its flower power which rates pretty low especially in warm climates. Give this perfect drainage to promote a longer life. Collect and sow seed or take cuttings. 90cm (3ft). Z6.

S. blancoa is a lovely hardy grey plant often incorrectly seen as S. lavandulifolia. It bears attractive lavender flowers. Suitable for cold winters and dry summers. 60x60cm (2x2ft).

S. canariensis has a whitish undersides to its leaves. This long blooming, adaptable shrub has red-violet calyces and lavender flowers. Z9.

S. candidissima has basal silver leaves on a drought and frost tolerant sage with white flowers. 50cm (20").

S. canescens v daghestanica bears small, tight rosettes of white-felted leaves against blue-purple flowers. Good for rock garden or container. 30cm (12").

S. chamaedryoides is an evergreen perennial from Mexico which goes by the common name of germander sage. With its running rootstock and upright stems, small grey foliage and sky blue flowers, this sage has year-round appeal. Flourishing in dry conditions and not halted by drought, it does not do well in wet English winters though it will tolerate some frost. A nice edger which is good for beginners. 30cm (12"). Z8.

S. chionophylla is one of the most charming Mexican silver sages. The creeping stems make good groundcover and can cover 1.8m (6ft) in one season.

Salvia daghestanica

Salvia cyanescens above, S. leucophylla centre

Salvia multicaulis below

In spring and autumn pale blue flowers appear but never detract from the main feature of the foliage. It is good in hanging baskets. 10cm (4"). Z7-9.

S. cyanescens like *S. argentea* is a short-lived species. Basal pubescent, silvered leaves are topped with spikes of small blue-mauve flowers all season long. Drought and frost tolerant. 30cm (12"). Z7.

S. discolor is a favourite sage with me for its near black flowers held in pistachio green calyces, a striking effect. However, the leaves are handsome too, sage-green-grey on top and silver beneath. One of its common names is Andean Silver Leaf sage. This can be had in flower well into winter in a cold greenhouse. A scandent climber, it needs to be in an elevated postion so that the flowers can be appreciated. 60cm (2ft) Z9.

S. frigida is a perfect example of nice things coming in small packages. Its small stature is perfect for a trough or rock garden. A handsome silver blush adorns the leaf surfaces. The small inflorescence comprising of white or pale lilac flowers can easily be missed in early summer.

S. indica bears grey basal leaves which are loosely scalloped. This Middle Eastern species carries lavender blue flowers on 60cm (2ft) long stems with intricate purple and white markings on the lower lip. Z9.

S. lanceolata bears lanceolate, grey leaves on this much-branched shrub. An attractive combination of calyces which turn pink and lengthen and brownish, rosy flowers are found sparingly from May to November. A colouring which mixes well with similar rosy to apricot tones. Drought hardy and superb in sun.

S. lavandulifolia from Southern France and Spain, this species has long, grey leaves with long, leafless stems bearing light blue-purple flowers in early spring and summer in the dry garden. Z5.

S. leucophylla is a Californian grey species requiring excellent drainage and full sun. The foliage is pleasant smelling, drought and frost tolerant and is accompanied by small mauve flowers. Makes a superb silver accent. 80x80cm (32").

S. multicaulis (S. acetabulosa) is similar in shape to *officinalis* but the leaves are covered in tomentosum on both sides giving a silver sheen. It is a spreading, evergreen, prostrate shrublet making mats to 60cm (2ft) across. It is frost hardy to -10°C but dislikes wet. Violet flowers and deep purplish, persistent calyces are borne on erect stems in May to June and again in autumn.

S. 'Newe Ya'ar' (S. officinalis x S. fruticosa) means good plant in hebrew and aptly describes this good silver cross. This low-growing shrub has square, woody stems covered in white wool. The downy leaves grow to 7cm (3") long. Blue-lavender flowers appear in February and continue to bloom in spring. It has a mild, pleasant flavour when cooked.

S. nipponicum 'Fuji Snow' the deep green, arrowhead leaves are 10cm (4") long each having a broad white edge.

Santolina chamaecyparissus

The exquisite foliage is topped by pale lemon flowers. 45cm (18"). Z5-10.

S. officinalis 'Berggarten' (Herrenhauser) is a compact sage whose oval leaves start off fresh green becoming soft, downy grey as they age. This aromatic variety is shy-flowering but handsome for the leaves alone and for an *officinalis* cultivar it is relatively long-lived. 35x35cm (14x14"). Z5-9.

S. officinalis 'Compacta' bears small grey-green leaves looking handsome all year round. Z5-9.

S. officinalis 'Grete Stolze' has pointed, pale grey leaves. Z5-9.

S. officinalis 'Holt's Mammoth' has long, wide, grey-green leaves and is a compact form. Z5-9.

S. officinalis 'Sturnina' has white-grey leaves. Z5-9.

S. taraxacifolia this perennial species from Morocco has foliage which looks like a dandelion when young. The grey, sweet-smelling rosettes send up spikes of palest pink flowers from late spring to autumn. 45cm (18"). Z9.
Cool Companion: *Ballota, Perovskia, Artemisia*

SANTOLINA

A good component of the dry garden, this Southern European shrub needs little water. It is useful as a small, evergreen hedge and if left untrimmed until after July you can enjoy flowers as well as foliage; like having your cake and eating it!

HOW TO GROW
A sun lover. Once established all that is required is one deep watering a month. Poor soil is preferred and well-drained soil is essential. Z6-9.

S. chamaecyparissus the cotton lavender is grown for its white stems and silver-grey, aromatic leaves. Small, fragrant, yellow flowers appear in midsummer. It is useful for attracting beneficial insects into the garden. Dried leaves can be used as an insect and moth repellent. This is a good choice for coastal gardens forming mounds which are kept neat by clipping. Looks good in summer and winter. Z5-10.60x60cm (2x2ft).

S. chamaecyparissus 'Lambrook Silver' is the best silver form making an attractive dwarf dense hedge of well silvered leaves or making a nice mound. 75cm (30").

S. chamaecyparissus 'Pretty Carol' is a little gem bearing dark grey leaves. 30cm (12").

S. chamaecyparissus v nana (S. incana 'Nana') is a perennial with finely dissected silver foliage useful for edging and in containers. It bears closely-set, saw-edged, thread-like aromatic leaves. 40cm (16").

S. pinnata ssp neapolitana 'Edward Bowles' is one of the nicest cotton lavenders. Its finely divided, ferny foliage is wonderful beneath the palest primrose yellow button flowers in July. A rounded, dwarf shrub.

S. pinnata ssp neapolitana 'Sulphurea' is admirable for its sulphur button flowers atop grey-green foliage.
Perfect Companion: *Lavandula, Perovskia, Ballota.*

Santolina chamaecyparissus left,
S. chamaecyparissus v nana below

Santolina pinnata 'Sulphurea'

Saxifraga fortunei 'Silver Velvet'

Saxifraga stolonifera

Schizophragma hydrangeoides

SAXIFRAGA

Silver suits the saxifrage family, they enjoy shimmering in shade. For some reason the species name goes after the cultivar name in brackets, a practice I do not always follow.

HOW TO GROW
Many of the alpines are best in scree, shade from hot afternoon sun.

S. 'Bridget' bears tight, silver rosettes in domed mounds and numerous pink flowers.

S. burseriana (crenata) is a neat tuft of silver foliage and white flowers on red stems in very early spring. 8cm (3").

S. callosa bears pearly leaves making cushion mounds with panicles of white flowers in May. 7x25cm (3x10").

S. callosa ssp callosa v australis (S. callosa v lantoscana 'Superba') has beautiful large, heavily encrusted, silver rosettes. Arching sprays of white flowers are borne in profusion in summer. 15x30cm (6x12").

S. 'Caterhamnis' (cotyledon) bears white flowers and broad, silvered rosettes that are most handsome. 10x10cm (5x5").

S. crustata is small and neat. Trim, dark silver-green rosettes are lime-encrusted at leaf edges giving the appearance of a white edge. Subtle cream flowers are borne on this easy to grow saxifrage. 10cm (4").

S. 'Cumulus' forms grey cushions with very attractive white flowers turning pink, massed like a cloud. 5cm (2").

S. 'Dr. Ramsay' Irving has silver rosettes with white flowers in spring. 15cm (6").

S. fortunei 'Silver Velvet' known as Strawberry Begonia and looking like a *Begonia rex* has large, velvet-looking dark leaves banded with silver with striking, rosy pink flowers in late summer and early autumn. An unforgettable sight, this is one of my all time favourite plants. Neutral soil in part shade in moist, humus, well-drained soil. This amazing woodland jewel was brought back from Japan by Dan Hinkley. 35cm (14"). Z6-9.

S. hostii ssp hostii bears mats of lime-encrusted leaves with panicles of white flowers having red spots.

S. longifolia this symmetrical, silvered beauty grows to 20cm (8") wide then puts forth wands of white blooms vying for attention. Monocarpic.

S. luteoviridis is one of the most silvered. Rosettes are slow to form a tiny hummock. Chartreuse blooms are carried in spring. 10cm (4").

S. x macnabiana is a giant silver, floriferous saxifrage with some *cotyledon* ancestry. 50x25cm (20x10").

S. 'Monarch' is a lime-encrusted variety with vigorous, green rosettes forming loose cushions and bearing panicles of white flowers.

S. 'Mother of Pearl' bears very silvered grey leaves with pink flowers carried just above the foliage.

S. paniculata is the most widespread of the silver saxifrages from the Alps. Many forms are available including the most common *Minutissima* forming tiny rosettes of just 2cm (1") high. 20cm (8").

S. paniculata 'Cockscomb' has the name for its crested central leaves. Crowded, silver rosettes bear white flowers on this form which originated in Frank Cabot's garden.

S. paniculata 'Dr. Clay' is a distinct cultivar with intensely silver-grey hairy rosettes.

S. paniculata 'Hi Ace' is a Scottish selection with extra white tiny rosettes.

S. paniculata 'Rex' is a very silver form with mahogany stems and creamy white flowers.

S. 'Pilatus' (x boydii) makes a neat, grey-silver tufted mound with yellow flowers.

S. porophylla has silver encrusted rosettes and large, wine-coloured flowers.

S. scardica bears very silver rosettes with comparatively large, white flowers in early spring. Heat tolerant for its type. 10cm (4").

S. sempervivum bears silver, flat rosettes. Purple flowers and purple velvet clad stems make for a showy specimen.

S. 'Silver Cushion' has pink flowers almost nestling amongst the hairy, silver-variegated foliage in March to May, which gives it a soft look. 7cm (3"). Z5-9.

S. stolonifera 'Hime' is a beautiful green-leaved, carpeting perennial with fine, creamy silver venation on the leaves. Pink flushed. Irregular white flowers appear in August to September. Partial shade and moist but well-drained soil. 15cm (6").

S. stolonifera 'Hsitou Silver' (BSWJ1980) bears rounded rosettes of mid to dark green handsomely overlaid with strong silver venation. 30cm (12").

S. 'Wisley' (federici-augustii ssp grisebachii) bears superb grey foliage plus the most incredible flowers which terminate in darkness. 15cm (6").

SCHIZOPHRAGMA

An attractive, deciduous climber with aerial roots. A lovely ornamental in both flower and foliage and beats climbing *Hydrangea* for me.

HOW TO GROW
In sun or partial shade, site to avoid early morning sun in spring. Best in a moist, acid soil. Z5.

S. hydrangeoides 'Moonlight' is a delightful climber similar to climbing hydrangea with cymes of ivory white flowers to 20-25cm (8-10") across having conspicuous, heart-shaped cream coloured bracts which make the heart beat a little faster in July. Takes a little time to settle in but is also well worthwhile for the fabulous, heart-shaped silvered foliage. Excellent on north-facing walls or growing up a tree trunk.

SEDUM

Attractive succulents for little nooks and crannies in the garden and as edgers or in the rock garden.

HOW TO GROW
Short stem pieces of *S. spathulifolium* root easily in garden soil. Divide March to May. Z4.

S. burrito is like a string of pearls. It is known as donkey's tails. The pendent stems carry small, pearl-like, white-grey succulent nuggets of leaves. This evergreen enjoys well-drained soil and must be kept frost free. Appreciate its qualities in a hanging basket. 20cm (8").
S. cauticola 'Coca Cola' bears silvery grey, ovate foliage with masses of soft pink flowers in July and August. 20cm (8").
S. lineare 'Pachyclados' is a reliable silver foliage succulent whose rosettes make an admirable carpet. White flowers are borne in July to August. Superb on any rock garden or scree. Not sure on the nomenclature here, *S. pachyclados* is a species now classified under *Rhodiola*. 10cm (4").
S. spathulifolium 'Cape Blanco' bears near white tiny rosettes, as if carved from icing for a wedding cake. The powdered rosettes are held on short pinkish stems. It is one of my favourite plants. So valuable in the garden as an easy undercover story to *Ophiopogon* and so many other low-growing perennials. The star-shaped yellow flowers in summer are secondary to the foliage. This carpeter likes a little shade and any well-drained soil. It dislikes wet. Excellent for nooks and crannies where there is no foot traffic and just perfect nestled in cracks in dark stone walls. A choice Oregon and N. Californian native. This is a superb winter evergreen and an easy beginner plant. 5cm (2") with a spread of 30cm (12"). Z5-9.
S. 'Silver Moon' looks like another *spathulifolium* hybrid with soft green foliage covered in a white powder, yet it is larger and more vigorous than the *spathulifolium* types making ground hugging rosettes. 5cm (2"), 25cm (10") spread. Z5-9.
Perfect Companion: *Ophiopogon p. 'Nigrescens'*.

SEMPERVIVUM

Houseleeks are a personal favourite, but you cannot choose just one, it is impossible. From pearly grey to contrasting near black, these are a collector's joy.

HOW TO GROW
Bright light or full sun in very free-draining soil, I always add extra grit especially around the neck of the plant. Frost hardy and once established, very low maintenance. They put up with severe conditions, but do enjoy more comfortable living when they respond with even more colourful rosettes.

S. arachnoideum can be grown for its spiderweb covered rosettes giving a whitish appearance.
S. 'Grey Dawn' bears purplish grey leaves with a downy appearance on medium to large rosettes.
S. 'Grey Lady' when mature displays its lavender, grey-green colouring on broad rosettes to 15cm (6") wide.
S. 'Grey Ghost' the large, wide leaves of this variety are in dull grey tones.
S. 'Jack Frost' is a green variety with heavy silver frosting provided by the silver marginal hairs.
S. 'Lavender and Old Lace' I grew some years ago and admired greatly for its stunning purplish grey tones on wide rosettes to 20cm (8").
S. 'Shirley's Joy' bears grey-green rosettes with a white felted look especially in the centre. 25cm (10") width.
S. 'Silver Jubilee' bears greyish green rosettes covered in silvery hairs.
S. 'Silver Thaw' bears small, greyish green rosettes that are intensely hairy.
S. 'Spider's Lair' is a green *arachnoideum* covered in white webs.

Sedum spathulifolium 'Cape Blanco' left
Sempervivum below

Senecio crassissimus above, S. leucophyllus below

SENECIO

You might know the foliage type better by one of its synonyms *Cineraria maritima* or by its common name of dusty miller, a name shared with many other plants. Much used as annuals, these Mediterranean natives are easy to keep perennials that can be cut back if they get leggy. I have kept mine as a non-flowering white accent plant here in Z7 in containers outdoors from one year to the next. An easy plant anywhere except in deep shade. They often lose their silver dusting in rain.

The succulent Senecio are something else.

HOW TO GROW
Well-drained light soil in full sun. Take cuttings. Perennial Z9-10, annual 3-8. Tip: Cut off the flowers.

S. cineraria is almost white. Beloved by city councils it is worthy of inclusion in the garden. There are many forms all with the same near white-coloured foliage. 60cm (24").
S. cineraria 'Cirrhus' this form has very white, rounded leaves. 30cm (12").
S. cineraria 'New Look' has lovely white, oak-shaped leaves for great contrast in the garden or containers. 25cm (9").
S. cineraria 'Silver Dust' has finely divided leaves. Slightly hardier than the species, uniform and compact. A popular variety which is more grey than white. 30cm (12"). Z8-10.
S. cineraria 'Silver Lace' is shimmering silver; delicately cut foliage is the star here. Less hardy than others but admirable wherever it is used. 20cm (8").
S. cineraria 'Snow Storm' ('Silver Cloud') has broad, strap-like white leaves. 20cm (8").
S. cineraria 'White Diamond' is a spectacular white variety, compact and uniform. 25cm (10").
S. haworthii has foliage densely covered in silver hairs.
S. leucophyllus is one of the best European species, nice white tomentose basal leaves are good for trough or scree. Usual yellow daisies.
S. viravira (leucostachys) bears silver leaves and cream button flowers in full sun in June to September. An evergreen scrambler, highly attractive and soft-looking. Very fine, lacy foliage makes an alternative to *Artemisia*. Comes through most winters in the Cotswolds. 50cm (20").
Succulent Senecio
S. aizoides is a distinct succulent with blue-grey leaves and small, white flowers in summer. This evergreen needs protection from frost and will be happiest in a sunny, well-drained position in a pot or in the rock garden. 10cm (4").
S. crassissimus is a spectacular succulent. Well-spaced leaves rise on purplish stems. Leaves are silvery when young, maturing more green.
S. ficoides grey slender foliage like a mini succulent tree.
Cool Companion: *Phlomis lanata, Ballota pseudodictamnus, Lavandula.*

Senecio cineraria

SERIPHIDIUM

Used to be classified under *Artemisia* and looks like it.

HOW TO GROW
As for *Artemisia* full sun, very little water. Z4-9.

S. canum is a small, rounded shrub with narrow, grey-green leaves and a spicy aromatic scent. Known as white or hoary sagebrush. Leaves have a pungent odour when crushed. Older stems become dark brown and fibrous and can layer when in contact with soil. In August-September, tiny yellow flowers appear in 20cm (8") spikes.
S. maritimum is an attractive form with finely divided foliage. An English and Northen Ireland native with sweet-scented foliage.
S. tridentatum makes a mound of aromatic, silver leaves. A slow to moderate grower which makes a low care, evergreen shrub. Sagebrush is found in semi-desert and foothill regions in western U.S. Pleasantly sweet foliage releases its scent into the air upon touch or rainfall. In September, numerous tiny yellow flowers adorn the plant. 2.8m (9ft)x1.8m (6ft).

SINNINGIA

South American gesneriads attractive in both foliage and flower. This one hails from Brazil and is truly silvered.

HOW TO GROW
In full sun, gritty soil. Bright light is important. Tubers can be dried at the end of the growing season and started into growth in spring. Can be propagated from seed or cuttings. Z7.

S. canescens (leucotricha) is a most handsome silver leaved variety with silver hairs giving a furry appearance. Long, narrow, hairy tubular apricot-orange flowers are borne in summer. It is caudiciform, the thick, hairy stalks rising from a tuber which is usually proud of the soil level, although it can be buried. It looks at its best when young as the pubescence is lost with maturity. It has been grown as a bonsai.

STACHYS

A hardy beginners' plant and a favourite with children. A must-have for its soft, felted foliage. Originally from the Middle East, especially Turkey and Iran, it likes it dry. An ideal edging plant to form a soft, textured, silver carpet.

HOW TO GROW
Well-drained, light sandy soil in full sun. Reasonably drought tolerant and clay tolerant once established. Divide in spring. Do not crowd, allow air to circulate. Will usually self-seed. Grow it as a short-lived perennial in Z8 and above and avoid wetting leaves. Z4-9.

S. bacanica bears very hairy, grey-green leaves coupled with white flowers tinged pink in summer. 30cm (12").
S. byzantina is one of the best known silver plants. Lamb's ears are so strokeable, so soft. Looks like drowned rats when wet, but we won't talk about that. Small mauve blooms in spring, beloved by bees. Not truly evergreen but foliage does persist in mild areas into autumn. Spring is the best season for this softie. Flowers can be pinched off and this can form large colonies. 35cm (14").
S. byzantina 'Big Ears' ('Countess Helen von Stein') has larger leaves, around twice the size of the norm and rarely flowers. It is known for better heat and humidity tolerance than the species. No Noddy in sight.
S. byzantina 'Cotton Boll' instead of flowers this variety has little cotton wool balls on spikes! Very effective over the grey felted leaves. 45cm (18").
S. byzantina 'Silver Carpet' is a non-flowering form and if you are not planning a pink-mauve colour scheme, you may prefer this low carpeter.
S. byzantina 'Striped Phantom' is a variegated form with bold splashes of white and cream on the same soft, fuzzy leaves. Vigorous with purplish flowers.
S. candida bears small, grey felted leaves with pale pink, freckled flowers.
S. lavandulifolia is a refined alpine of downy, silver-green leaves with spikes of lavender-pink, spider-like flowers. This Turkish native is happy in scree. 10cm (4").
Cool Companion: *Rosa glauca*.
Hot Partner: *Clematis 'Niobe'*.

Stachys byzantina

Stachys 'Silver Carpet'

Stachys byzantina

Stachys 'Phantom'

Stachys 'Big Ears'

135

Tanacetum leontopodium

STAEHELINA

An uncommon member of the *Asteraceae* family hailing from Spain.

HOW TO GROW
Its normal habitat is dry, stony, sunny southern Spain.

S. dubia bears slender, upright, greyish green, linear leaves that are more silvered on the underside. The narrow, cylindrical white flowers are tipped light mauve and held in a reddish brown involucre. They remind me of the fibre-optic false Christmas trees, as the flower blossoms out in little rays. It forms a small, rounded dense subshrub which is quite attractive in flower.

TANACETUM

An excellent contender for the dry, Mediterranean garden are these natives of the Canary Islands. Better known to many under the former classification of *Chrysanthemum* and other botanical names, and also by the common name, Tansy. The botanists have been having great fun. Ornamental silver tansy has its place in dry gardens. Not much used these days medicinally or in the garden either. Easy maintenance and easy to grow. Deadhead if you do not want them to seed. They are great performers in heat.

HOW TO GROW
Performs well in dry areas, dislikes wet soils. Full sun in well-drained, sandy soil. Z6-9.

T. albipannosum is one of those delicate, filigree tansies suitable for the rock garden. Silver-grey foliage beneath white daisies with yellow centres. 25cm (10").
T. argenteum often seen as *Achillea argentea* bears narrow, serrated, silver leaves in low mounds. Clusters of small, white daisies are borne in May to June. 10cm (4").
T. argenteum canum is even whiter, quite ghostly.
T. capitatum is now known as *Sphaeromeria capitata*, I know you are jumping up and down at the thought! It bears minute, silvery leaves in tiny mounds which love a hot, dry spot. It is topped by gold flowers. 1x10cm (.5x4").
T. cineariifolium bears finely divided, grey leaves with white daisies in spring. Adaptable as to soil and situation. It is the source of the insecticide, pyrethrin. 25cm (10").
T. densum ssp amani is known as partridge feather and has really white, fern-like leaves. Small daisy flowers appear in summer. It is good for xeriscaping and often remains evergreen in winter months. Very similar to *T. haradjanii*.
T. haradjanii is grown primarily for its evergreen, silver foliage which is deeply incised. Yellow daisies in June to July, but infrequently. Plant in exceptionally well-gritted soil or it will succumb to botrytis. Also known as *Chrysanthemum haradjanii*. 20x60cm (8x24"). Z6.

T. herderi is an excellent rock garden plant with silver, thick, forked leaves. Correctly classed as *Hippolytia*, it is similar to *T. argenteum* for making silver rosettes topped by golden daisies. 10cm (4").
T. huronense makes a solid block of attractive, ferny, silvery foliage. Threatened in its native habitat, this might spread rather too much in fertile soil and is much better in poor soil. The usual yellow daisies. 60cm (2ft).
T. leontopodium (Pyrethrum) is a small alpine with feathery, divided leaves in a grey-green tone. Leaves and stems are downy and it bears snow white daisies with yellow centres on short stems. (Yes, I do love these daisies too, very refined). Any alpine lover would beat a path through 10 foot of snow to get it, usually only seen on the show bench. Any plant lover would go for this too.
T. marshalliana makes a neat mound of silver-white, lacy foliage with yellow daisies in summer. 15cm (6").
T. niveum is similar to the more widely available species below. Fragrant leaves are almost entirely obscured by small daisy flowers in midsummer. Presents a cloud of white daisies admirable in the white garden beneath roses. Excellent for mass planting and suitable in full sun in coastal areas or part shade. Probably the most attractive tansy you could plant. 90cm (3ft).
T. niveum 'Jackpot' is a record breaker, capable of having over 1,000 white blooms open at the same time. A stunning plant for the border. 30cm (3ft).
T. praeterifium makes good clumps of filigree, white small mounds with showy daisies. Hailing from Turkey, this is excellent for a scree or rock garden. 30cm (12").
T. ptarmiciflorum 'Silver Feather' elegant, feathered grey-silver leaves add much needed texture to the garden. An extremely attractive, silver-leaved perennial with touchable, lacy and feathery foliage on stiff branches. 90cm (3ft).
T. vulgare 'Silver Lace' could adorn the back of a Victorian armchair like an antimacassar with its beautiful filigree foliage. Very similar to the above but variegated. An excellent ladybird or ladybug farm, larvae, adults and pupae will love this plant.
Perfect Companion: *Artemisia, Perovskia, Salvia*.

Tanacetum haradjanii

Tanacetum argenteum canum above left
T. densum ssp amanii below left
T. vulgare 'Silver Lace' above
Teucrium fruticans below

TEUCRIUM

Shrubby germander is a perfect choice for the rock garden or for topiary. It also makes a useful low hedge.

HOW TO GROW
Tolerates poor, rocky soil in full sun. Best in a sheltered site in neutral to alkaline soil. Z8-9.

T. fruticans is an evergreen, shrub with grey-green foliage that is whiter on the reverse. Stems are white too. Attractive blue flowers can be borne almost all year, but are at their best in summer. Up to 1.8m (6ft).
T. polium ssp capitatum is a sub-shrub from Greece with white-felted leaves. Almost stemless, large, soft purple-blue flowers are carried in summer. An alpine suited to trough culture. 5cm (2").

TOWNSENDIA

North American silver alpines with needle-like foliage and the coolest, large, sumptuous daisy flowers in spring and you know I am not that fond of daisies, but these are so fine, a kind of upper-class daisy. Give me more!

HOW TO GROW
Rocky ground in their natural habitat. Grow in well-drained, gritty soil in full sun. Z3-4.

T. condensata has furry, greenish leaves with pinkish daisies over a long period. This is sumptuous.
T. exscapa bears stemless white daisies, still good ones, over narrow, silvery foliage. Very long lived in a trough. 5x10cm (2x4").
T. hookeri makes compact mounds of silver, linear leaves and stemless white flowers. Delicious daisies, I take back all I said about not liking daisies. I do love daisies, I do.
T. jonesii v lutea beautiful daisies with creamy petals that are exquisitely pink-backed, nestle into the narrow, grey-green foliage.
T. leptotes is a Californian native that makes domes of silvered grey leaves with stemless pinkish flowers.
T. spathulata catches the eye with its rounded rosettes of hairy, silvered leaves and stemless, pink flowers. Pink flower power. The Pryor Mountains Form is highly attractive.

TRADESCANTIA

Soft and furry leaves are sheer delight on this silvery perennial from Northeastern Mexico. It looks great in baskets. It is one of those beauties that almost thrive on neglect; perfect for the forgetful gardener.

HOW TO GROW
Light shade to full sun in sandy soil. Moderate water and is best kept on the dry side through winter. Overwatering will rot the rhizomes. Trim and repot in winter or early spring. Cut back to the ground every two years. Take cuttings of growing shoots or divide. Frost hardy to 0°C (32°F). Z10-11.

T. fluminensis 'Albovittata' (T. albiflora 'Albo Vittata') giant white inch plant makes a handsome plant trailing from a basket. Its white striped green leaves and white flowers are elegant.
T. fluminensis 'Quicksilver' has silver variegated leaves.
T. sillamontana little wonder that this is known as white velvet or white gossamer. It makes a slow-growing, trailing plant that is covered in white hairs. Rose-magenta flowers are borne from summer to autumn. It is perfect for window boxes and restrained groundcover. A highly attractive species. 20x40cm (8x16").
T. zebrina is a glossy-leaved plant and one that is a study in colour. A dark central stripe is bordered by silver stripes with a definite sheen and finally edged in a thin green margin. The underleaves are purple and the stems mottled. Keep moist but not soggy. 45cm (18").
Perfect Companion: Grow with dark foliage plants such as *Ipomoea batatas 'Black Heart'*.

Tradescantia sillamontana

Townsendia condensata above
T. hookeri below

Townsendia jonesii v lutea above
T. spathulata below

VERBASCUM

Charming spires of attractive flowers and silvery foliage are superb in herbaceous borders. Dainty species are superb in the rock garden.

HOW TO GROW
Full sun and good drainage, poor soil.

V. bombyciferum 'Silver Lining' the silver leaves and stems of this dynamic looker are bombshell quality, combined as they are with rich yellow blooms. The species itself is known as silver mullein; the fabulous leaves are large and silver. The show starts in the first year with the elephant grey leaves followed by those yellow flowers in the second year; it is a spectacular biennial. Z4-8.
V. dumulosum is a must-have species from Turkey. Not one of the towering *Verbascums*, this is a daintier species for a rock garden. Silvery, velvet-like, pointed foliage with gorgeous veining sits beneath a mass of yellow flowers with a lavender eye. A shrubby, trailing and prostrate plant which makes an eye-catching specimen in the rock garden. 30cm (12") with a spread of 90cm (3ft).
V. nevadense has large, basal leaves covered in silver hairs. It bears white or yellow spikes of flowers with reddish purple filaments in July to August. Native to the Sierra Nevada in Andalucia, Spain. 1m (4ft). Z9.
V. olympicum makes large basal rosettes of silver, felted, wavy leaves which are eye-catching in winter. From July to September spires of silver candelabras soar heavenwards with cheering, yellow flowers. Feature this mullein in your dry Mediterranean border. Grey gargantua, grand and strong, dramatic and aromatic. An easy, self-seeding biennial in open sites. 1.8-2m (6-8ft). Z3-8.
V. olympicum x V. bombyciferum makes large, evergreen, white felted rosettes with tall strong spires of yellow flowers in May to September. A naturally occurring hybrid which self seeds as a biennial.

Verbascum dumulosum

VERONICA

Undemanding speedwell adds summer colour to the border with its blooming spikes and silvery, felted foliage like garden sage. Deadhead to keep this flowering all summer long.

HOW TO GROW
Easy in sunny, well-drained sites with good drainage. Drought tolerant. Z4.

V. bombycina ssp bolkardaghensis has tiny, white-felted leaves which make a neat, tight mat with clear blue, stemless flowers in lean and mean scree. 5cm (2").
V. spicata ssp incana has deep blue flower spikes which make a great contrast to the silvered leaves. 35cm (14").
V. spicata ssp incana 'Sarabande' has handsome foliage which will stand up to frost and is handsome in late spring to summer with porcelain blue flowers.
V. spicata ssp incana 'Silbersee' deep violet spikes grace the silvery sea of sage-like foliage in June to July. The dense mats are mostly evergreen; this is handsome by a path. Easy from seed. 30cm (12").
V. thymoides ssp pseudocinerea tiny, toothed silver leaves are matched by blue flowers. 8x20cm (3x8").
Perfect Companion: taller types associate well with *Salvia, Ballota, Tanacetum*.

WESTRINGIA
An uncommon Tasmanian seaside shrub.

HOW TO GROW
Well-drained soil in sun, little water.

W. fruticosa 'Wynyabbie Gem' silver rosemary foliage on this Tasmanian shrub is a delight in summer with its large lavender flowers. 120cm (4ft).

BARK

ACER

I can always find room for this incredible genus in my books. See how to grow in the main section.

A. x conspicuum 'Silver Vein' has such amazing, silver-streaked bark, it is worthy of inclusion in your garden as a valued ornamental. 8m (35ft).
A. x conspicuum 'Silver Ghost' has green peeling bark that reveals white patches.
A. saccharum the silver maple is so called for its silvery bark. This is the fastest growing of the native American maples, especially in moist soils. Admirable for its graceful habit and its tolerance of a wide variety of soils. In 4 to 5 years it will reach 3m (10ft).
A. 'White Tigress' bears grey, silver and white striped bark. Green leaves show attractive yellow autumn colouring. Often a multi-trunked shrub or tree to 10m (30ft).

CASTANOSPERMUM

The Australian native Black Bean is a suitable container subject.

C. australe this medium to large tree has smooth grey bark, dark green leaves and fabulous yellow-red pea flowers. Slow growing and subject to frost damage when young, it resprouts in spring. It is grown in many parts of California.

RHUS

Those silvered stems are a plantsman's treasure.

R. aromatica has many attributes, not least the silvery stems which along with the leaves are pungent when rubbed. Early, tiny spring flowers in yellow with light green slightly serrated leaves, red berries that taste of lemonade and brilliant fall colour are all reasons to grow the aromatic rhus.

Right: Betula papyrifera
Left: Betula pendula

BETULA

The most wonderful silver and white bark is found in *Betula*, the silver birches. Planted in groups these can take your breath away. *B. pendula* and its cultivars make handsome and such graceful drooping branchlets as a single specimen in the garden. Upright forms such as *B. utilis v jacquemontii* are superb alone or magnificent in a group. They make a nice and underused hedge planted 60cm (2ft apart). Delicate in feature but tough trees. Choose the right variety and in naked winter, bare against the elements, birch handles its nudity with finesse and flirts its white bark. Narrow and upright crowns cast little shade, even the pendulous ones are highly garden friendly.

HOW TO GROW
Suitable for most soils and sites but best on deep, well-drained loam and not performing well on shallow chalk. Full sun to partial shade. Remove low branches to emphasise the beauty of bark colour and the fascination of peeling bark in winter coupled with the tracery of naked branches. Easy from seed following stratification. Cultivars must be grafted. Z2.

B. ermanii has white peeling bark. It can be grown as a multi-stemmed tree. Found wild on the Kamchatka peninsula in the Pacific Rim.
B. 'Fetisowii' grow this for its peeling, chalky white bark.
B. medwedewii is a stout, wide spreading shrub or tree with silver bark and lovely autumn colour.
B. papyrifera is one of the loveliest of birches having white peeling bark on mature trees. Bark is variable in colour and ranges into the pinks. 7.5x3.5m (25x12ft) in 20 years.
B. pendula known as the silver birch. This hardy British native is suitable in exposed sites, for chalky soil and is even tolerant of wet sites. Needs good light. Rapid growing and gracefully drooping, with age the silver bark fissures into black channels. Peeling bark is another attractive feature of this tree. Its elegance has led to the name of 'lady of the woods'. Its poise sets the stage for an understory of bulbs and perennials. 7.5x3m (25x10ft) in 20 years.
B. pendula 'Dalecarlica' (B. alba) was discovered in 1781 in Sweden and is still considered to be the best of the silver birch. Finely cut foliage and a gracefullly pendent form add to its charm but it is not weeping. Stake when young.
B. pendula 'Laciniata' try this for a slower growing cultivar, with more deeply cut leaves and the same attractive white bark. 12m (40ft).
B. pendula 'Youngii' is an extremely graceful specimen. Compact and suitable for small gardens. It often lacks a central leader and has a mushroom shape.
B. populifolia is similar to silver birch but its leaves are longer and elegantly pointed.

B. pubescens has bark which reflects light and appears silvery. It remains smooth for a long time, then begins to flake in layers. Glabrous leaves and young twigs are warty, thin and pendulous.
B. pubescens ssp microphylla is the Scottish mountain birch with small leaves and white bark.
B. 'Royal Frost' is an improvement over 'Crimson Frost' with its purple leaves against striking white bark.
B. utilis 'Ramdana River' collected in Uttar Pradesh has exceptionally white bark even when young and possesses highly glossy foliage.
B. utilis v jacquemontii is variable and all have whitish bark, some better than others, which often curls into scrolls. It appears milky white and luminescent in winter sunshine rendering it a very handsome subject in the winter garden. I often think of it as the snow scene tree.
'Doorenbos' is a particularly good selection.
'Grayswood Ghost' appears as apparitions in the woods. Ghostly white trunks with heads of glossy green leaves. The white colouring extends to outer branches.
'Jermyns' is a reliable cultivar with mahogany bark peeling to brilliant white.
'Silver Shadow' is a striking cultivar for the whiteness of its bark. Aptly named, it appears as silver shadows in the winter garden.
Hot Partner: *Fagus sylvatica 'Purpurea', Cornus alba 'Kesselringii', Bergenia cordifolia 'Purpurascens', Epimedium.*
Cool Companion: *Galanthus nivalis, Helleborus foetidus.*

NEW GROWTH

Some *Rhododendron* have a silver effect from the white bloom, the tomentosum on new leaves.

R. macabeanum bears large, ribbed dark leaves with a silver flush and felted silver on the underside. A little shy of flowering, the flowers appear maybe only every second year but are well worth the wait. Heavenly, large deep creamy, primrose-yellow bells with a basal maroon blotch hang in trusses. Hardy in most areas, this Himalaya species is most at home in open woodland with protection from strong winds.

R. yakushimanum makes a neat, dense mound of deep green leaves covered in a silvery bloom. Quite an early flowering species with white to pale pink flowers from deep pink buds which sit well in a silver garden.

Tetrapanax papyrifer is a very tropical looking plant with its large, handsome green leaves. New leaves appear silvery and are quite exquisite in their unfurling state.

Rhododendron macabeanum above
Rhododendron yakushimanum below

Tetrapanax papyrifer left

145

HIDDEN BEAUTY

Look under leaves for a silvery side.

BUDDLEJA

Every gardener has encountered the butterfly bush, but the species are often quite rare and certainly under-used. They are nothing like *B. davidii*; many are very attractive shrubs, far superior to the latter.

B. agathosma is distinct and free growing. Striking, white-felted leaves with deeply toothed foliage and scented lilac flowers in spring. It is best grown against a warm wall. It is often found classified under *B. crispa* but is untypical of this species.

B. alternifolia 'Argentea' this species is my favourite especially when grown as a standard. It is capable of initiating a love affair with the genus. I adore the arching branches and in this form the silvery, willowy leaves smothered in June with fragrant lilac flowers.

B. crispa bears soft, woolly stems and leaves with serrated edges. Fragrant lilac-pink flowers are carried in profusion in August to September. It is best against a wall.

B. crispa 'Moon Dance' bears pale pink flowers and heavily felted, silver leaves. Dance by the light of the moon.

B. davidii 'White Ball' is a must for the white garden with its delightful silver foliage combined with fragant white flowers. For the best flower show, cut back heavily in spring.

B. davidii 'White Harlequin' has white-edged foliage teamed with white flowers.

B. fallowiana v alba has silver woolly stems and leaves and terminal panicles of sweet-scented white-cream flowers.

B. loricata is a rough textured, bushy shrub with smallish, ovate dark green leaves, which are white to silvery on the reverse. Creamy white flowers with an orange eye grow in clusters in spring. Each possesses a peach scent. A hardy, evergreen shrub from South Africa for a sheltered spot. Z7.

B. 'Silver Anniversary' is love at first sight. This is a sophisticated, grown-up version with beautiful silver, evergreen leaves teamed with charming, white flowers having a mustard eye and a wonderful honey scent. Raised in 1997, this is a cross between *B. crispa* and *B. loricata*. Unless hand-pollinated, this will not produce seed, so it is perfectly safe in the garden; it will stay where you put it and not pop up everywhere in the garden. Flower arrangers will find that stems stay fresh for two to three weeks. I saved the best until last!

Cheilanthes argentea is a sweet fern with silver undersides to the finely cut green leaves.

Olea europea with its gnarled rheumatic trunk and handsome foliage, silvery green on the upper and silver on the lower surface, the olive is a symbol of the Mediterranean. Hardy types are now available for cooler climates. The graceful foliage contrasts with the rough, twisted limbs of its branches and trunk.

Populus alba is the European White Poplar. The undersides of this leaf are silver-white woolly and often visible in the wind. The bark is also silver-white and smooth for many years, later on developing dark splits and ridges.

Tilia tomentosa the silver linden is a stately tree with the silvery underside of its leaves in evidence in the breeze. 30m (90ft). Z4.

Buddleja 'Silver Anniversary'

SILVER SPARKLERS

Variegated plants in white and green add a fresh quality to the garden

Alocasia 'Hilo Beauty'

ACER

Beautiful trees and shrubs in any disguise, there are some particularly handsome variegated forms.

A. crataegifolium 'Veitchii' is extremely attractive, its white and green variegated leaves also show some pink tones. This shrubby tree possesses purple bark and horizontal branching. 2m (8ft). Z6.

A. negundo 'Flamingo' bears handsome foliage edged in white with some pink hints on red twigs. A spectacular specimen from spring through to autumn. Prune to control size. 6m (20ft).

A. palmatum 'First Ghost' is a selection made by Talon Buchholz of Buchholz Nursery. Narrowly irregular-shaped leaf segments are creamy white with green veins, each being edged in pink. 1.8m (6ft). Z6.

A. palmatum 'Harry's White' is another very attractive shrubby tree with white veined leaves.

A. palmatum 'Ukigomo' is one of the most elegant variegated plants known as the floating cloud maple. It will stay green for two years but in its third year it will start to display its white and pink marbling. From a distance it appears white. Only room for one white variegated plant in your garden? I would choose this. Z4.

A. 'Silver Cardinal' confetti in pink and white on this small, Asian species. 3m (10ft) in 10 years. Z7.

Actinidia kolomikta 'Arctic Beauty' is as pure as driven snow in the white tips of its green foliage. Some deep pink appears and young leaves show colouring of purplish tints on green. Fragrant white flowers are an added bonus.

If you need vigorous ground cover en masse, make room for the beautiful variegated leaves of **Aegopodium podogaria 'Variegatum'** but do remember that this is not one to be satisfied with a small role in the garden. It likes centre, left and right stage; it will take over. It works well under shrubs and trees. 40cm (16").

Acer crataegifolium 'Veitchii'

Acer palmatum 'Harry's White'

The rare Aeonium arboreum 'Albovariegatum' has waxy leaves and grows like the better known black one, 'Zwartkop'.

Agave americana 'Mediopicta Alba'

AGAVE

Add a tropical touch to the garden with these admirable tender succulents.

Agave americana 'Mediopicta Alba' is extremely striking in its variegation. Broad leaves have a wide, white stripe edged in green.

A. parviflora has beautiful white markings and filaments on compact, small rosettes.

AGLAONEMA

Here I go with my Aroids again, and no-one can deny that these fabulous foliage plants make a great indoor plant. Known as silver evergreen, one of the houseplants reputed to clean air. In the past few years, interest has increased in *Aglaonema* with many new cultivars being introduced, these newer cultivars are capable of tolerating colder temperatures.

HOW TO GROW
Quite tolerant. Excellent in shade, as long as they are out of draughts. Light porous soil with good aeration. Propagate from tip cuttings. Keep minimally moist, never wet, but never allow to dry out completely. This is most important with young plants. They rarely flower in cultivation. Require 21-25°C (70-85°F). Z10-12.

A. 'Cassandra' is an upright variety with glossy, silver-green leaves having dark, random spots, a light green to white midrib and white petioles.

A. 'Cecilia' bears silver mottling to most of the leaf surface. Midrib and some veins are green on large, wide leaves.

A. 'Christina' looks similar to *'Silver Queen'* but has a shorter, rounder leaf.

A. commutatum itself is a handsome plant with dark green leaves attractively splashed with silver markings. *A. commutatum* is the most widely grown species and has given rise to many cultivars which differ in their markings.

A. commutatum 'Alumina' is so called for its aluminium look. Like silver foil the leaves are heavily silvered.

A. commutatum 'Silver Queen' is a perfect interiorscaping plant, in medium light. It also makes a good choice in warmer climes outdoors. This older variety is still popular even though it is especially sensitive to cold. This one bears silvery green, glossy foliage with dark green markings. Minimum temperature 17°C (55°F).

A. 'Deborah' is one of the most striking cultivars. Not only does it possess silver markings on the leaf surface, but silver-white veins on the leaf back. However, the most amazing characteristic of this plant has to be the white stems. Unusual dense, upright growth on this showy form.

A. 'Illumination' has leaf surfaces illuminated with a silver sheen. White, showy petioles.

A. 'Jubilee' is similar to *'Pattaya Beauty'*, with silver to white centred, green margined leaves.

A. nitidum 'Ernesto's Favourite' and likely to be everyone's favourite as it is a pretty plant. However its downfall is that it is extremely cold sensitive and needs careful watering too.

A. 'Parrot Jungle' bears lanceolate leaves which are heavily silvered on dark green.

A. 'Patricia' has long pointed leaves, well-silvered with green midveins. Compact growth and spiky apperance. Handles lower temperatures without damage.

A. 'Pattaya Beauty' if anything is more silvered. The dark green margin is set alight by the silver centre of the long, pointed leaves. Suffers from brittle leaves. Good for a low trough and tolerates office conditions well.

A. 'Queen of Siam' bears white stems with upright growth and leaves are marked in grey-green.

A. 'Silver Bay' is equally handsome, the silver-white, broadly lanceolate leaves are margined in dark green and white stripes. This new cultivar is capable of withstanding lower temperatures. Heavy suckering and compact growth.

A. 'Silver Frost' is extremely sensitive to cold. Its attractive leaves are silvered with green midribs and mottling.

A. 'Silver King' like *'Silver Queen'* but more highly variegated with irregular green markings and not as well-branched. Larger leaves than many to 30cm (12"). Suckers well but is not very vigorous.

A. 'Silver Ribbon' is another newer cultivar. Long, narrow wavy leaves are predominantly silver with two shades of green.

A. 'Silverado' is a very elegant cultivar having handsome silver leaves with a green tinge.

A. 'Tropic Snow' is a favourite with me, diminutive yet powerful. Wonderful strap-like foliage in silver-green with mid green edges, veining and undersides. Its size makes it ideal for a table top plant or display on a jardiniere. 5cm (2").

A. White-leaf Group is simply knockout. Leaves appear white and gradually become green speckled as they mature. This is a terrific plant.

A. 'White Lance' bears narrow, pointed leaves, nicely silvered with a green edge. Compact.

A. 'White Rain' bears silvered, rounded leaves with a white mid vein and variegated green edging. A milky white look.

Aglaonema 'Silver Bay'

Aglaonema 'Silver Queen'

ALOCASIA

Stunning ornamentals with large, elephant ears leaves make a definite statement with their variegated leaves. These boldy go where no plant has gone before. Enjoy the tropical look.

HOW TO GROW
Humus rich soil direct in the ground or in pots in dappled shade. Keep moist. Protect from frost.

Alocasia 'Frydek' fabulous, arrowhead black-green leaves have thick white veins. Pale stalks have purplish banding. This is a stunning plant. Z9.
A. 'Hilo Beauty' apple-green leaves are bedecked with white splashes. This has a delicate look to it for such a large leaved plant. Prefers shade but takes heat. Z8.
A. odora 'Okinawa Silver' you might reel from the price this beauty is fetching or simply from the fetching and stunning leaves. Rounded leaves are variegated in silvery grey, cream and white. Introduced by Dr. Masato Yokoi in Japan. Z8.

Alocasia 'Frydek'

AJUGA

In sun to part shade, the bugleweeds are handsome perennials in spots which never dry out. The silver types tend to spread slower than the darker bugles and have the reputation of being more difficult to grow.

HOW TO GROW
Likes soil on the rich, moist side. Z3-8.

A. 'Arctic Fox' is quite stunning with a small grey-green heart surrounded in bright, cream-white having a green, wavy edge. Blue flowers appear in April to May. Z4-8.
A. reptans 'Gray Lady' bears small grey-green leaves and blue flowers from April to May. 15-20cm (6-8").
A. 'Silver Beauty' ('Silver Carpet') bears grey-green leaves edged in silver-white topped by blue flowers.
A. 'Silver Queen' is mottled cream on blue-green foliage which fades and has purplish hints in winter. 15cm (6").
A. 'Silver Shadow' is the most attractive to my eye in this colour range. Bears silvery grey foliage with blue flowers.

Arisaema sikokianum silver leaf

ARISAEMA

Silver leaved *Arisaema* are such a treasure in the garden. Some of my very favourite plants to grow for those fabulously intriguing spathes. As if that is not enough, many have interesting and handsome leaves too. These with silver markings are real treasures in the garden.

HOW TO GROW
Light shade is necessary, but do not overdo it as plants will become leggy.

A. consanguineum silver leaf has the most amazing leaflets with silver centres. This beauty is touched by a silver wand! Fourteen or more leaflets cascade from the stem like an umbrella. Emerging in late July, this aroid takes the silver screen by storm. Silvering can vary and a broad silver-centred clone is being offered too. 1.2m (4ft).
A. consanguineum 'Poseidon' makes large leaflets up to 60cm (2ft) across. The blue-green leaves have a silver patterning to the handsome, wavy leaves with good substance. Stems are snakeskin pattterned.
A. consanguineum 'The Perfect Wave' the wave rises in a rush of energy and at its height appears a silver crescendo, the leaves of this beautiful form are almost a perfect grey and definitely a superb foil to other plants particularly of purple foliage. 1.2m (4ft).
A. kishidae 'Silver Center' has striking foliage; a large silver centre and silver dots adorn the two divided green leaves. Spathes are brownish. Z5-9.
A. lobatum is another that often sports silver splashed leaves. The spathe is hooded. The most striking part is the bright turquoise-coloured tubers.
A. serratum 'Silver Center' is just as striking with its silver centred leaves, snakeskin stem and striped spathes.
A. sikokianum 'Silver Center' has those incredibly beautiful and elegant spathes combined with foliage having a silver streak.
A. taiwanense silver leaf form selected at Heronswood in the Pacific Northwest of the U.S. with each leaf having a pewter overlay to enhance the beauty of the dark spathes.

ARUM

Foliage from late summer, but a real star in the winter garden. Spathes are followed by berries and then it sleeps all summer long, perchance to dream. Dreams sure are made of this!

HOW TO GROW
Tolerate dry shade or part sun. Z4-9.

A. italicum ssp italicum 'Marmoratum' (A. italicum 'Pictum') produces large leaves beautifully silver marked, which are superb in winter. Glossy, arrowhead leaves. Greenish-white spathes appear in summer. The plant then goes dormant. There is a larger leaved version called **'Cyclops'**. However, if big is not your thing, there is a smaller version called **'Tiny'**.
A. italicum 'White Winter' is one of the hardiest and has deep silver veining, more pronounced than usual.
A. italicum 'Tresahor Beauty' is an excellent marbled version selected at the nursery of the same name.

Arum italicum 'White Winter'

ASARUM

Turn shade wild with totally ravishing shiny leaves bespeckled in silver. From cute, heart-shaped leaves to large arrowhead foliage, there is an *Asarum* to suit you in a wide variety of patterns - speckled, spotted, marbled and washed in silver or pewter. These woodland natives known as wild gingers after the aromatic roots, should be on your list of favourites. Most are evergreen and many have remarkable foliage and very unusual flowers. A little slow to make a clump, but when they do so, they are spectacular plants. They tend to dislike disturbance. Used in pots in Japan where these plants are rightly revered. In this way, both foliage and flowers can be fully appreciated. In general, the American species are the easiest to cultivate and in Texas and Georgia, *Asarums* can put on a year-round show. Often variable patterned leaves can differ and plain leaves can occur in some species noted below.

HOW TO GROW
Humus-rich soil in light shade with excellent drainage. Needs must be satisfied to keep these happy, but most are not too difficult. Divide in spring. Provide slug protection. Z5-9.

A. arifolium bears densely pubescent, triangular green leaves marked and splashed in silver. An easy and tough wild ginger making attractive ground cover in time. It bears numerous dark flowers in spring. 20cm (8").
A. arifolium v ruthii is native to the East coast of the USA. Triangular green leaves are marked in dull silver. When crushed they give off an anise scent. Dark purple flowers are hidden under the foliage. 15cm (6"). Z5-9.
A. asaroides is a clump-forming, Japanese species with clouds of silver patterning on grey-green leaves to 15cm (6") long with a rosy blush in winter. This makes easy clumps and has large tubby brown flowers in spring. Z6-9.
A. asaroides album has exceptional leaf patterns and a sought-after jade green flower. Z6-9.
A. asperum is a beautifully marked Japanese plant making a good garden plant, often seen in Kyoto gardens. Sage green leaves are nicely pattened in pewter. It bears brownish flowers. Z6-9.
A. blumei has delicate silver veining and lovely purple flowers.
A. 'China Mirror' (Ozzie Johnson) has dark near black glossy leaves with distinctive, almost pure white veins. Good groundcover for south-eastern U.S. states. 15cm (6"). Z7.
A. chinense can often have silver markings. There is also a stoloniferous form of this species which bears attractively marked, pointed leaves.
A. delavayi can bear pewter marked, deep green leaves. Black and white flowers are large and showy.

A. epigynum 'Kikko' bears soft, hairy leaves with a tortoise-shell silver patterning. Z8-10.

A. epigynum 'Silver Web' (BSWJ3442) the dark green, arrow-shaped leaves of this delightful species are dramatically webbed in silver veins. A very choice foliage specimen plant. It is one of those plants you will covet and guard jealously or want to tell the world about. I want to shout about it, go and buy it! Originally collected by Bleddyn and Sue Wynn Jones in Taiwan. Possibly hardy to Zone 10, but if in doubt, contain it and hide when friends come around. 5cm (2").

A. forbesii is remarkably handsome with long, arrowhead foliage marked in pewter. Chunky, chocolate-purple flowers have a white throat.

A. 'Gosho Zakura' by gosh! Blue-green leaves are washed in silver with random markings of blue-green. Superb! Z6-9.

A. 'Haku Cho' bears silver-grey leaves with a broad, dark green central stripe and patches of green. The name means swan. Z6-9.

A. hartweggii bears deep green, shiny evergreen leaves with wonderful silver-white veining. This U.S. rhizomatous species has a citrus scent if leaves are crushed or bruised. It bears brown flowers. Full shade. 20cm (8").

A. hartweggii 'Sterling Silver' is one of the most silver of this genus, leaves are margined in silver and mottled towards the centre.

A. hexalobum has beautifully marked leaves reminiscent of *Cyclamen.*

A. hexalobum 'Asteroid' is a Japanese species bearing matt, silver leaves with a central green stripe. Makes an exceptional garden plant. 15cm (6"). Z5b-9.

A. hexalobum 'Tapestry' has dark green, semi-glossy foliage heavily marked in silver and a lighter green. Z5-9.

A. infrapurpureum B&SWJ bears dark, evergreen, heart-shaped leaves with purple undersides and silvery upper surfaces. Maroon flowers are borne at ground level.

A. kiushianum v tubulosum is a Japanese species bearing silver-mottled foliage and white owl-eye flowers.

A. kumageanum bears well-silvered leaves in summer with dark purple flowers appearing in August to October.

A. kumageanum 'Frosted Jade' is a selection of a Japanese species made by Tony Avent, Plant Delights Nursery. Large, pointed, glossy, dark green leaves are well-speckled with silver. Easy and vigorous. 15cm (6"). Z6-9.

A. maculatum as its name suggests, has leaves spotted silver, they are glossy and long. This beautiful, deciduous clumper from Korea bears almost black flowers. Z4-8.

A. magnificum with heart-shaped, green leaves heavily clouded in silver. Flowers are just as dramatic, charcoal to violet with a white ring and an inner tinted violet throat.

A. marmoratum is the virtually evergreen, marbled wild ginger of West Coast USA. Deep green, polished leaves have incredible silver zones. The inner ring to the flowers is maroonish.

A. maximum will give maximum delight in the woodland setting. Its flowers are nothing short of show stopping; its leaves nicely and quietly patterned on an elegant species.

A. maximum 'Ling Ling' has two silver blotches on either side of the large, glossy green leaves. In late spring, those large black and white panda eye flowers will astound visitors to the garden. It makes an imposing garden plant for warm gardens. Truly a wow plant. 15cm (6"). Z7b-9.

A. minamitanianum is the most widely cultivated species in Japan, but hardly known here in the U.K. It bears evergreen, heart shaped foliage which is glossy and well-silvered. Purple, starfish-like flowers are out of this world even though you will encounter them borne near ground level, they are not really of this earth. It will need protection in a shady, moist site.

A. minor 'Honeysong' (Alex Summers) has very attractively marked, silver-marbled leaves. Heart-shaped leaves almost hide the white and maroon spotted flowers in spring. This East Coast native makes a clump to 90cm (1ft) across, 13cm (5") tall. Z5-9.

A. naniflorum 'Eco Decor' (Don Jacobs) is a selection made in South Carolina bearing dramatic silver venation on dark green shiny leaves. It has a spreading habit and yellow flowers are hidden beneath the foliage. A cutie, one of the smallest of the genus. 7cm (3"). Z5-9.

A. nobilissimum silver-foiled, evergreen leaves to 20cm (8") long over caramel-brown flowers to 7cm (3") across.

A. porphyronatum has fantastic large leaves to 15cm (6"), incredibly silver-blotched. Dark purple flowers with a white eye are borne in spring. Another form of this Chinese species, *A. porphyronatum v atrovirens* has green backs. 15cm (6"). Z 7b-9.

A. rigescens bears leaves which are well-silvered.

A. sakawanum is a strong-growing Japanese species. Its glossy, evergreen leaves are usually nicely patterned. Z7-9.

A. sakawanum 'Emerald Dragon' (Ozzie Johnson) bears arrow-shaped foliage with an intricate pattern in greens and silvers, capable of making vigorous clumps. A good performer in warmer areas. Z6-9.

A. 'Sekkyo' bears dark blue-green foliage and is included here for its remarkable white central stripe. Its name means snow bridge. It also bears green flowers. Z5-9.

A. 'Setsu Getsu ka' meaning snow moon flower, this selection bears medium green leaves mottled with dark green and silver over pale green flowers. It has a watercolouring effect. Get set to get it! Z 5b-9.

A. shuttleworthii is a semi-evergreen with dark green leaves patterned in silver. A North American native with some of the largest leaves of the American species, makes good clumps bearing dark flowers in spring. This is grown at Durham Botanic Garden. 15cm (6"). Z5-9.

A. shuttleworthii 'Callaway' is a compact, small-leaved variety marked in pewter. Brown flowers in spring selected by the late Fred Galle at Callaway Gardens in Georgia. Needs excellent drainage. 12cm (5"). Z5-9.

154

A. shuttleworthii 'Carolina Silver' (We-Du) bears leaves which are marked with silvery cream. 12cm (5"). Dark purple contrasting flowers are hidden by the foliage. Z5-9.

A. shuttleworthii v harperi 'Velvet Queen' makes a fine clump of rounded leaves, marked in silver. On this selection, the flowers are almost twice the size of those on the species. 12cm (5"). Z5-9.

A. speciosum 'Buxom Beauty' (Kitto/Fret) bears larger leaves than the species which are silver marbled to 25cm (10") long with larger flowers too. 25cm (10").

A. speciosum 'Woodlanders' Select' (Bob McCartney) the 15cm (6") arrowhead green leaves of this native Alabama wild ginger are marked with pewter like a *Cyclamen*. Owl eye flowers are borne in spring. 15cm (6"). Z5-9.

A. splendens is aptly named, for this Chinese species will make easy and spectacular ground cover accompanied by dark purple flowers to 6-8cm (3") across in spring. Large, handsome leaves are boldly splashed in silver. Choice in containers, very effective, first class ground cover. 15cm (6"). Z6b-9, although has been known to overwinter in Z4.

A. splendens 'Quicksilver' has marbled, arrow-shaped leaves to 15cm (6") long. Z5-8.

A. subglosum 'Mariner' (Ozzie Johnson) possesses glossy green leaves to 12cm (5") long, with silver etchings.

A. taipingshanianum bears heart-shaped, *Cyclamen* like spotted leaves and incredible brownish owl eye flowers.

A. takinoi 'Galaxy' is a selection of a Japanese species. 5cm (2") rounded leaves are blotched with silver. This clumper works hard in the garden and can look as good in late winter as it does in spring, taking 5 years to make a clump 30cm (1ft) wide. 7cm (3"). Z5-8b).

A. takinoi 'Ginba' is another fabulous selection completely covered in a silver wash. Its small leaves are like the old fashioned silver sixpences. Z6-9.

A. virginicum has leathery, glossy leaves well marked in silver. No two leaves are quite the same and this is similar in leaf to *Cyclamen coum*. Z5-8b.

A. virginicum 'Little Silver Treasure' (Parker Lewis Little) bears leaves which are mostly silver with deep maroon flowers. 15cm (6").

A. virginicum spp virginicum 'Silver Splash' (Charles Oliver) is it the neat, rounded leaves that get you, or the exceptional silver markings? More silver than the species. A handsome selection, usually evergreen and easy in woodland. 15cm (6"). Z5-9.

A. wulingense is a newly introduced species from China with pubescent stems bearing narrowly ovate leaves to 25cm (10") long. On the deep green background, the silver-white veining stands out, the leaves are also covered in pubescent, brownish felted hairs below. Purple flowers have a white ridged interior and a dark inner ring.

Cool Companion: *Cyclamen, Trillium luteum, T. grandiflorum.*

Hot Partner: *Trillium chloropetalum, Arisaema.*

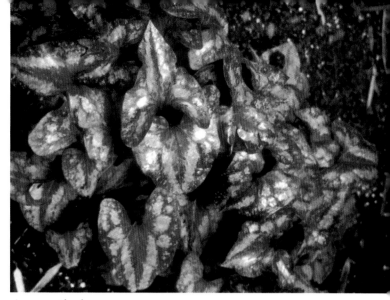

Asarum splendens

Athyrium 'Branford Beauty'

Athyrium niponicum v pictum 'The Ghost'

ATHYRIUM

Victorians loved ferns so why should we use them in the modern garden? Ferns have entered the millenium in shades of silver and purple. They are ideal in shade offering excellent colour and texture. Do you want more reasons to be fond of fronds?

HOW TO GROW
Part to full shade in moist, humus soil. Heat and humidity tolerant. Z4-9.

A. 'Branford Beauty' has tall, upright, clump-forming growth. Muted tones of green and silver adorn this elegant fern and make it a good partner for the darker *A. niponicum v pictum* and the paler *'Ghost'*. 50cm (20").

A. 'Ghost' displays vigorous, upright, arching fronds tinged silver grey. This is a cross between *A. niponicum v pictum* and *A. filix-femina* and like you want your children to do, it exhibits the best of its parents. Allow the remarkable, deciduous silver fronds to brighten the woodland floor. From the Virginian garden of Nancy Swell. 75cm (30").

A. niponicum 'Applecourt' comes from Roger Grounds and Diana Grenfell. It has two exciting features, the colouring, green, silver and purple and the crested fronds which twist at the end. 60cm (2ft).

A. niponicum v pictum a good clone of this is one of my favourite plants and certainly my favourite fern. Metallic greys and silvers are beautifully 'painted' on each leaf, but not all are alike, and selection is the key.

A. niponicum v pictum 'Cristatoflabellatum' can cause a stir with its unusual crested fronds. Cool, silvered crispy foliage with some red and green tones. As we all know the best things in life are unfortunately rare.

A. niponicum v pictum 'Pewter Lace' (PPAF) a metallic offering, not as attractive to my eye as a good *A. niponicum v pictum*.

A. niponicum v pictum 'Silver Falls' (Ballantyne PVR) is stunning with silver fronds tinged with red. Colour develops with age to a shimmering lustre. Named after the famous Oregon waterfall, that I have had the great pleasure to visit with my friend, David Vala, a landscape designer. 40cm (16").

A. niponicum v pictum 'Soul Mate' is a selection of the Japanese painted fern from Angelo and Carol Randaci of the Fernery. The same silver colouring of the species but with added zest in the form of the lacy crests at the tip of each fern. 30cm (12").

A. niponicum v pictum 'Wildwood Twist' is a smoky grey-green. Its upright fronds twist slightly.

Cool Companion: *Hosta, Arisaema.*
Hot Partner: *Trillium woodwardii.*

Top to bottom: Athyrium 'Wildwood Twist', A. 'Silver Falls', A. niponicum v pictum

BRUNNERA

Forget the plain green-leaved Siberian bugloss which is not much more exciting than the ordinary forget-me-not, *Myosotis*, which incidentally I believe has nicer blue flowers if you want those tiny things; they are an enchanting blue. Plant instead, a spectacular silver-leaved perennial and outstanding shade-loving foliage plant. Sparkling silver for shade.

HOW TO GROW
Shaded spot in rich, moist soil. Will take morning sun, keep moist. These certainly loathe hot sun and dry sites and leaves can turn ugly brown. Z3-8.

B. macrophylla 'Dawson's White' tends to brown less on the edges but is superceded by newer cultivars.
B. macrophylla 'Jack Frost' (PBR) was spotted at Walters Gardens in the U.S. in a tray of *B. 'Langtrees'*. The large, heart-shaped, silver leaves are veined in mid-green with a distinctive tracery. Tiny clusters of clear blue flowers like forget-me-nots appear in spring. Cool, frosted ice for summer. 30x30cm (12x12").
B. macrophylla 'Looking Glass' (PPAF) beats *'Jack Frost'* for me, a silver looking glass with the faintest light green veins teamed with the usual blue flowers. Sterling silver. 30cm (12").
B. macrophylla 'Silver All Over' Bob Brown of Cotswold Garden Flowers is pushing this as an all-silver version. 50cm (20").
B. macrophylla 'Silver Wings' is a recent introduction from Naylor Creek Gardens in the U.S., another sport of *'Langtrees'* with large, heart-shaped green leaves overlaid to varying degrees with silver. Shows more silver than its parent. Topped by the usual blue flowers.
Hot Partner: *Athyrium niponicum v pictum, Heuchera 'Obsidian', Tiarella 'Black Snowflake'*.

Brunnera 'Jack Frost'

Caladium humboldtii above, C. candidum below

CALADIUM

White light in the garden, what an addition this is to the white garden and how it will glow. Fancy leaves with fancy colour, alright I was trying to fool you, but I'm drooling, they are aroids, I know it's an addiction of mine. South American showman's plants perfect for shade or semi-shade. Newer varieties are being bred for more sun tolerance. They make good pot plants indoors or out just like *Begonia rex*. Striking as mass plantings but one single white will draw the eye.

HOW TO GROW
Not outdoors for cool climates unless in the heat of summer. I jest, how can an English woman think of the heat of summer. Ideal for a mini white garden in the conservatory. Water well and spray leaves. Fertilizer can affect the colour, low fertilizer is best for whites. Dig roots and store in a frost free place overwinter. Start into growth at 21°C (70°F) minimum. Keep evenly moist. Z10-11.

C. **'Aaron'** is a white-leaved variety with green margins which bleed attractively into the white and it shows some sun tolerance. 30-60cm (12-24").
C. **'Caloosahatchee'** is a white lance-leaved type with a broad, wavy, green margin.
C. **'Candidum'** is an older cultivar with white leaves and green veins, still very attractive. 30-60cm (12-24").
C. **'Candidum Jr.'** is a dwarf, white lance-leaved variety with green veins like its big daddy. 15-30cm (6-12").
C. **'Florida Fantasy'** has a white base with red veins sometimes with a green or pinkish-red overlay, sometimes with a green edge.
C. **'Florida Moonlight'** proving the moon is best viewed by day, this white-leaved, white-veined *Caladium* with just a touch of green around the edge, was developed by the University of Florida's Institute of Food and Agricultural Sciences. Petioles are light purple with black marbling. 45-55cm (18-22").
C. **'Florida White Ruffles'** is a white, strap-leaved *Caladium* for small pots or hanging baskets. It will tolerate quite a bit of sunshine.
C. **'Galaxy'** is proof that better things can be found on a different planet. Take off with the green, hotter than hot leaves with intricate central veining arrowing out from the centre and pink spots. A favourite. 60cm (24").
C. **'Gingerland'** is a white, lance-leaved form with red blotches and a green margin. Grow this well it has some beautiful markings. Slightly upright, even and bushy. Makes a certain splash.
C. **humbodtii** is a small *Caladium* with immense presence in its green and white variegated leaves. 15-20cm (6-8").
C. **'Jackie Suthers'** is a strap-leaf white with a green edge producing smaller leaves. 15-30cm (6-12").

C. **'June Bride'** is white with a green margin. A good sun tolerant variety which tends to exhibit rather a lot of green in its first year, from the second year on it can produce almost pure white leaves. 30-60cm (12-24").
C. **'Marie Moir'** is whitish green with red spots. Interesting, it looks like someone has dropped strawberry jam on it, but I love strawberry jam.
C. **'Mrs. Arno Herling'** is often classified as a white, but has more of a mottled green effect with central red veins.
C. **'White'** has white leaves with a green border. Delectable. 30-45cm (12-18").
C. **'White Christmas'** has large, showy heart-shaped, white leaves, with green veins and a green edging. Sun tolerant. 30-45cm (12-18").
C. **'White Queen'** is if anything more spectacular with its white-green leaves having vivid pink veins. Veins can bleed into the white background colour on young plants. Some sun tolerance, it will appear more red in shade. Follow that one. 30-45cm (12-18").
C. **'White Sim'** has white leaves with red veins, green minor veins and a green edge.
C. **'White Wing'** is a white lance-leaved variety with a green margin. This is delightfully fresh-looking with its wavy, medium-sized leaves. Sun tolerant. 25-45cm (10-18").

Caladium candidum 'White Christmas'

158

CHAMAECYPARIS

Handsome in winter, false cypress shine in light shade.

HOW TO GROW
Well-drained soil in partial shade. Size can be restricted with moderate pruning.

C. lawsoniana 'Barry's Silver' bears silvery white foliage on a compact, dwarf upright form. It is best in partial sun out of winds, although it will take full sun despite its delicate colouring. Found by Roly Barry on a mutation of 'Silver Queen'. Slow growing to 1.8m (6ft). Z5-9.

C. lawsoniana 'Ellwood's White' is a dwarf upright bearing splashes of real white foliage amongst its variegated leaves. Found as a sport off 'Ellwood' in the 1960's. 1.8mx60m (6x2ft). Z5.

C. lawsoniana 'Fletcher's White' is a large growing shrub with green-blue leaves speckled in white. Best in full sun. Mature plants reach 4m (16ft). Z5.

C. lawsoniana 'Konijn Silver' bears silver tips to its green foliage, fairly loose but full conical.

C. lawsoniana 'Pygmaea Argentea' is a small, flat-topped bush with the outer leaves in creamy white.

C. lawsoniana 'Silver Queen' is a large growing upright with dark green leaves being variegated white, particularly towards the tips of the sprays. Best in full sun. A mature plant will reach 6m (24ft). Z5.

C. lawsoniana 'Snow Queen' bears soft yellow sprays turning light blue and each stem twisting slightly to show the silver underside. Found at M&J Kristick Nursery, Pennsylvania. Fine in full sun, making a broadly conical conifer. 2mx1.5m (8x5ft). Z5.

C. lawsoniana 'Snow White' (PBR) displays white tips on new growth and is very attractive in tubs with its dwarf, broadly conical form and blue juvenile foliage. A mutation of 'Ellwoodii' which originated at Allandale Nursery, Yorkshire. 1mx30cm (4x1ft). Z5.

C. lawsoniana 'Summer Snow' bears white leaves on underlying green adult foliage. A semi-dwarf that is best with some shade. Grows around 15cm (6") a year. Z5.

C. lawsoniana 'Variegata Ed Rezek' is a dwarf, upright loose plant with green foliage splattered with white in full sun. Z5.

C. lawsoniana 'White Spot' has white new foliage turning blue on a columnar upright. Best in full sun, growing 15-30cm (6-12") per year. Z5.

C. lawsoniana 'White Wonder' has adult white foliage with a dark green interior. Fast growth up to 30cm (12") a year in full sun. Z5.

C. obtusa 'Snowflake' bears adult foliage which is all white against blue-green offering a two-tone effect. An upright plant which stays miniature. Z5.

C. obtusa 'Snowkist' has the tips of its sprays kissed by snow with best colour in full sun. Remains small reaching around 30cm (12") in ten years. Z5.

C. pisifera 'Iceberg' was introduced from New Zealand in 1991 as a sport from 'Snow'. It grows larger than its parent and makes a nice dwarf, rounded globe of white foliage which is best in partial shade. 90x90cm (3ft) Z4.

C. pisifera 'Silver and Gold' has green, flattened foliage marked with both silvery white and gold variegation in an upright form. Z5.

C. pisifera 'Silver Lode' was found as a mutation of 'Minima Aurea'. A mini bun of grey-green foliage with white specks. An excellent choice for the rock garden in partial shade. At maturity it reaches 15x90cm (6x36"). Z4.

C. pisifera 'Snow' makes its whitest foliage in shade, sun makes it appear greener and it will burn. This dwarf was introduced from Japan. 45x45cm (16"). Z4.

C. pisifera 'White Beauty' is another dwarf form with white foliage best in partial shade. 30x60cm 91x2ft). Z5.

C. pisifera 'White Pygmy' bears white new growth on a green background making a flat little bun of a dwarf form. 7x30cm (3"x1ft). Z5.

CORNUS

Handsome shrubs that have to be a part of the garden.

Cornus alba 'Elegantissima' makes an attractive hedge for exposed or windy sites. Its green leaves are edged in white.

C. alternifolia 'Argentea' is sometimes seen as 'Variegata' and pulls out all the stops with its green foliage neatly edged in icy white. Clusters of small white flowers are borne in spring at the tips of branches.

C. contoversa 'Variegata' is one of the loveliest of variegated shrubs, a real choice variety. Handsome and elegant, it is highly worth growing.

C. 'Ivory Halo' is a compact form with dark green leaves having wide ivory borders. Deep red twigs make a show in winter. 1.2-1.5m (4-5ft).

C. kousa 'Snowboy' is attractive with white edges showing strong pink tones in cooler weather. Attractive white flowers make this stunning in light shade. 3m (12ft). Z5-9.

C. kousa 'Wolfeye' is a handsome dogwood, a small tree with exfoliating bark when mature. White flowers and sun-resistant, elongated leaves with a white margin.

Cornus and Hydrangea

Corydalis 'Silver Scepter' above
Cornuskaempferia left

CORNUSKAEMPFERIA

This will certainly make a stir in the garden. Foliage does not come much more handsome. John and Tim Oakland of Oakland Nurseries brought this back from Thailand.

CORYDALIS

A Corydalis that can take some southern heat. Grow this for the silver splashed foliage.

HOW TO GROW
Best in light shade to shade in moist, humus-rich soil with good drainage. Do not use chemical sprays or fertilizers. Z5.

C. 'Silver Spectre' is a Heronswood selection collected in China in 1996 by Dan Hinkley with initially a silver streak to the lacy, handsome, olive-green leaves, which develops into a fairy dusting of silver. Extremely handsome in foliage, it is topped by charmingly fragrant light lavender flowers in spring. Though dormant in summer, foliage will return in autumn and remain where it is mild. According to Tony Avent where it has made a 90cm (3ft) clump at Plant Delights Nursery, this performs in the Southeast of the U.S. where *Corydalis* usually curl up their toes in the heat. 25cm (10").
Cool Companion: *Dicentra, ferns, Podophyllum, Tiarella, Arisarum.*

CRYPTANTHUS

Earthstar bromeliads bear strap-like or slightly broader leaves often banded in silver. These are real stars for the warm climate garden or indoors in cooler areas.

HOW TO GROW
Loose soil-less mix and bright, indirect light. A houseplant in all but tropical and semi-tropical areas.

C. 'Alberta' (Jim Irvin) is a sculptural delight, a rosette of succulent leaves elegantly and intriguingly 'painted' in black and silver.
C. 'Alpine Frost' (Jim Irvin) is just as exquisite and even more silvered. Beautiful patterning. This would be my choice if I could only have one.
C. 'Alternating Current' (Jim Irvin) has a silver sheen to its striped and non-striped leaves.
C. 'Angel Dust' (Jim Irvin) is truly from heaven, very well silvered, plain leaves. See it, fall in love, want it.
C. 'Archaic Expression' (Antle) has black leaves with silver banding.
C. 'Arrogance' (Jim Irvin) is black-maroon with silver-grey zoning shimmering down the length of its leaves.
C. 'Audacity' (Jim Irvin) has metallic grey foliage with black and silver-white chevrons.
C. 'Bone Chiller' (Jim Irvin) radiates in icy silver with thin black bands. Beautiful cultivar like pure snow driven fields with black lines.

C. 'Circuit Breaker' (Jim Irvin) has black and silver banded foliage and it is electric.

C. 'Cosmic Storm' (Jim Irvin) has beautiful grey and silver foliage on a very handsome cultivar. This has quiet colours and yet is undeniably stunning.

C. 'Frostbite' (Jim Irvin) feel the nip on this chilly, icy cultivar in stunning shades of silver with black heartbeat lines. Fantastic.

C. 'Ice Age' (Jim Irvin) is a handsome chevron pattern of black and silver that has you begging for the next ice age to come right into your garden.

C. 'Iceberg' (Jim Irvin) is not as icy as some, so this must be just the tip of the iceberg, in metallic grey and silver, with sometimes just a hint of green coming through. I love these silvered grey tones.

C. 'Peaches' (Fred Sparrow) is an unbanded variety with green leaves, speckled completely in silver on very attractive, slightly broad foliage.

C. 'Razor Back' (Jim Irvin) another nicely striped black-maroon and well-silvered variety. The maroon is almost vertically striped in places.

C. 'Silver on Burgundy' (G. Goode) bears metallic leaves on a burgundy background. Very dark and effective.

C. 'Silver Sheen' (Foster) has some of the broadest leaves on this genus, with a silver sparkle on each leaf.

C. 'Silver King' a King it is, a superb silver sheen with a slight pink tone beneath. An outstanding cultivar with broadish leaves.

C. 'Silver Zones' (G. Lawn) bears black-maroon leaves with nice silver chevrons.

C. 'Snow Rose' (Hummel) bears broadish silver banding on green foliage.

C. 'Tranquility' (Jim Irvin) is the best green and silver form I have seen. Mid green leaves with silver markings and patches.

C. 'Unabashed' (Jim Irvin) is remarkable for its upright leaves displaying undersides in whitish silver. Upper leaves are remarkable too for black and silver chevrons.

C. 'Vanity' (Jim Irvin) bears maroon-purple foliage with silver heartbeat lines. I am not sure vanity is permissible, but when you are this good looking, well who knows.

C. 'White Lace' (G. Goode) is a green form with irregular silver chevrons.

C. zonatus 'Silver' bears broadish leaves with deep black and silver banding.

Cryptanthus 'Alpine Frost' top, 'Arrogance' above, 'Cosmic Storm' below

Cryptanthus 'Frostbite' above, 'Ice Age' below

Cryptanthus 'Razor Back' above, 'Tranquility' below

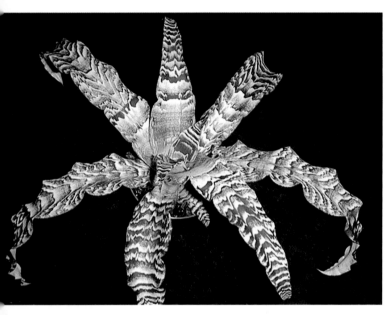

Cryptanthus 'Iceberg' below

Cryptanthus 'Vanity' below

CYCLAMEN

Needing no introduction, these plants are stars of the garden in flower and leaf. Many silver mottled or silver veined leaves abound, but I have concentrated on those that are almost wholly silver. *C. hederifolium* are often in flower from September, *C. coum* flowering from January. Ideal for cheering up the base of mature shrubs and trees. Also good at the base of a north-facing wall, in a rock garden or stone trough. Left undisturbed they form small colonies. They can be grown under beech trees.

HOW TO GROW
Cyclamen are hardy and half-hardy depending on species. The ones for the garden are happiest in light shade, planted in well-drained, leafy soil which is moist in autumn and late spring. *C. hederifolium* will seed happily in these conditions and *C. coum* will seed to a lesser degree. *C. persicum* needs to be under glass.

C. coum 'Blush' has soft pink flowers with rounded petals and silver leaves.
C. coum silver and pewter group. These are almost entirely metallic silver, usually with a dark green margin. The appearance is of silver dust. Mixed forms can tend to be less showy in their glittery capacity unless supplied by a reputable supplier who names the source such as Paul Christian's **C. coum pewter** which is from a BSBE collection made in or near Iran. Named forms such as 'Nymans' are more variable than one would expect and this form is slow to increase.
C. coum 'Maurice Dryden' is a silver-leaved form with white flowers having a magenta blotch at the base.
C. coum 'Tilebarn Elizabeth' is slightly tender and most suitable for the alpine house where its silvered leaves shine beneath two-tone flowers. This is a superb introduction from Peter Moore.
C. coum 'Tilebarn Graham' is a delicate pewter-leaved form with small dainty flowers having twisted, serrated petals.
C. elegans silver-leaf form originated in a batch of seedlings at Tilebarn Nursery, the midribs and edges to the leaves are mid-green, the overall leaf has a silver wash.
C. graecum f graecum 'Glyfada' was found by Brian Mathew near Athens. Pale magenta flowers above silver leaves. The species itself is usually well patterned in silver.
C. hederifolium silver leaf form is still sometimes found as **C. neapolitanum**. It is easy, hardy and vigorous making a great beginner's plant. Leaf shapes typically resemble *Hedera* (ivy) though they are variable in shape from broad to narrow. Leaf margins can be smooth but are more usually toothed or lobed. These forms have hardly any markings as found on the green leaved forms and are almost entirely metallic silver, often with a pale green margin. They bear strong pink flowers.

The hardiest of all *Cyclamen* which even self-sows in upstate New York. Leave seedlings for two years to see the full extent of patterns before you discard any. *C. hederifolium* is worthy in any garden, working hard for eleven months, so it deserves a month off. 10cm (4").
C. hederifolium 'Nettleton Silver' comes almost one hundred per cent true from seed. Silvery leaves are broken at the margin with veining.
C. hederifolium 'Silver Cloud' exhibits fabulous entirely silver leaves with deep veins. This is superb in dry shade and flowers in August to October. Pink flowers, the white flowered form is **'White Cloud'**. 10cm (4"). Selected by Phil Cornish. Similar to **'Bowles' Apollo Group'** which is one of its parents, in having a pink overlay on some leaves. The latter is distinguished by a double shield of silver. It is from this group that silver leaved forms are often selected.
C. mirabile 'Tilebarn Anne' bears overall silver leaves with pink flowers. It has marked leaf veins and a rose colouring when leaves first open.
C. persicum scented silver leaf is the well-known pot plant, most persicum are scented. Admirable in a pot, the striking ivy-like leaf has a green centre surrounded by silver and marked with beautiful silver veining. Can be grown from seed. It will withstand several degrees of frost in a cold greenhouse if kept dry.
C. persicum silver leaf form was originally collected by Jim Archibald in Lebanon.
C. purpurascens silver leaf form originated in Italy. The species bears pink flowers which are strongly scented.
C. repandum ssp peloponnesiacum silver leaf form was discovered by the Cyclamen Society in 1992 and introduced into cultivation.

The silver-patterned leaves of Cyclamen

DAPHNE

Sweet scent is always welcome and is provided by these semi-evergreen shrubs.

HOW TO GROW
Perfect drainage is essential in partial shade to full sun unless noted. Z5-8.

D. x burkwoodii 'Briggs Moonlight' is a favourite with me for its creamy white leaf is edged in dark green. A perfect combination on handsome, slender leaves. A sport from *'Somerset'* which needs shade. 90cm (3ft).
D. x burkwoodii 'Carol Mackie' has green leaves edged in white and maintains its vigour. 90cm (3ft).
D. x transatlantica 'Summer Ice' from the North Willamette experimental station in Oregon comes this dense rounded shrub which is evergreen in Z7, but semi-deciduous in colder areas. Grey-green leaves are edged in creamy white. Clusters of sweetly fragrant white flowers have a pinkish reverse and bloom on and off almost year round. 90cm (3ft) Z6.

Daphne 'Brigg's Moonlight'

DISPORUM

People who grow these woodlanders, and I am amongst them, are big fans. They are highly prized in Japan, particularly the variegated forms. Related to Solomon's Seal, they occur naturally in Asia and in the U.S.

HOW TO GROW
Light shade to shade in good, humus-rich, moist soil.

D. sessile 'Cricket' does not make me think of a Test Match with its exquisite white central leaf markings. This superb addition to a shade garden maintains vigour. Z4-9.
D. sessile 'Kinga' has broad, oval leaves which are striped and streaked in silver. 30cm (12"). Z4-9.
D. sessile 'Sunray' is streaked with yellow soon changing to white and it can have almost pure white leaves in summer. Small white bells appear in spring. Z5-9a.
D. sessile f stenophyllum 'Variegatum' narrow, green leaflets are striped white and the dainty white bells look wonderful against this fresh-looking backdrop. A strong grower and vigorous spreader which makes handsome groundcover. Z4-9.
D. sessile 'Variegatum' has green leaves edged in white, broader than the one above. Its arching stems are a wonderful addition to the shade garden. It bears yellow flowers. This spreads underground by stolons and is quite vigorous but not normally a nuisance. 40cm (16").
D. sessile 'White Lightening' is on the creamy side with a tiny green margin. Z5.
D. smilacinum 'Gunchiku' makes a small carpet of dark green leaves edged in white. 13cm (5"). Z4-9.
D. smilacinum 'Morning Glow' is an incredible plant with striking, wavy margined, almost white leaves with green streaks. A very attractive way to add light to a dark corner. 30cm (12").
D. smilacinum 'Rei Ho' has broadish leaves neatly edged in white.
D. smilacinum 'Streaker' is a quiet beauty with its green leaves marked in creamy streaks.
Perfect Companion: *Hosta*, ferns and woodlanders.

EPISCIA

Fantastic foliage with colours reminiscent of the hand of an artist, displaying the best foliage of any gesneriad. Used effectively in the hot house at Kew as groundcover. Quick and easy to grow. Known as flame violet, they are a good choice for grow lights or growing in a terrarium. Colouring is best at maturity.

HOW TO GROW
Warmth, humidity and moist soil are required for ideal growing conditions similar to African violets. Pebble trays increase humidity. Intolerant of strong sunlight and of water on their leaves.

E. 'Acajou' is a favourite for its quilted, silver leaves with green-brown edging, having a pinkish tinge to the edge of the underleaf. Similar to the newer cultivar 'Silver Skies', it differs in the edging.
E. 'Annette' has pink-silver foliage edged in bronze.
E. 'Country Cowboy' has a large, central silver streak and a chocolate margin combined with red blooms.
E. 'Faded Jade' bears deep green leaves veined with silver. Red flowers can be had almost all year round. It is similar to the one below, but has red flowers.
E. 'Frosty' is bright green covered with silver hairs and having a wide silver midrib.
E. 'Grey Lady' has white veining on slate grey leaves with red flowers making a striking combination.
E. 'Pearl Drops' is similar to the one below, but smaller in stature. Less of the pearly purple edging but more of a pearl to the leaves, mother of pearl. This is my favourite.
E. 'Pearl Passion' this Vincent Parsons hybrid is truly spectacular. If you choose just one *Episcia*, this might be the one to try. Vincent is working on making *Episcia* easier to grow for the inexperienced gardener. A fine cultivar with silver foliage edged in a pearly purple-mauve.
E. 'Sea Cliff' bears silvery, smooth leaves and orange-red flowers.
E. 'Shimmer' bears glistening, silver-green leaves bordered by copper-brown, and topped by red flowers.
E. 'Silver Lace' is an interesting form with silver foliage edged in mid green, giving a nice two-tone effect. Very cool.
E. 'Silver Skies' is a vigorous, small-leaved hybrid with predominantly silver leaves having a solid brown edge. Bears bright orange-red flowers.
E. 'Sylvan Beauty' is a smooth, silver-green with light brown perimeters.
E. 'Temiscaming' has silver leaves which shimmer against the dark edging and is teamed with red flowers.
E. 'Toy Silver' is a compact variety, quite miniature with the usual orange-red shocking flowers. An attractive brown patterning eats into the silver.
E. 'Westwood' is silvery with medium brown edging.

EUPHORBIA

Garden worthy spurges should be in every garden. They are my foliage Queen perennials. Easy to grow to say they give such a stunning show.

HOW TO GROW
Full sun and well-drained soil. Remember the milky sap is irritating and can spurt, protect yourself when cutting.

E. polychroma 'Lacy' is hardy with green-centred leaves with a broad, white border and long-lasting, creamy yellow bracts. 40cm (16"). Z4-8.
E. 'First Blush' (PPAF) has pink, white and green foliage in spring. The pink fades leaving a white edge to the green leaves in summer. Yellow bracts. Good in well-drained soil. 30-45cm (12-18"). Z4-7.
E. 'Tasmanian Tiger' has striking white leaves with a dark green centre. The cream-white to yellow bracts have a green blotch.
Annual, variegated spurge includes **E. marginata** which seems to go by many cultivar names, but the plant always looks the same. It is known as Snow on the Mountain.
E. virosa is one of the succulent types with vicious white spines.

Episcia

Euphorbia virosa

HEDERA

Well known ivy is most attractive in its variegated forms.

H. helix 'Glacier' has icy white edges and marks to its grey-green foliage. A controlled spreader to adorn tree trunks.
H. helix 'Henrietta' has some white variegation in its leaves making this an unusual, glossy ivy.
H. helix 'Thorndale' bears green leaves with white venation. A hardy, strong grower with subtle colouring.
H. helix 'White Knight' has a bold white centre befitting a knight. It is a selection from *'Kolibri'* but brighter.
H. helix 'White Wonder' has a broad, white margin.

IRIS

There are three varieties with sumptuous variegation. They offer a foliage treat for different situations in the garden.

I. ensata 'Variegata' is hard to beat for its beautiful, white-striped foliage. The handsome deep-purple to blue flowers in summer cannot take anything away from the foliage. Grow in full sun with ample water. 90cm (36"). Z4-9.
I. laevigata 'Variegata' bears cream to white variegation on this iris which stands in water. Purple flowers. 75cm (30"). Z 4-9.
I. pallida 'Albovariegata' is a delightful, drought tolerant variety with broad leaves having a white stripe. Lilac to blue bearded flowers in early summer. This one is a sun lover. Z4.

KOHLERIA

Gesneriads with their colourful leaves and flowers make superb houseplants.

HOW TO GROW
Growing conditions are basically the same as for African Violets. Careful watering is the key. Regular feeding is important.

K. 'Brazil Gem' is wonderfully netted and veined in silver on a background of green with a chartreuse mid-vein. Very attractive.
K. 'Brimstone' not only has some of the loveliest of gesneriad flowers, orange tubes covered in large red spots and densely covered in red-orange hairs, but the leaves stand up well to such flamboyant colour with their silvery sheen still allowing the flowers to shine.
K. 'Green Goblin' (John Boggan) is predominantly fresh green with a silver blush along the veins. A compact grower with orange-red flowers having a yellow throat that is spotted red. 20cm (8").
K. 'Regent' bears dark green velvety foliage adorned with silver veins. Fringed yellow flowers have purple spots.

LAMIUM

Dead nettle sounds so morbid and conjures up images of poisonous or dying plants. The dead refers to the fact that there is no sting. An excellent, shallow-rooted carpeter in shade, providing silvery mats of foliage in difficult sites even those with roots near the surface. Flowers are best produced in poor soils. Evergreen in milder climates and deciduous in cooler areas. It looks best in cool temperatures where it shines in shade.

HOW TO GROW
Moist but not wet soil, but will perform in dry to normal soils when established in part shade in cool climates. If growing in sun or warmer climates they will struggle. Take care to water well as they hate humidity and heat. Leaf scorch can occur. Sheer back in midsummer for fresh growth. Protect from hot sun in warm zones. Z4-9.

L. galeobdolon 'Hermann's Pride' (Lamiastrum) bears small, ovate green leaves with distinctive heavy silver streaking which is exquisite. Yellow flowers. Try yellow archangel at the edge of a path or amongst paving stones in shade. A slow spreader with truly spectacular foliage. 20x30cm (8x12").
L. galeobdolon 'Silberteppich' ('Silver Carpet') is more tolerant of dry soils. Silver leaves are etched with green veins. Yellow flowered and well-behaved. Cut right back to replenish.
L. galeobdolon 'Silver Angel' bears ovate to diamond or heart-shaped, silver leaves. Yellow flowers have brown marks flowering in summer.
L. maculatum 'Album' bears sought-after pure white flowers to dispel gloom in the shade and blue-green leaves with a white-silver central stripe enhancing the effect. No clouds permitted.

Lamium maculatum 'Beacon Silver'

L. maculatum 'Beacon Silver' bears silver-white leaves edged in green. It has red-purple flowers in compact heads, a pleasing colour link to purple foliage especially with the bronze-red stems of this variety. A sturdy, sterling silver evergreen in all but the coldest winters and superb in containers. This chance seedling was discovered in the mid 1970's and brought into cultivation by Beth Chatto. 20cmx1m (8x39").

L. maculatum 'Brocade' does justice to the pink flowers with leaves of silver and purple, this attractive groundcover flowers in summer. 15cm (6").

L. maculatum 'Chequers Board' is a seedling of 'Chequers' with a broader white stripe to the green leaves and red-purple flowers with the upper lip edge in white and dark red-purple bracts matched by purplish stems.

L. maculatum 'Dingle Candy' sports clear pink flowers that I love so much with white leaves having a dark green margin. The green stems blush bronze. Introduced by Dingle Nurseries in Welshpool.

L. maculatum 'Elizabeth de Haas' has a pebbly surface to the green leaves with a silver centre and purple flowers.

L. maculatum 'Forncett Lustre' has delightful salmon-pink flowers. The leaves curl under and are white with a green margin having a gold flush. On this compact and mounded variety, the green stems are flushed bronze. Found and introduced by John Metcalf of Four Seasons Nursery, U.K.

L. maculatum 'Hatfield' is a vigorous, fairly upright variety with red purple flowers and stems contrasting admirably with the white leaves having a green margin in winter which changes to green leaves with just a broad white stripe in summer.

L. maculatum 'James Boyd Parselle' the serrated edged leaves of this dense groundcover are attractively splashed with silvery white. Clusters of shell-pink hooded flowers top the foliage in spring. 15cm (6").

L. maculatum 'Orchid Frost' (Michael Bovio 1999) a great improvement on heat tolerance and vigour is this U.S. variety. This silver-leaved form is edged in dark bluish green. In late spring a profuse number of violet-pink flowers top the plant. 15cm (6"), with a spread up to 90cm (3ft). Z3-8.

L. maculatum 'Peck's Pink' displays the palest pink, delicate to behold against white leaves edged in green which curl under. Found by Phil Lusby.

L. maculatum 'Petit Point' with its fancy French name this sounds more demure and is quite a dainty selection. Silver leaves are accented with green margins and midribs. It bears bright yellow flowers. 20cm (10").

L. maculatum 'Pink Pewter' warm silvery, salmon-pink flowers are a perfect match for the dense, showy mats of green foliage splashed with silvery white. Delicate looking against the green stems flushed bronze. Spreads quickly and tolerates some drought. Found by John Metcalf of Four Seasons Nursery, Norwich, U.K. 15cmx1m (6x39").

L. 'Pink Nancy' bears salmon pink flowers to contrast with the well-silvered foliage primly edged in green. A compact variety which will not run amock. 15cm (6").

L. maculatum 'Purple Dragon' nice silver leaves have a neat green edge. The large purple flowers are very attractive. Z3.

L. maculatum 'Red Nancy' has dark rosy pink to red-purple flowers perfect over the reddish stems against silver-grey foliage edged in green. Bears the reddest flowers. 15cm (6").

L. maculatum 'Roseum' ('Shell Pink') pink flowers sit so handsomely with silver foliage making this a sure winner. 15cmx1m (6x39").

L. maculatum 'White Nancy' adds purity with its elegant silvery leaves narrowly margined in green and the immaculate white flowers. Low growing and compact. Try this cascading down a shady wall or running down a steep bank. Choice. Found as a chance seeding by Philip S. Levesley. 15cmx1m (6x39").

L. 'Wootton Pink' bears pale pink flowers and white leaves with yellow-green margins. Noted for its larger flowers and as a non-spreading, compact variety introduced by Bridgemere Nurseries.

Others with tiny silver streaks include **'Chequers'** which is noticeable for having the darkest flower amongst dead nettles, **'Pink Pearls'** and the golden **'Beedham's White'**, and variegated **'Golden Anniversary'**. **'Changeling'** is aptly named as its leaves are variable, but can be silver-streaked. **'Wild White'** is striped silver in winter. The species **L. maculatum** also shows a silver streak to its leaves. **L. orvala 'Silva'** bears a white streak.

Hot Partner: *Ophiopogon planiscapus 'Nigrescens'*, *Lirope muscari*.

Lamium 'Golden Anniversary' has a silver streak to its golden and green leaves

PTERIS

An interesting genus of ferns, natives to the tropics. For cool indoor situations or terrarium. Cretan ferns are also known as table ferns, where they grow in the shadowless light of a north window.

HOW TO GROW
Soil moist, humid sites in neutral to slightly alkaline soil. Bright to moderate light. Feed established plants every two months at half strength. Night temperatures of at least 10°C (50°F), 21°C (70°F). Propagate at any time by dividing the base.

P. argyraea is the silver brake fern with pinnate, dark green fronds having a silvery, central stripe. An attractive species, native of rock cliffs and hillsides. 1m (4ft).
P. cretica v albolineata is an easy to grow cultivar with a white, central band on light green fronds. 80cm (32").
P. cretica 'Alexandrae' has incised fonds with curled tips and is white-variegated.
P. cretica 'Mayi' is like *'Albolineata'* but with heavily crested tips. 40cm (16").
P. cretica 'Maxii' is also similar to *'Albolineata'* only dwarfer with pinnae.
P. ensiformis the sword brake fern has narrow, pinnate green fronds with grayish white midribs. Fertile fronds are 30-45cm long (12-18") with sterile fronds shorter.
P. ensiformis 'Arguta' is dark green with silver midribs.
P. ensiformis 'Victoriae' is the silver leaf fern with white bands parallel to the midrib. 60cm (24").
P. 'Evergemensis' has a silvery sheen to its dark fronds.

Pteris cretica 'Albomarginata'

THYMUS

Culinary but so useful as ornamentals. Tough and low maintenance evergreen perennials. Highly ornamental and good in troughs, borders, the herb garden as well as planters and hanging baskets. The most spectacular use of thyme is often on a bank, where cascading colour is unforgettable. Silver cultivars can be substituted for common thyme in culinary use.

HOW TO GROW
Likes lots of sun for best flavour and aromatic leaves and only a little water. Loose, fast-draining soil which is relatively poor. Shear over in winter and maintain by deadheading. Z4.

T. x citriodorus 'Argenteus' is the classic silver thyme. Tough and hardy. An upright thyme with tiny leaves edged in silver forming a 20cm (8") mound which will serve well anywhere you desire to plant it. This hardy perennial is covered in mauve flowers attracting bees to their nectar. Richly aromatic leaves. 30cm (12").
T. x citriodorus 'Silver King' larger and wider variegation than *'Silver Queen'* with mauve flowers.
T. x citriodorus 'Silver Queen' the white-edged leaves offer a nice contrast to other plants in the herb or thyme garden accompanied by lemon scent.
T. dzevanorski this Russian thyme was almost lost to cultivation and Rice Creek Gardens describe it as a silver 'fog hugging the ground'. Plant this creeper between rocks and on slopes. 2cm (1").
T. 'Hartington Silver' ('Highland Cream') bears cream-white variegated leaves with shell pink flowers on this mat forming type. Raised by the Lawleys of Herterton House Garden Nursery.
T. lanuginosus woolly thyme makes a gray, downy blanket for a slope. 1cm (.5").
T. neiceffii bears grey-green foliage with trailing stems and pink flowers.
T. 'Peter Davis' has greyish foliage with pink-mauve flowers on a compact bush.
T. serpyllum 'Pink Chintz' bears grey-green foliage with soft pink flowers.
T. vulgaris 'Hi Ho Silver' is silver-variegated. An attractive evergreen with pink flowers, its silver moon (sun is shining) will shine no matter where it goes, but it is obvious that we shall not make a fuss about it. I never did understand the words to the song, but it was a good one to sing along to. I'll have people calling me the Kareoke garden queen next. 30cm (12").
T. vulgaris 'Silver Posie' bears scented, silver variegated leaves.
T. 'Yugoslavia' is a Rice Creek introduction with masses of tiny grey leaves like a mist covering the ground. This little ground hugger bears pink flowers. 1x20cm (.5x8").

Aralia elata 'Silver Umbrellas' is smaller than the species in all respects, with stunning white variegation. Z5-9.

Armoracia rusticana 'Variegata' is highly prized for its white variegated leaves which begin to show after the first year. Horseradish makes an unusual specimen in full sun. 90cm (3ft). Z5.

Brugmansia 'Snowbank' is very desirable with its elegant grey-green leaves edged in white. Large, fragrant peach-coloured trumpets hang in July to September. A superb container plant for the patio. Overwinter this tender beauty under cover. 1.5m (5ft). Z8-10. If you want white flowers with variegated foliage, try **B. suaveolens 'Variegata'**.

Bukiniczia cabulica sounds so awful, but few plants are as beautifully variegated as this. The 12cm (5") wide rosettes of leathery, bluish-green are astoundingly mottled in grey. Loose heads of small pink flowers are borne in September to May. A choice, hardy alpine from Pakistan which needs to be kept on the dry side. It has also been known as *Aeoniopsis* and *Dictyolimon macrorrhabdos*. If it flowers before it has formed offsets, that is the end of the plant, so allow it to form offsets first. It does self-seed.

Canna 'Liberty Sun' has paddle-shaped foliage edged in ivory white. Yellow flowers have pink dots on this patio variety to 90cm (3ft).

Caryopteris 'Snow Fairy' bears green leaves with wide, white borders contrasting well with the dark blue flowers in late summer. A very pretty front of border shrub in light shade. 60-90cm (2-3ft). Z5.

Catalpa speciosa 'Pulverulenta' is a beautiful variegated tree with speckled green leaves. It does not seem to be very highly thought of, but I find it attractive. I have a thing about oddballs; I like the unusual.

Cercis canadensis 'Silver Cloud' bears fresh green leaves with white margins. Some strong pink tones come through. Purplish pink flowers adorn the delicate branches. 3m (12ft).

Chirita are handsome in their veined leaves, those marked with silver are like flashes of lightning.

From top to bottom:
Armoracia rusticana 'Variegata'
Brugmansia 'Snowbank'
Bukiniczia cabulica
Caryopteris 'Snow Fairy'

Chirita above
Chiastophyllum 'Jim's Pride'

Hacquetia epipactis 'Thor'

Chiastophyllum 'Jim's Pride' is a superb foliage plant with its succulent, green leaves edged in white. An evergreen perennial which flourishes in full sun in wet but well-drained sites and banks. In late spring to late summer, it bears bell-shaped, yellow flowers on long stems. It makes good rhizomatous groundcover to 15cm (6") high.

Dieffenbachia 'Pacific Rim' is included for its white variegated leaves with a white rim. Easy, indoor plant but remember they are poisonous. Z11.

Dracaena 'Indonesian Whiteout' what a stunner this easy indoor plant is with its broad white margin to the green leaves. Z10.

Elegant beauty is found on **Eleutherococcus sieboldianus 'Variegatus'**, this slow growing shrub dazzles with its green leaves having wide cream-white borders. Stunning from a distance when it appears virtually all-white. 1.8m (6ft).

Fagus sylvatica 'Albo Marginata' is a showy beech with broad, irregular white margins to the green leaves. It is not the beech I would choose to grow, I prefer the purple beeches, but I had to fit one beech into my book.

Fallopia japonica 'Devon's Cream' is similar to *'Variegata'* but has superior foliage colour of white and green with some hints of pink. A real splash of non-running colour to 1.2m (4ft). Z5-9.

Farfugium are such showy, such must-have plants. True performers of the stage, they grow naturally along streams and moist meadows in Japan, Korea and Taiwan. They dislike too much fertilizer and humus rich, moist soils suit best. Shelter from cold, drying winds and mulch well before frosts. Good container plants. Often killed to the ground by severe frosts. Divide in spring. Z7-10.
F. japonicum 'Argenteum' bears broad, thick, leathery cream and green variegated, round evergreen leaves. The creamy-white colouring is in broad bands or wide stripes, sometimes half the leaf, in an altogether captivating manner. Unfortunately not as hardy as the yellow spotty type. If grown in a conservatory in cooler climates, small, yellow-orange, ligularia-like flowers might appear between December and January. 35cm (14").

Forsythia 'Kumson' has to be one the loveliest forsythia in existence. Its dark green leaves are beautifully silver-veined making this an absolute gem in shade. Usual yellow flowers. 1.2-1.5m (4-5ft). Z5.

The plain green *Hacquetia epipactis* is always welcome in my garden, but the variegated **'Thor'** is a knock-out. I first saw this exhibited by Edrom Nurseries. It is one to covet and adore.

Hemerocallis kwanso 'Variegata' bears stunning white-striped variegation combined with double orange flowers having a red eye zone. Very attractive. 60cm (24"). Z4-8.

Hydrangea macrophylla 'Maresii Variegated' a distinct wide white margin haunts each grey-green leaf. Z6.

Lonicera nitida 'Silver Beauty' has silver margined leaves on a shrub which can be pruned to shape. Attractive all season, it bears small foliage like the better known golden varieties of the shrubby honeysuckles. The effect is a shimmering fountain. 1.8m (6ft).

Metasequoia glytostroboides 'White Spot' is an accurate description of the foliage on this new variety.

Oxalis regnellii 'Fanny' (triangularis) bears olive-green leaves with a large silver blotch accompanied by pink flowers in late spring. Patterning retreats in summer, to return on cooler nights. Well-behaved. Z7b-10. 15cm (6").
O. 'Silver and Gold' is a neat pot plant to attract attention to a sunny windowsill. Almost non-stop, fragrant golden flowers sit just above the silver-variegated foliage. 7cm (3"). 16°C (60°F) minimum. Z9.

Pachysandra terminalis 'Variegata' bears bright, showy leaves with a white border. This evergreen, shiny groundcover spreads by stolons. It is very attractive in the right, shady spot where it can roam. Z5-9.

Parthenocissus quinquefolia 'Variegata' is a climber that will make you stop and stare. Its attractive leaves are striped, mottled and splashed in creamy white. Longer than your arm to 11m (35ft).

Philodendron ilsemannii 'Whitewash' from Thailand bears new leaves of pure white or white flecked with green, slowly maturing to all green. Stable and easy in well-drained soil in moderate light. Z11.
P. 'White Knight' eat your heart out sweetheart, lush green leaves are boldly variegated with bright white patches. It will trail or climb a pole. A beautiful and rare plant. Z11.

Phlox 'Norah Leigh' has white-cream, bordered green leaves with pink flowers. 75cm (30"). Z3-8.
P. paniculata 'Creme de Menthe' has a white edge to the green leaves with hints of pink. Pink flowers have red eyes in June to September.

Phytolacca americana 'Silverstein' is a very showy form of the American native pokeweed. Superior to *'Variegata'* in every way, it bears striking green leaves heavily overlaid with creamish white. Large clusters of purple berries on red stems in autumn. Give this huge plant lots of space. 1.8-2m (6-8ft). Z4.

Pilea cadieri

Pittosporum tenuifolium 'Silver Sheen'

Scrophularia auricula 'Variegata'

Selaginella

Pilea cadieri bears deep glossy green leaves painted in silver. The aluminium plant is a sprawling evergreen which makes handsome groundcover. 16°C (60°F). 30cm (12").

Pittosporum are handsome trees or shrubs with usually glossy foliage. They appreciate deeply worked soil with added humus. **P. tenuifolium 'Silver Sheen'** bears small, pale green silvery leaves against dramatic black stems. Each leaf has a silver streak. Fragrant red flowers. Dense and leafy, it is capable of providing a quick screen. Clip if bushy growth is required. This New Zealand native is naturalised in parts of California. It is frost tolerant. 3x1.5m (12x5ft).

Polemonium 'Brize d'Anjou' the dark green and white leaves on this jacob's ladder set it apart from the rest. Blue flowers in spring. 45cm (18"). Z5-9.
P. caeruleum 'Snow and Sapphires' (PPAF) is very similar but claims to be more vigorous and longer lived.
P. caeruleum 'White Ghost' is a taller variety with white and purple leaves and fragrant blue flowers.

Polygonatum falcatum 'Variegatum' this Solomon's Seal has beautiful white flowers over the clean green foliage neatly edged in white. Graceful, making attractive colonies in light woodland. 90cm (3ft).
P. multiforum 'Variegatum' is just as attractive with its two-tone green foliage, edged in white and accompanied by dainty white bells. 60cm (2ft).

Salvia 'Fuji Snow' is a wonderful variegated white and green leaved form I found at Crownsville Nursery.

Scrophularia auricula 'Variegata' bears rough leaves with a green centre and creamy margin. It is topped by unusual maroonish flowers.

Selaginella, club moss is an interesting plant, and no more so than in its white tipped, fan-like display.

Silybum is another thistle relegated to weed status in parts of the U.S. but an elegant ornamental nevertheless. It is valuable in herbal medicine. **S. marianum** has numerous common names amongst them milk thistle, but whatever you wish to call it, it is grown for its highly distinctive foliage. Handsome dark green leaves with silver veining. The prickly foliage is unsuitable by a path.

Silybum does seed madly, so cut off flowerheads of the pinkish purple scented thistles which appear in early summer before they seed. Distinctive spiny bracts surround the flowers. Use it as an impenetrable hedge to wild land. It enjoys cool weather. 1.8m (6ft).

Solenostemon (Coleus) the white-centred leaves of this Coleus are stunning. They emerge with creamy markings.

Syneilsis acontifolia is one plant I fell in love with as soon as I saw it. Called the shredded umbrella plant. The white woolly leaves emerge like a rocket opening to a stunning, umbrella like-leaf, much-divided into 15-20 leaflets. Large 20cm (8") leaves are breathtaking, flowers are insignificant. In time, it colonizes by rhizomes. Z5.

Spiraea thunbergii 'Mt. Fuji' is dense and slow growing with dark pink flower clusters over the narrow green and white leaves on delicate, willowy stems. Z5.

Tellima 'Forest Frost' try this silver splashed variety in full shade to bring light to dark areas. Turns deep bronze in autumn to winter. Chartreuse flowers appear in spring and fade to pink. Z5-9.

Thuja occidentalis 'Beaufort' is a dwarf, conical bush with white variegated leaves. On established plants this can account for almost fifty per cent of the leaf.

Tricyrtis 'White Flame' has white leaves with green stripes and border. White flowers have lavender speckles. Z5-9.

Tsuga canadensis 'Abbott's Dwarf' the silvery undersides are often on view on this tightly congested, upright growing plant.
T. canadensis 'Betty Rose' is a very slow-growing cushion with white variegated leaves. Quite rare.
T. canadensis 'Little Snow' makes a miniature two-tone cushion of dark green inner foliage against the white of the new growth. Best in a shady position.

Veronica spicata 'Noah Williams' bears deep green leaves with pure white borders with spikes of white flowers from June to September. 50cm (20"). Z3-8.

Viola 'Green Jade' bears distinctively splashed green and ivory leaves with blue flowers. Z5-9.
V. 'Koreanna Stylettas' looks like a silver-patterned *Cyclamen* with purple undersides to the leaf. Small light purple flowers. A prolific self-seeder forming ample groundcover. Z3-8.
V. 'Silver Cloak' bears pure silvery green leaves from Yunnan.
V. 'Sylvia Hart' is similar to *'Koreanna Stylettas'* and spreads rapidly by self-seeding. Z5.

Yucca filamentosa 'Variegata' long, evergreen leaves have white margins on what has become a classic garden plant.

Solenostemon

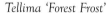

Tellima 'Forest Frost'

Carex comans 'Frosted Curls'

GRASSES

Many grasses have fine silver-white variegation. Often they appear almost wholly white from a distance. Others have silvery plumes adding a great attraction in late season.

Agrostis canina 'Silver Needles' is a fully hardy, mat-forming, evergreen grass with linear green leaves having silver-white margins. From early to late summer, reddish-brown spikelets are produced. 6cm (3"). Z5.

Arrhenatherum elatius spp bulbosum 'Variegatum' is quite a mouthful for such a pretty white-striped grass. Tuber oat grass hardly depicts its beauty either. It is a cool season, clump-forming, fine foliaged fellow. It is best in moist to wet, but well-drained soil. It tolerates acid soil in part to full shade and dislikes hot, dry conditions.

Arundo donax v versicolor ('Variegata') makes a statement in green and white variegation. Although not as tall as the species, it forms a cool background to an herbaceous border. Frost tender and semi-evergreen so mulch and protect in cold areas. In cool areas this starts into growth in summer. Cut back to 40cm (16") in the last week in February. One of the most handsome variegated plants. 1.5m (5ft).

Calamagrostis x acutiflora 'Overdam' is a variegated white and green deciduous grass with feathery, pinkish plumes. The very upright foliage is impressive in an open, sunny spot. 1.5m (5ft).

CAREX

Carex are probably my favourite grass-like plants, these sedges come in gold and silver forms as well as those with black seedheads.

C. comans 'Frosted Curls' displays extremely fine texture in its evergreen, silver-white foliage. This New Zealand sedge has a lovely habit and is suitable for so many garden situations where it will shimmer. Prefers a moist site in sun. Large specimens are breathtaking. Z7. 35cm (14").

C. 'Ice Dance' is semi-evergreen and has white edges to its grass-like leaves. This form introduced by Barry Yinger spreads by stolons in shade; making welcome groundcover. Z5-9.

C. morrowii v temnolepis 'Silk Tassel' makes silvered clumps of hair-like silken threads. White and green striped leaves have a silver shimmer looking at its best in the woodland garden or by a pond. From Barry Yinger.

C. muskingumensis 'Ice Fountains' is sought after for its almost pure white leaves which sway in the slightest breeze. 75cm (30").

C. muskingumensis 'Silberstreif' is known as palm sedge, its fine textured, arching green leaves are striped in white. This attractive, compact deciduous grass makes good ground cover. Requires moist soil and partial shade. 50-60cm (20-24"). Z4.

C. phyllocephala 'Sparkler' bears bold, white-striped green foliage, leathery in appearance. Not as hardy as the green form, so provide protection in Z7 and below out of direct sun or in a cool greenhouse. 45cm (18").

C. riparia 'Aurora' emerges pure white and ghostly, greening up by midsummer. This vigorous European bog lover grows in shallow water. Enjoy in a container without drainage. 1.5m (5ft).

C. siderosticha 'Spring Snow' has pure white edges to the green foliage. Another superb introduction from Japan.

C. siderosticha white center (I retain the American spelling) was brought back from Japan in 1997 by Dan Hinkley of Heronswood Nursery, the leaf centre is white. Emerging foliage is almost wholly white, quite startling in the springscape.

C. 'Silver Sceptre' makes rhizomatous clumps of green foliage with white margins. Silver silken strands make outstanding inflorescences. Best in moist to fertile soil, dislikes hot sun. Looks great in a pot and is equally stunning in the border in part shade with hostas and ferns. 25cm (10"). Z6.

CORTADERIA

Placed well, these spectacular grasses really make a display, but they are often used in gardens that are far too small for them. Eye-catching when the sun falls on plumes or on the foliage of variegated types.

HOW TO GROW
Moist but well-drained soil in full sun to partial shade. Z8-11.

C. richardii is the most ornamental of the pampas grasses. Tall and graceful, its nodding flowers make a majestic statement especially by water. 3m (12ft).

C. selloana 'Albolineata' ('Silver Stripe') does one grow this for the large, silvery plumes or the white striped leaves? You decide. 1.2m (4ft).

C. selloana 'Silver Comet' bears narrow leaves with white stripes. Medium-sized, white plumes appear in late summer in warm weather. A fast-growing variety, smaller and finer than the type with arching foliage. Since the plumes are barely higher than the foliage, it is often best to remove them and just enjoy the cascading foliage. 2m (8ft).

C. selloana 'Sunningdale Silver' is considered to be the best form for superbly silvered plumes on strong culms. 1.5m (5ft).

C. selloana 'White Feather' has the longest, whitest plumes.

Deschampsia cespitosa 'Northern Lights' makes dramatic foliage in creamy white and green sometimes suffused pink. It does not normally flower. This deciduous grass is best in an open, sunny site. 25cm (10").

Hakonechloa macra 'Albolineata' is like the golden version only the variegation is cream to white. Truly stunning. Soil not on the dry side in sun or part shade.

Miscanthus sinensis 'Gracillimus'

Holcus mollis 'Albovariegatus' bears almost wholly white leaves with thin green stripes. Purplish white flower spikes in summer. Evergreen. Full sun to part shade in moist soil. 20cm (8") and quite a spread.
H. mollis 'White Fog' has bright white variegation. It looks best if the flowers spikes are removed before flowering. 30cm (12") and a spread of 45cm (18").

Lagurus ovatus bears silvery bunny tail plumes. A pleasant annual grass grown from seed in a sunny, open spot. A good edger by a path. 40cm (16").

MISCANTHUS

Miscanthus are excellent, deciduous grasses offering great late season structure to the garden with airy silver plumes. Think specimen and mass planting. Think where best to show off those airy plumes to catch late afternoon and early evening sun. Variegated forms do not normally flower in the U.K.

HOW TO GROW
Full sun for maximum performance and moist, well-drained soil. Divide in early spring. Z4.

M. floridulus is big and I mean BIG as in giant. A huge plant with spectacular green foliage turning reddish in autumn and topped by silvery plumes to 3.5m (14ft).
M. x giganteus bears white striped, wide, pendulous foliage on tall, vigorous clumps. Pink flowers turn silver in late summer. Makes a good screen in an open, sunny spot. 2.4m (10ft).
M. malepartus is known as silver grass for the silver stripe to its leaf. This is striking in August as flower plumes gradually fade to silver. 1.5m (5ft).
M. saccharifolius is the silver banner grass. A large, clump-forming perennial which is not invasive with dark, linear green leaves having a central white stripe which make a sure foliage statement. This does not normally flower in the U.K. 3m (12ft).
M. sinensis 'Adagio' is a miniature form with silvery grey leaves and pink to white plumes. An early flowering variety which may become invasive. 120cm (4ft).
M. sinensis 'Cabaret' has a broad leaf and a central broad white stripe. Sturdy, upright clumps are spectacular in container or garden in sunny, well-drained soil. 2m (8ft).
M. sinensis 'Cosmopolitan' has slender blades edged in white. Copper-red plumes in September provide a focal point and good contrast in a silver border. 2m (8ft).
M. sinensis 'Cosmo Revert' is a reversion of *'Cosmopolitan'* with bright, green foliage topped with silver plumes in late summer. 2m (8ft).
M. sinensis 'Dixieland' bears wide, white striped leaves. A compact form ideal in large containers. 1.5m (5ft).

Outstanding plumes create a silvery haze in the garden; these are often combined with white striped leaves in Miscanthus

M. sinensis 'Graziella' makes upright clumps of green foliage which turns orange-red in autumn paired with initially pink plumes which turn silver by the time the foliage changes colour. Plumes are held high above the foliage in late summer. 1.8m (6ft).

M. sinensis 'Grosse Fontaine' is a notable selection made by Pagels for its large panicles of weeping silvery plumes over large, broad green leaves. 2m (8ft).

M. sinensis 'Haiku' bears bright green foliage in strong, upright mounds with graceful, pendulous silvery pink plumes in late summer. 1.8m (6ft).

M. sinensis 'Huron Sunrise' bears profuse blooms and has a central silver line to the foliage. Burgundy flowers grab the attention in late summer.

M. sinensis 'Malepartus' makes silver veined foliage topped by dark red plumes which fade to silver. 2m (6ft).

M. sinensis 'Morning Light' is one of the most attractive of Japanese silver grasses. A tidy cultivar, admirable in form and shape. The narrow, variegated foliage makes neat clumps with reddish plumes turning to silver. Aptly named for its bright silver light. Light and airy, this tall specimen looks silvery from afar and is suitable for the small garden or a courtyard. 120-150cm (4-5ft).

M. sinensis 'Sarabande' bears narrow green and white striped foliage. A statuesque statement with coppery golden plumes from late summer onwards. 2m (6ft).

M. sinensis 'Septemberrot' is a tall grower with green leaves having a silver midrib. Red flowers are borne in late summer. 2.4m (10ft).

M. sinensis 'Silberfeder' has fine, light-green and silver midrib, arching leaves topped by pink panicles in late summer which fade to silky silver. 2m (8ft) stems last long into winter giving structure to the garden at this time of year. One of the best for flowering effect.

M. sinensis 'Silberpfeil' is a silver arrow grass having silver-green, stiffly ascending, erect leaves with a white margin which develops tan hints in winter. Exceptional plumes from August to October. An excellent Ernst Pagels selection. 1.2-1.5m (4-5ft). Z5-9.

M. sinensis 'Silberturm' is another Pagels selection with wide green foliage and silver plumes from high summer onwards on a tall growing, erect plant. 2.5m (10ft).

M. sinensis 'Sirene' was selected by Pagels for its pinkish plumes which turn to silver. 2.2m (9ft).

M. sinensis 'Undine' makes upright mounds of narrow, white striped foliage with pink to purple flowers. 2m (8ft).

M. sinensis 'Variegatus' is a distinctive plant having green and white variegated stripes on upright stems. 1.5m (5ft).

M. sinensis 'Vorlaufer' is distinguished by being one of the earliest to flower and its pinkish plumes do turn silver as they age.

M. sinensis 'Yaku Dwarf' is useful in the small garden for its buff white fluffy flowers. 1.5m (5ft).

PENNISETUM

Favourite deciduous grasses for their silky plumes which are irresistible to touch.

HOW TO GROW
Sunny, well-drained spot. Pick flowerheads for display on a dry day and hang to dry in a light, airy place.

P. alopecuroides 'Little Honey' is a real sweetie with its narrow green and white foliage and furry flowers in summer. 25cm (10").

P. alopecuroides 'Weserbergland' makes mounds of narrow, green foliage with many cream to white flowers in late summer. 1m (over 3ft).

P. caudatum is attractive for its large, white flowers over deep green foliage in summer. 1.2m (4ft).

P. 'Malibu' pencil thin white flowers over dark green foliage distinguish this borderline hardy variety. 1m (over 3ft).

P. orientale bears mounds of striking green foliage and pink-white plumes in summer. 60cm (2ft).

P. orientale 'Tall Tails' makes attractive green mounds with foxtail like plumes in summer. 1.2m (4ft).

P. villosum bears grey-green leaves and silky silver plumes in late summer, which turn purple. The hardy feather grass makes large hummocks and looks superb in first frosts. It is used as an annual. Discard or cut back hard and pot up and keep under cover over winter. 60cm (2ft).

Phalaris arundinacea 'Feesey' is a ribbon grass that is more white than green with pink hints. Best planted in pots sunk into the ground. A vigorous beauty though said to be better behaved than most . Z4-9.

Pleioblastus Tsuboii makes semi-evergreen, narrow foliage in white and green stripes on compact slow growing mounds in sun or part shade. 1.2m (4ft).

Schoenoplectus albescens is a clump-forming rush with foliage striped in green and white. Best in damp, wet ground in a sunny spot. 1.2m (4ft).

Pennisetum villosum

STIPA

Handsome grasses and easy to grow, they just seem to blend almost anywhere in a sunny border.

HOW TO GROW
Full sun, dryish soil.

S. barbata is one of my favourite grasses. I actually first saw **S. barbata 'Silver Feather'** at Sissinghurst in the white garden. A graceful beauty, I fell in love at once. However, plantsman and friend Tim Fuller of Plantsman's Preference regards this as no different from the species. I have to agree, I think it to be one of those cases where the common name of silver feather grass becomes used incorrectly as a cultivar name but that does not take anything away from the plant itself. Over low clumps of pale green mounds, deliciously long up to 20cm (8"), delightfully feathery white awns grace this plant in June to July and persist into autumn. Perfect for flower arranging, and a slender, arching beauty for the border. 60cm (2ft).
S. capillata bears grey-green foliage and silver awns, allow this one to catch the sun for a breathtaking sight. 1m (over 3ft). Z6.
S. filiculmis was the name I found this plant under, it has the most silver-white plumes.
S. tenuiflora is mixed in commerce with *S. tenuissima*. Angel's hair bears silvery plumes.
S. tenuissima bears green tufts of foliage with graceful, fluffy silver plumes in summer. This performs best in full sun in a light soil. Grow this for beautiful movement in the slightest breeze. 60cm (2ft). Z7.

Stipa filiculmis

GRASS-LIKE PLANTS

To all intents and purposes the following plants appear like grasses and are often called such.

Acorus calamus 'Variegatus' is a striking plant with its handsome upright foliage striped in green and white. Grows in regular, humus-rich soil or in bog. All parts of this plant are fragrant. Looks like a grass but is actually a member of the Arum family.

The grass-like umbrella sedge, **Cyperus involucratus 'Variegatus'** bears white-striped, shiny deep green leaves with chartreuse flowers. A real stunner when grown in a pot without drainage or by a pond. Easy and eye-catching when soil does not dry out. Z9.

JUNCUS

Designer rushes are very trendy for their unusual foliage. True rushes are natives of Florida where they are found growing in the wetlands. Highly original and decorative.

HOW TO GROW
Usually preferring to have their feet in water; those listed here will tolerate drier conditions. Hardy to 32°C (0°F). Z4-10.

J. inflexus 'Afro' has grey-green spiralling stems. Intricate, like knitting wool when the cats have played. On the blue side of grey. This is being sold as seed. Introduced by Joe Sharman of Monksilver Nursery. 60cm (2ft).
J. patens 'Carman's Gray' makes steely grey upright columns in moist soil. Broad, arching evergreen tufts. Good by a pond but will tolerate drier sites. 60cm (2ft).
J. patens is known as the California grey rush.
J. 'Silver Spears' the pointed knitting needle leaves make stiff clumps radiating from a central rosette. Tolerant of dry soils and another superb container plant. 60cm (2ft).

Typha latifolia 'Variegata' is a most uncommon form of the deciduous bullrush. Attractive cream and green slender foliage with typical flowers. Best in water in a sunny site. 1.5m (5ft).

LIRIOPE

Like *Ophiopogon*, this is a member of the lily family, known as lily turf. Clumping, grass-like evergreen natives of Asia make soft, attractive mounds and superb groundcover in shade. Flowers are followed by berries. A wonderful companion for green and white hostas. Its neat habit is suitable for small gardens or use in irregular masses in Japanese style.

L. muscari 'Monroe White' bears white flowers over green strappy leaves. 40cm (16"). Z5-10.

L. muscari 'Okina' is out of this world. I would give this the honour of the number one white-foliaged plant. Neat, compact habit with broad, strap-like leaves. The paper-white new growth later develops green tips and a greenish tinge in warmer areas. Lilac-purple flower spikes contrast beautifully. Z6-9.

L. muscari 'Silvery Sunproof' is green and white variegated, a handsome addition to the edge of a path in part sun or shade. Lilac flower spikes in summer. 60cm (12").

L. muscari 'Variegata' bears white and green striped foliage and purple flowers in summer.

L. spicata 'Silver Dragon' the strap-like leaves of this beauty look silver from a distance, the effect of the white-striped green leaves. It can be planted under trees where nothing else will grow and as a variegated form should not choke other plants out unlike the species. 25cm (10"). Try in Z5 in a sheltered area. Z 6-9.

OPHIOPOGON

Ophiopogon provides lovely silver grass-like plants to mix with that blackest of foliage *O. planiscapus 'Nigrescens'*. Whilst it is a common practice to shear over O. japonicus as a lawn substitute, I do not recommend that you follow this practice with the black variety. Flowers are followed by berries on these long-season performers.

O. japonicus 'Nanus Variegatus' is a dwarf form with bright green and white leaves. 10cm (4"). Z5b-10.

O. japonicus 'Silver Dragon' (PPAF) is an evergreen mondo grass with green and white striped foliage. 30-40cm (12-16"). Z5.

O. japonicus 'Silver Mist' is more white than green and makes superb edging. A bright addition to the garden, capable of taking more sun in the north but hot sun in warm climates will cause leaf burn. 15cm (6"). Z6-9.

O. planiscapus 'Silver Ribbon' bears dark green leaves striped in grey-green with white flowers in summer. 20cm (8").

Ophiopogon japonicus 'Nanus Variegatus'

WHITE VARIEGATED HOSTA

We are used to *Hosta* in green, blue and gold and the many variegations thereof, but white hosta are that little bit different and a good addition to the white garden. The good news is hosta are getting whiter. Beautiful in the shade garden. Lacking a little in vigour, but what a splendid sight these are.

HOW TO GROW
Do not place these in sun, they will burn. Give them a shady spot in moist, humus soil. Z4.

H. 'Amazing Matthew' (Asch) has a wide white brim to fresh green centres.
H. 'Cascades' (Lachman 1993) is one of nurseryman and breeder, Tony Avent's favourites. White centred, green margined leaves taper and cascade to 30cm (12") long. Arching clumps make a fine specimen. 65cm (26").
H. 'Cherry Berry' is another great Lachman introduction (1991) much favoured again by Tony Avent. Narrow, dark green leaves have a white central streak. In midsummer, violet flowers arise on red spotted stems. Best in morning sun. 70cm (28") scapes and 40cm (16") wide clumps.
H. 'Dancing In The Rain' I would dance in a thunderstorm to have this delightful selection in my garden. Pure white leaves are beautifully edged in green. A sport of *'Blue Umbrellas'* introduced by Walter's Gardens.
H. 'Eternal Flame' (Hansen 1999) a sport of 'Whirlwind' this is indeed a flame which will eternally ignite the garden. Deeply veined, dark green leaves are the perfect colour to display the ice white which does not fade. 40cm (16") spikes of lavender flowers in midsummer. 60cm (2ft) wide.
H. 'Fire and Ice' is a favourite with me for its icy white centre edged in green. An incredible sport from 'Patriot' with good, heavy substance. Lavender flowers are carried on whitish stems.
H. 'Flame Stitch' the smallish leaves are white centred with a streaky green border, whitish stems and purple flowers.
H. 'Grey Ghost' emerges almost white changing through yellow to end blue-green in summer. The thick leaves are slug resistant. Near white flowers appear in late June to July.
H. 'Ice Castle' (Hansen) is a spectacular cultivar bearing slightly creamy white centres with blue margins.
H. 'Janet' has heart-shaped, white leaves with a green edge. Lavender flowers appear over the compact foliage. 40cm (16").
H. 'Loyalist' (Walters Gardens 1998) a reverse sport of *'Patriot'* offering a sharp contrast in darkest green margin and brightest white centre. Very good substance and very similar to 'Fire and Ice'. Light lavender flowers in summer. 60cm (2ft) wide.

H. 'Moonstruck' this small variety bears long, narrow, white leaves with a streaky, narrow, blue edge. Despite the amount of white, it shows good growth.
H. 'Mostly Ghostly' bears new foliage emerging pure white in spring, gradually greening up in summer. Delectable.
H. 'Mountain Fog' is a different type with long narrow leaves in creamy white and narrowly margined in green. In the heat of summer the centre becomes more green. Lavender flowers in summer. 45cm (18") wide.
H. 'Night Before Christmas' (J Machen 1994) is a sport of *'White Christmas'* with a central white stripe to the largish green leaves. In late summer, older leaves turn green. Lavender flowers on 75cm (30") scapes, making clumps 75cm (30") wide.
H. 'Pandora's Box' (Hansen) bears clear white centres with a two-tone, green-blue variegated broad margin. Tiny lavender flowers are borne on miniature stalks in summer. Outstanding mini variety, a sport of *'Baby Bunting'*, give it tender loving care. 15cm (10").
H. 'Paul Revere' to be revered, this is a truly beautiful sport of 'Patriot' with slightly puckered white leaves and an attractive green margin.
H. 'Remember Me' (Walters Gardens) is one for your sweetheart, or one to write home about. Beautiful white leaves edged in green. A small to medium variety with good substance and slug resistance. This fine mutation of my favourite hosta *'June'*, is named after former Walters Gardens employee, Sandy de Boer. 50cm (20").

Hosta 'Whirlwind'

H. 'Revolution' (PPAF, Walters/G. Van Eijk Bos/Dirk Van Erven 2000) is quite remarkable for its white-cream flecked leaves, broadly margined in dark green. This sport of *'Loyalist'* has leaves which are pointed and twisted. Light lavender flowers on 60cm (2ft) long scapes. 60cm (2ft) wide clumps.

H. 'Savannah Supreme' bears fragrant lavender flowers over heavily streaked, green and white foliage having a white margin.

H. 'Silver Streak' has a white center to its foliage.

H. 'Snow White' (Arett 1983) bears white leaves with a green, undulating margin.

H. 'Summer Music' is a beautiful form with a white centre and a broad green margin. Lavender flowers on short stems. 75x50cm (30x20").

H. 'Surprised By Joy' long, narrow, white leaves and a neat green edge makes a beautiful clump topped by white scapes of pinkish lavender flowers. Best with morning sun only or filtered light.

H. 'Whirling Dervish' is a reverse sport of *'Whirlwind'*. The large foliage features a very dark centre highlighted with wide, white margins.

H. 'White Bikini' (Whitmore) bears a white central stripe on pointed, green leaves with a fairly upright, vase habit.

H. 'White Christmas' (Krossa/Ruh 1999) keep on dreaming, this one is as smooth as Crosby's voice. A fine hosta with white leaves irregularly margined in dark green. Leaves are slightly wavy and are topped by lavender flowers. 30-45cm (12-18").

H. 'White Colossus' (Aden 1978) is an off-white with a mid-green margin and pale lavender flowers.

H. 'White Feather' (Heemskerk) take your breath away. This is an unusual sport from *undulata* with wavy margined leaves. Creamy, all-over white upright growing devastating beauty. It turns greener later in the season. Pale purity. Will take two hours morning sun, then is best in dappled shade for the rest of the day.

H. 'White Hot' (Walters Gardens 1998) is an unusual variety having white centres with yellow and a hint of green edging.

H. 'White Magic' (Aden 1978) bears tricolour leaves. The centre of the foliage is white with a green edge and some yellow streaking.

H. 'White Ray' (Minks 1974) is an attractive plant mainly in dark green with a real icy white centre.

H. 'White Trouble' (W G Schmid) is white as driven snow. Nicely shaped leaves with deep veins enchant.

H. 'White Vision' (Aden 1978) bears flattish foliage, well veined in a yellowish white.

H. 'White Wall Tires' (Avent 1995) bears simply incredible white foliage.

There are many hosta with white flowers and some with very pale silver to white undersides to their foliage.

Hosta 'Amazing Matthew'

Chrysanthemum 'Paulard White'

WHITE FLOWERS

The purity of white is what attracts the soul, the eye is attracted by the freshness, the heart by the echo of innocence. It cools the temperature to icy white.

Leucanthemum

White looks crisp against green and clear against purple and black which enhance its purity. The starkness of white is diminished by yellow stamens or cones and by conrast.

Abutilon vitifolium 'Album' is one of those cannot resist plants with the purity of white flowers. Hanging bells of pure white are stunning. Makes a large shrub or small tree with greyish green leaves. 5m (20ft).

Achillea ptarmica 'The Pearl' is a sweet white pearly flower almost like little roses and not at all like the usual flat plated heads of *Achillea*. This is a vegetatively propagated plant which is well-behaved and not the variable and often weedy, seed-raised version. 75cm (30") tall with a spread of 60cm (2ft). Z6.

Agapanthus 'Silver Baby' is a lovely dwarf form from New Zealand with a slight blue tinge to this extremely floriferous form. 30cm (12"). **A. 'Snowdrop'** has more than a drop of white in its huge flowerheads from July to September. 50cm (20"). **A. 'Seafoam'** is a pretty dwarf with 10cm (4") white flowers. (30cm) 12". Z6-9.

Allium 'Ivory Queen' step into the ivory tower with this wonderful member of the onion family. Ivory ball flowerheads are backed by glaucous foliage in April to May.

Anemone japonica 'Honorine Jobert' is still the best white of the Japanese hybrids, crisp and pure with a central boss of yellow stamens. Very floriferous in partial shade in humus, moist, but well-drained soil. 90cm (36"). Z4-8.
A. nemerosa 'Vestal' what a pure beauty this is, and understated too. Early to rise, it displays its pom-pom multi-petals before many plants have come into flower. Shiny, palmate leaves are handsome beneath shrubs. Summer dormant. Z5.
A. trullifolia alba mats of small, basal toothed leaves make a handsome foil for the pretty white flowers in May to June. In sun or partial shade, this sweet anemone makes ideal groundcover under trees. 15cm (6").

Anthurium have such incredible spathes and are very handsome in white. **'Paradiso'** is a nice form. There are also others with green and white spathes and spadices vary from pink to reddish to purple. Z9b-11.

Astilbe 'Snowdrift' I admire for its cool, white plumes and finely serrated green foliage. Prefers moist ground and mixes well with *Rheum* and *Hosta*. 50cm (20"). Z3-8.

Calochortus gunnisonii is a favourite for its pure white petals teamed with a greenish throat and deep purple eye.

Campanula persicifolia 'Moerheimii' is a snowy white double on a long flowering cottage garden flower. Z4-9.

Anemone trullifolia alba above, Anthurium 'Paradiso' below

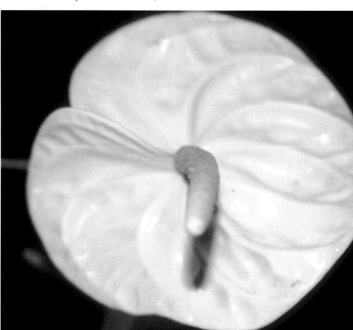

Astilbe 'Snowdrift' below

Cistus

Cardiocrinum giganteum exotic white lilies with intoxicating fragrance make this a must-have despite the long wait. 7 years to bloom, you need patience in capital letters but it will be amply rewarded by an unforgettable sight. Bulbils are left around the parent as the plant dies after flowering. 3m (10ft). Z8.

Cistus x cyprius is chosen for its long summer display of crinkly white flowers with a basal blotch of maroon and a central boss of yellow stamens. Rock roses are frost hardy and withstand cold though they look exotic. 1.5m (5ft). Z7.

Clematis montana alba is a breathtaking sight in full flower in May. This needs plenty of room to grow, it will climb to 10m (30ft). **C. florida 'Sieboldii'** is a bold flower, not clinically white but very attractive and possesses purple stamens giving another colour echo.

Clematis florida 'Sieboldii'

Colchicum speciosum 'Album' graces the autumn garden like a spring crocus only larger flowers. They have the common name of naked ladies as the flowers appear before the leaves. 15cm (6"). Z6.

Cornus kousa v chinensis an avalanche of white flowers are found on this beautiful small tree or large shrub. Best in sun to partial shade. Z5-9. Up to 10m (30ft). **C. 'Eddie's White Wonder'** is admirable too.

An attractive annual filler is easily found in **Cosmos 'Sonata White'**. Its feathery foliage makes a perfect foil for the clean white flowers with a central boss of yellow.

Convolvulus, noxious weed it may be, but it is a beautiful flower. I am not suggesting that you plant it, but if you see it in a hedge on your travels, stop to admire and say a word of thanks that it is not in your garden.

A white haze is an admirable quality in the garden found in **Crambe cordifolia** or **Gypsophila**, a beautiful foil for more solid plants.

Crinum x powellii 'Album' this white form is more sought-after than the usual pink. It has an almost transparent quality to its white flowers.

Dahlia 'Fusion' and **D. 'Twyning's Chocolate'** both bear sumptuous dark foliage and cream to white flowers.

Datura metel is a beauty for its showy, white trumpets.

Davidia involucrata 'Sonoma' improving on the beauty of the species is not easy, but here it is, in this form the bracts are up to 25cm (10") long. A very floriferous form of the dove tree where the 'handkerchiefs' wave goodbye to your sweetheart in May.

Cornus kousa v chinensis

Top: Cosmos 'Sonata'
Centre: Crinum x powellii 'Album'
Below: Dahlia 'Fusion'

Top: Dahlia 'Twynings' Chocolate'
Centre: Dicentra spectabilis 'Alba'
Below: Doritaenopsis 'Dutch Starlight'

Dianthus 'Musgrave's Pink' is a fringed white flower with a green heart. A single pink introduced in 1750. Full sun in well-drained neutral to alkaline soil. 10cm (4"). Z4.

Diascia 'Iceberg' is welcome in containers and makes a delightful summer bedder with its tiny, icy white flowers.

Dicentra spectabilis 'Alba' bleeding hearts are delightful in any colour, but there is an attractive innocence about the white form. Little lockets dangle from the arching stems most gracefully. If you have planted silver and pink in the garden, use **D. spectabilis** for its pink and white lockets. Best in partial shade in moist soil. Sun results in the plant going dormant earlier in the season. 1m (39"). Z3.
D. formosa 'Aurora' is worthy too for its dainty white hearts over greyish foliage. Vigorous. 30cm (12"). Z3.

Dodecatheon dentatum is a pure beauty with its swept-back white flowers with dark purple stamens. Small rosettes of toothed, heart-shaped leaves clump up quickly to make attractive groundcover in spring. Z5.

Doritaenopsis 'Dutch Starlight' this orchid shines brighter than any star with its purer than pure white flowers.

Echinacea purpurea 'White Lustre' off-white petals hang down from the prominent raised burnt gold cone. A superb native from North America. A stalwart of the late summer garden. Appreciates humus-rich, well-drained soil in full sun. 1.2m (4ft).
E. purpurea 'Kim's Mophead' is a dwarf variety with white petals and a gold-green cone. 45cm (18"). Z3-8.
E. 'Fragrant Angel' is a sweet thing to plant in your white borders or in any colour border. Great with orange to yellow to echo its vivid centre.

Echinops spaerocephalus 'Arctic Glow' is a handsome plant with its steely white globes, spiky at first then softening with age. Vigorous thistle-like plants. Unfussy as to soil but does prefer full sun. 80cm (32"). Z3-8.

Echinopsis huascha is a cactus bearing superb large, white flowers.

Epilobium glabellum bears white bell flowers in June to September on a subshrub which is good in the rock garden in moist soil. Found from the East Cape southwards. 30cm (12").

Epimedium grandiflorum 'White Queen' makes handsome groundcover with fresh green leaves and pure white, elegant flowers.

Echinacea 'Fragrant Angel' above, Echinopsis huascha

Hemerocallis 'Gentle Shepherd' above
Hydrangea 'Love You Kiss' centre

Eryngium above
Gaura lindheimeri below

Hydrangea below

ERYNGIUM

Eryngiums make an excellent garden plant and are much used as a decorative when dried. The sea holly belongs to the carrot family but this description belies its value in the garden. Try it in an annual bed with darkest *Scabiosa* for a wicked combination and a magnet for butterflies. It is best in well-drained soil in a sunny area with good drainage. Will tolerate dry conditions. Basically the poorer the soil, the better the plant performs. Propagate by seed, division or root cuttings. Z6-8, annual in Z4-5.

Eryngium giganteum is a short-lived perennial which seeds around. Known as Miss Wilmot's ghost after the English gardener's habit of taking seeds to friends' gardens, and unbeknown to them, sprinkling them where she walked. They would appear as ghostly reminders of Helen's visit. It also has a ghostly appearance especially at dusk. The largest of all Eryngo flowerheads appear in July to August surrounded by an Elizabethan ruff of luminous, spiky silvery bracts, with silvery-blue-green leaflets in tow. It can survive very low temperatures but needs summer heat. 1.2m (4ft).

E. planum 'Silverstone' bears attractive, toothed leaves. Branched stems carry silvery thistle flowers tinged green in July and August. 90cm (36").

E. proteiflorum is a most attractive sea holly, with silvery bracts and whitish flowers tinged green. 75-90cm (30-36"). Hardy to 10°F.

E. 'Silver Ghost' is a biennial form of *E. giganteum* with very silver bracts. 60cm (2ft).

E. variifolium is a compact, low-growing species with prickly, white-veined leaves having contrasting, pale blue-grey flower cones.

Hot Partner: *Cotinus coggygria 'Royal Velvet'*.
Cool Companion: *Stipa barbata, Athyrium niponicum v pictum, Artemisia 'Powis Castle'*.

Erythronium 'White Beauty' is aptly named with its large white flowers and pale green centres flecked with red appearing in April. It looks like a small flowered turkscap lily with its swept back petals. Mottled light green leaves are attractive too. Easy to grow and increases well in humus-rich, moist but well-drained soil in partial shade. 25cm (10"). Z5.

Fragaria vesca is purity none can touch. Dainty flowers and sweet fruit are found on the wild strawberry.

Fritillaria meleagris 'Alba' is a white delight, naturalise in grass and for contrast plant with the purple hues of the desirable *F. meleagris*.

Epilobium glabellum above,
Eryngium giganteum 'Silver Ghost' below

191

Magnolia kobus above, M. wilsonii below

Miltonopsis above, Narcissus below

In any garden, the year starts with **Galanthus nivalis**, snowdrops, but these are an absolute must in the white garden. There are dozens of choice forms from reliable bulb suppliers. The species **G. elwesii** has broad, grey leaves. They are often planted in full sun but appreciate a partially shaded site in humus-rich, moist but well-drained soil. 15cm (6"). Z4.

Galtonia candicans is most attractive. Its neat white tubular flowers are sheer purity against the green stems and strappy leaves. These South African bulbs need a well-drained soil in full sun. Mulch in winter in Z7 or lift after flowering and store. 1.2m (4ft). Z7.

I am extremely fond of **Gaura lindheimeri 'The Bride'** a pure delight in its flight of white flowers against green foliage I still think this far outstrips new varieties for its sheer purity.

Same cultivar name but a different plant is found in **Gladiolus 'The Bride'** with its wonderful white flowers having faint green stripes.

Grow **Helleborus 'Mrs. Betty Ranicar'** for its double white flowers, breathtaking in late winter. 45cm (18"). Z4-9.
H. niger is also very attractive and valuable for it is in flower in the depth of winter.

Hemerocallis 'Gentle Shepherd' is a must. This tremendous daylily has a delicate beauty that is wonderful.

Hyacinthus 'L'Innocence' is recommended for its purity and its heady scent so welcome in early spring. Grow in full sun in well-drained soil. 25cm (10").

Hydrangea paniculata 'The Swan' (PPAF) is a superb hardy form to grow as a shrub or tree with immense white flowers. Z4. **H. 'Love You Kiss'** might have a strange name but it is a superb beauty edged in pink. This is my absolute favourite *hydrangea*.

Ipomoea alba, the white morning glory is wonderful in the white garden and opens its startling petals at night. It is known as moonflower.

Iris sibirica 'Snow Queen' is a snow-white rebloomer with yellow shoulders. Best in sun or light shade in slightly acidic, moisture retentive soil. 75cm (30"). Z. 3-9.

Lilium the Queen of white flowers, L. regale 'Album' top, Asiatic lily bottom and centre

Phalaeonopsis 'Brother Goldsmith'
white Rhododendron and Nectaroscordum below

Phalaeonopsis 'Brother Passat'
Rose grown in the white garden Sissinghurst

Rosa 'The Fairy'

Jasminum sambac Arabian jasmine is a pure beauty in light shade to sun and makes a handsome indoor plant. The waxy, white petals are used to flavour foods. My favourite scent. The double flowers of **'Grand Duke of Tuscany'** look like miniature gardenias. Blooms throughout the summer, almost all year round in warmer areas. In Z8 it can be grown outside and cut back by first frosts given a good mulch, it will re-sprout in spring but probably not flower until late summer. In warmer areas it is evergreen. Easy in moist soil. Arabian jasmine is the national flower of the Philippines. 1.8-3m (6-10ft). **J. officinale** is also very sweet in flower and perfume. The scent transports me like no other. I simply cannot and will not live without Jasmine.

Lathyrus 'White Supreme' is one of the purest sweet peas. Bold and beautiful with excellent vigour.

Lavatera 'White Satin' is a soft white on very hardy plants. Well-drained soil in full sun. 1.75m (6ft). Z5-8.

Leucojum aestivum 'Graveteye Giant' is known as the summer snowflake even though it flowers in spring. The drooping white bells are most attractive against the green stems and leaves. 50cm (20"). Z4.

Lilium is hard to beat for purity. Top of the list is **Lilium 'Casablanca'** but I also always grow **L. regale 'Album'** (1.2m, 4ft. Z.5). **L. martagon 'Alba'** (1.5m, 5ft. Z.4) is much coveted for its turned back, waxy petals are exquisite. Superb in partial shade in well-drained soil. These are virgin whites in the garden. Some of the Asiatic lilies are favourites too. *Lilium* create colour echoes.

Magnolia are truly magnificent for their stately form even catches the eye of the non-gardener. I love the bowl cup shapes of many of the hybrids. **M. kobus** is an admirable species with large flowers. **M. stellata** is a must with its strappy petals and it has the advantage of flowering when young. **'Waterlily'** is an admirable cultivar of this deciduous shrub to 3m (10ft). Z5.

Miltonopsis perhaps has almost as much pink and maroon in its petals as white, but I would find a spot for this orchid in the conservatory.

Muscari botryoides 'Album' the humble grape hyacinth becomes elegant and sophisiticated in its white form. This is not an invasive form and is particularly handsome in mid-spring. 15cm (6"). Z3.

Narcissus poeticus recurvus is the old fashioned pheasant's eye with pure white flowers swept back from a tiny yellow cup edged in red in May. Excellent for naturalising. There are many fine white daffodils. 40cm (16").

Osteospermum 'Danden White' above
Paeonia 'Ben Kaku' below

Sparrmannia africana above, Stephanotis floribunda centre,
Sutera Cabana below

Viburnum plicatum 'Mariesii' above
Yucca outside Sheffield Botanic Garden

Sanguinaria canadensis above
Sarracenia alata x leucophylla below
Spiraea japonica 'White Gold' bottom right

I doubt the existence of silver flowers, but **Nectaroscordum bulgaricum** bears silvery pink flowers in silvery green calyces.

Nicotiana alata spreads its fragrance from its delicate white trumpets, a real treasure in the evening garden when it glows and its scent is much appreciated. Looks great by moonlight. Sow seed in autumn. **N. sylvestris** is equally handsome, tall and elegant.

Nymphaea grace any pond with a white waterlily and transform an area to a higher level.

Odontoglossum 'Pumistar' is a magnificent white orchid.

Ornithogalum saundersiae is an attractive bulb bearing white flowers.

Osteospermum the beautiful South African daisies look at their best in white with their contrasting dark centres.

Paeonia lactiflora is another gorgeous white flower. Simple purity is found in its single flowers. **'Avalanche'** is an admirable cultivar with double, very fragrant flowers. Best in partial sun. Z3-8. 90cm (3ft). **P. 'Krinkled White'** is a single having large, textured, wavy petals. Green pistils show through the yellow centre. 60cm (2ft). **P. 'Bai Yu Lan'** is a white tree peony with large, single flowers having a pink blush to the base. Vigorous and floriferous, early blooming beauty. 1.2m (4ft). Z5-8. Full sun and good soil. **P. 'Ben Kaku'** makes a glorious addition to any garden.

Papaver orientale 'Black and White' is stunning in its simplicity and contrast. Full sun in well-drained soil.

Phalaenopsis orchids **'Brother Goldsmith'** and **'Brother Passat'** are similar but both are highly desirable.

Philadelphus 'Beauclerk' what an enchanting variety this is in its white petals with just a hint of pink in the centre. An admirable and easy shrub in well-drained soil in sun or partial shade. 2.5m (8ft). Z5.

Schizostylis

Phlox divaricata 'White Perfume' is outstanding in groundcover for woodland and makes an attractive edging plant. Very fragrant, white, narrow-petalled flowers. Appreciates sun in humus soil. 25cm (10").

Prunus ornamental cherries are a breathtaking sight in spring.

Pulsatilla vulgaris 'Alba' the pasque flower is a shy, coy plant. These silky, hairy plants are very attractive in spring. Feathery seedheads are handsome after flowering. Best in full sun in a rock garden or on a dry bank. Drought tolerant in cooler climates, needing some shade in hot climates. 25cm (10"). Z5-8.

Rhododendron are fabulous in any colour, white is pure. These superb woodland plants really give their all.

Romneya coulteri is a desirable, fragrant white flower. Difficult to establish in heavy soils, it can spread its way in light soils a little too much. Its silky, papery white blossoms are exquisite with their boss of yellow stamens. Known as Matilja poppy, be aware of the underground runners and indefinite spread. 1.8m (6ft). Z7.

Rosa 'Iceberg' is a favourite and the fantastic white rose with startling yellow-orange stamens grown at Sissinghurst in the white garden is knockout. This looks equally good in the yellow to orange border. It is not at all stark staring white.
R. 'The Fairy' is a miniature double, white blooms emerge from pink buds. A very floriferous form from June to October that is superb in a container. I have enjoyed this on the patio for many years, it never fails to please.

Rubus 'Benenden' I admire for its purity, hard to beat, the flowers are truly beautiful with a boss of yellow stamens, add to this the silvery-white stems and you have an attractive, ornamental bramble. Thornless, arching stems can be cut back immediately after flowering. Grow in well-drained soil in sun or partial shade. 3m (10ft) height and spread.

Sanguinaria canadensis is a real favourite, a superb pure white flower perhaps superceded by the double form, but either will suit me just fine. Plant in humus-rich soil in light woodland or shade. 15cm (6"). Z3.

Sarracenia alata x leucophylla with its purple veined white flowers this will steal the show in boggy ground.

Schizostylis coccinea f alba this white form is sought after and is almost transparent.

Spiraea 'Arguta' few could plant a white garden without including bridal wreath. The arching, wiry stems are covered in clusters of tiny white flowers looking like seafoam. This easy to grow deciduous shrub needs pruning immediately after flowering. Full sun in moist, well-drained soil. 2.5m (8ft). Z4.
Spiraea japonica 'White Gold' can be grown for its sprays of white flowers over gold foliage.

Stephanotis swoon at the perfume and the sight of pure white, waxy flowers.

Sutera (Bacopa) pretty little white flowers adorn this plant which makes a suitable subject for hanging baskets and containers in summer.

Thunbergia alata is attactive in its white form having a central black dot.

Trillium grandiflorum is admirable in the spring garden. Its white flowers are stunning beneath shrubs in partial shade. 40cm (16"). Z4.

Trollius albiflorus is little seen but much preferable to the usual garish yellow.

Viburnum sieboldii 'Wavecrest' is an amazing sight in May in full flower. Its white blossoms are followed by orange berries. 6m (20ft). **V. plicatum 'Mariesii'** is an outstanding beauty, its white flowers are carried on tiered branches almost to ground level. It makes a most impressive sight in May.

Wisteria floribunda 'Longissima Alba' this pure white form of wisteria is exquisite. The long racemes are very fragrant. 6m (20ft).

Yucca have some of the most attractive creamy white flowers.
Y. baccata is usually available, **Y. harrimaniae** is even more attractive.
Y. smalliana bears exquisite flowers in creamy white.

Zantedeschia aethiopica 'Crowborough' bears pure white flowers. This has to be the all-time floral symbol of elegance. Large white cup shaped flowers with contrasting yellow spadices are beautiful by water.
Z. 'Green Goddess' has a white heart to its green cupped large spathes.

Yucca gloriosa above in the glorious setting of St. Michael's Mount, Cornwall, Y. smalliana below

Zantedeschia 'Green Goddess' above Z. aethiopica 'Crowborough' below

INDEX

Photograph Credits

All photographs are copyright 2004 Karen Platt unless noted below. t-top, b-bottom, r-right, l-left, c-centre.
Joshua Coventry:P8,P17,P39tr,P40,P52r,P67,P71br,P106, P107tl,P108 all, P109br,P142,P149,P177br,P188tl,P199
Jim Mercer: P1,P5,P74,P99b,P112
www.bcss-liverpool.pwp.blueyonder.co.uk
Dan Heims: P39bl, P95br,P96tr,tl,cr,br,P119br,P120bl, P121 all,P153,P156t,c,P157bl,P160tr,P169t,ct,b,P173, P180,P181,P189tr
DS Cole: P56tl,tr.P57br,P60,P64,P65tr.
Bob Skowron: P71cr,P79bl,P80tr,P81cl,P140 all,P203
www.rmrp.com
Josef Hlasek: P83br. www.hlasek.com
Hebe Society: P87t. www.hebesoc.vispa.com
Downderry Nursery: P100tr,tl,cr,cl,P102
EuroAmerican Propagators: P105br,P196tl,P197bl
Juan Enrique Gomez: P116bl http://waste.ideal.es
Tim Oakland: P116br,P117 all
www.oaklandnurseries.co.uk
Wayne Boucher: P118bl,P139br,P169cb(Bukiniczia)
Joan Ribera: P132br www.floradelpirineu.net
Farplants: P146
Agristarts: P147,P150,P151,P157tr
Jim Irvin: P161,P162
Stuart Asch: P183

Acknowledgements

My grateful thanks go to all those who play a part in my work. With especial thanks to the team at Euro American Propagators and friends and colleagues in the U.S. Also to colleagues in the U.K. and all those who help to get the books out there in shops and stores around the world.

To my son who maintains my websites and is always there ready to help when my computer does its own thing and with brilliant design ideas.

To my family for their support, and friends on both sides of the Atlantic.

A special thanks to those who have loaned images for this book, I am grateful to all of you.

Below : Helichrysum basalticum

ILLUSTRATIONS

ILLUSTRATIONS

Apple Court Nursery
Hordle Lane
Hordle. Lymington
Hampshire SO41 0HU
www.applecourt.com
Hosta, grasses

Avon Bulbs
Burnt House Farm
Mid-Lambrook
South Petherton
Somerset TA13 5HE
www.avonbulbs.co.uk
Galanthus

Beeches Nursery
Village Centre
Ashdown. Saffron Walden
Essex CB10 2HB
www.beechesnursery.co.uk
wide range

The Beth Chatto Gardens Ltd
Elmstead Market
Colchester
Essex CO7 7DB
www.bethchatto.co.uk
drought tolerant

Bridgemere Nurseries
Nantwich. Chesire CW5 7QB
info@bridgemere.co.uk
good range

Dibley's
Llanelidan
Ruthin. Denbighshire
Wales LL15 2LG
www.dibleys.com
Begonia, Solenostemon

Downderry Nursery
Pillar Box Lane
Hadlow. Tonbridge
Kent TN11 9SW
www.downderry-nursery.co.uk
Lavender

Duchy of Cornwall Nursery
Cott Rd
Lostwithiel
Cornwall PL22 0HW
www.duchyofcornwallnursery.co.uk
ornamental trees and shrubs

Edrom Nurseries
Coldingham
Eyemouth
Berwickshire
Scotland
TD14 5TZ
www.edromnurseries.co.uk
Anemone, woodland plants

Glenhirst Cactus Nursery
Station Rd
Swineshead.
Nr. Boston
Lincs PE20 3NX
www.cacti4u.co.uk
cactus and succulents

Ingwersen's
Birch Farm Nursery
Gravetye
East Grinstead
W. Sussex
RH19 4 LE
www.ingwersen.co.uk
hardy alpines and rock garden

Oakland Nurseries
147 Melton Rd
Burton-on-The -Wolds
Loughborough LE12 5TQ
www.oaklandnurseries.co.uk
Caladium, Plectranthus

Fernwood Nursery
Fernwood
Peters Marland
Torrington
Devon EX38 8QG
www.fernwood-nursery.co.uk
Sempervivum

Plantsman's Preference
Lynwood
Hopton Rd
Garboldisham. Diss.
Norfolk IP22 2QN
www.plantpref.co.uk
Geranium, grasses

Shirley's Plants
6 Sandheys Drive
Church Town
Southport PR9 9PQ
www.stbegonias.com
Begonia

Silver Leaf Nurseries
Charmouth Rd. Lyme Regis
Dorset DT7 3HF

Viv Marsh Postal Plants
Walford Heath. Shrewsbury
Shropshire SY4 2HT
www.PostalPlants.co.uk
good range

White Cottage Alpines
Sunnyside Nurseries
Sigglesthorne
East Yorkshire HU11 5QL
www.whitecottagealpines.co.uk

Winchester Growers Ltd
Varfell Farm
Long Rock. Penzance
Cornwall TR20 8AQ
www.wgltd.co.uk
Dahlia

Esveld
Rijnveld 72
2771 XS
Boskoop Holland
www.esveld.nl

Jim Almond (alpine seed)
http://freespace.virgin.net/almond.
jim/Seed.htm

Asiatica
PO Box 270
Lewisberry. PA 17339 USA
www.asiaticanursery.com
Asarum, woodlanders

Cloudy Valley Nursery
8005 Rowell Creek Rd
Willamina OR 97396 USA
http://begonias.com

Geraniaceae Nursery
122 Hillcrest Avenue
Kentfield. CA 94904. USA
www.gerianaceae.com

Glasshouse Works
Church St. PO Box 97
Stewart. OH 45778-0097. USA
http://glasshouseworks.com
Begonia

Kartuz
1408 Sunset Drive
Vista. CA 92085-0790. USA
www.kartuz.com
Begonia

Logees Greenhouses Ltd
141 North St
Danielson. CT 06239. USA
www.logees.com
Tropicals for containers

Plant Delights Nursery, Inc.
9241 Sauls Rd
Raleigh. NC 27603. USA
www.plantdelights.com
excellent range

The Primrose Path
921 Scottdale-Dawson Rd
Scottdale. PA 15683. USA
www.theprimrosepath.com

Rocky Mountain Rare Plants
1706 Deerpath Rd
Franktown. CO 80116-9462. USA
www.rmrp.com
Incredible alpine plants and seeds

Spring Hill Nurseries
PO Box 330
Harrison. OH 45030-0330. USA
Drought garden plants

Squaw Mountain Gardens
PO Box 946
Esdtacada.OR 97023. USA
www.squawmountaingardens.com
Succulents

Windmill Outback Nursery
4583 E. Old Mountain Rd
Louisa
VA 23093-2420. USA
www.australiaplants.com
Drought tolerant

Seeds
Seedhunt
PO Box 96.
Freedom.
CA 95019-0096. USA.
www.seedhunt.com

Wholesale only
www.agristarts.com
www.dscolegrowers.com
www.euroamprop.com
www.smgrowers.com
www.terranovanurseries.com

CANADA
Alpines Mont Echo
1182 Parmenter Rd
Sutton, Quebec
Canada J0E 2K0
www.alpinemtecho.com

AUSTRALIA
Cactusland
PO Box 2567
Cheltenham
VIC Australia 3192
www.cactusland.com.au

Kangarutha Nursery
Evans Hill. Tathra. NSW
www.kangarutha.com.au
Australian natives

Lambley Nursery
'Burnside'. Lesters Rd
Ascot VIC 3364
http://lambley.com.au
silver foliage plants

Paradise Distributors
27a Bonney St
Nambour. Qld 4560.
paraplants@iprimus.com.au

Sydney Flower Nursery West
241 South St. Marsden Park.
NSW 2765
www.australian-natives.com

NEW ZEALAND
Texture Plants Ltd
315 Marshes Rd
Christchurch
www.textureplants.co.nz

Helichrysum thianschanicum

Watercolours, Cards and Photos

All Karen Platt and Joshua Coventry photographs in this book are available as cards or photographic prints.
Cards are 14x14cm and are blank inside.
Photographic prints are 15x20cm.
Other sizes are made to order.
To order, please visit our website
www.karenplatt.co.uk
or telephone +44 (0) 114 2681700

Watercolour paintings are available of many of the silver plants in this book. Commissions are gladly undertaken.
To order see above.

Watercolour right: Begonia 'Martin Johnson'
Below: Leucanthemum x superbum
Card below right: Echeveria subridgia

www.karenplatt.co.uk